MINGMING
& the Tonic of Wildness

BY THE SAME AUTHOR:

Voyages of a Simple Sailor
Mingming & the Art of Minimal Ocean Sailing

ROGER D. TAYLOR

MINGMING

& the Tonic of Wildness

Yet More Voyages of a Simple Sailor

F

THE FITZROY PRESS

Published by The FitzRoy Press 2012.

F

The FitzRoy Press
5 Regent Gate
Waltham Cross
Herts EN8 7AF

ISBN 978 0955803 536

A catalogue record for this book is available from the British Library

Publishing management by Troubador Publishing Ltd, Leicester, UK
Printed and bound in the UK by TJ International, Padstow, Cornwall

MIX
Paper from responsible sources
FSC www.fsc.org FSC® C013056

In memory of my father
Angus D. Taylor
(1920 – 2011)
Seaman, raconteur, survivor.

In order to minimise the cost and ecological impact of this book, colour photographs have been omitted. Photographs and video clips linked to this text can be found at www.thesimplesailor.com

Contents

Preface xi

PART ONE
STORMS 1

PART TWO
MOUNTAINS 139

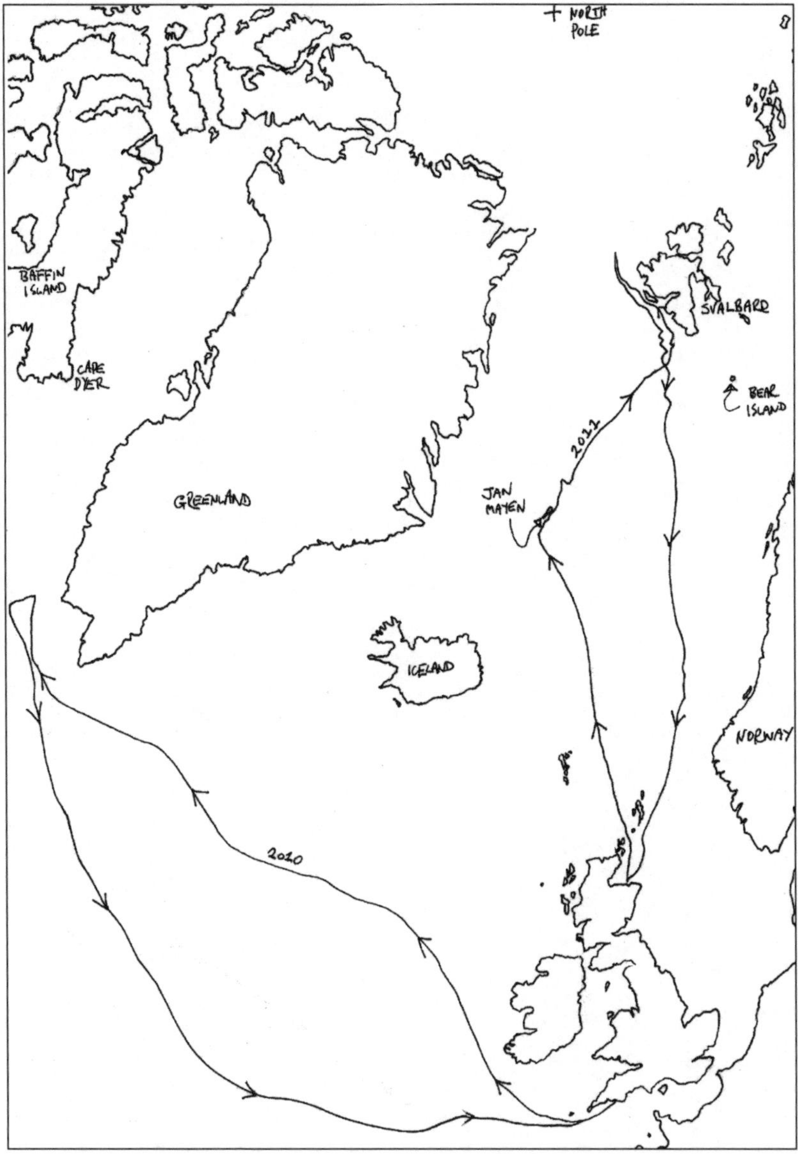

Mingming's *Voyages 2010-2011*

Preface

'We need the tonic of wildness... We need to witness our own limits transgressed, and some life pasturing freely where we never wander.'

Henry David Thoreau, *Walden.*

My first book, *Voyages of a Simple Sailor*, described how I arrived at the notion of simple sailing. The second, *Mingming & the Art of Minimal Ocean Sailing,* attempted to explain both the philosophy and the practice of this kind of pared-down voyaging. This third volume tries, in my usual halting and roundabout way, to explore the much more fundamental question: why go ocean sailing at all? Whilst it is first and foremost a narrative of two long voyages in a tiny yacht, it is also an attempt, therefore, to uncover the deeply-hidden motivations behind such voyages.

I approach this problem somewhat obliquely, and am still not sure whether I know or understand the answers. The underlying theme is not just the attraction of wild places and the life that thrives in those places, but also the growing imbalance between the untainted and the civilised. The fragile purity of the wild places contrasts with the over-stressed agglomerations of human habitation, and only heightens the sense of unease.

Spending long periods at sea can alter one's perception of those two mantles of the earth – the land and the ocean. As land-based and therefore terra-centric creatures we tend to view the sea as a strange and alien adjunct to the rock and soil on which we live. The more time one spends at sea, particularly in the kind of unmediated proximity that only a small and slow-moving cruising yacht can engender, the more one realises that it is the land which is the oddity, the geological aberration; perhaps it should not be there at all. This is a startling thought, and one that invites a total reassessment of our own place in the world.

I try to keep my narratives fast-moving and entertaining, and so my darker ruminations are, I hope, woven only lightly into the warp and weft of the stories. There are many aspects of our relationship with that other world, the timeless world of innocent creatures unburdened by self-awareness and crippling intelligence, which evoke sadness and anger and an overwhelming pessimism. I have tried as much as possible not to let these feelings intrude into the narrative. I hope, nonetheless, that I will be forgiven the occasional moment where I have expressed my thoughts without restraint.

PART ONE

STORMS

1

For nearly a year I struggled. I was supposed to be sailing in the 2010 Jester Challenge from Plymouth to Newport, Rhode Island. This is the hallowed route for all single-handed sailors, second only to a circumnavigation via the great southern Capes. However much I tried I could not raise any enthusiasm for the voyage. I had developed too strong a taste for the wild and the obscure, for the path less trodden. Departure was scheduled for the twenty-third of May. I thought that perhaps, as the day approached, I would find the necessary spark to fire me up, but it refused to appear. This worried me; to take a twenty-one foot yacht across the North Atlantic, against the prevailing winds and currents, requires a cast-iron commitment. I had by now sailed my little yacht *Mingming* twelve thousand miles or so, mainly in high latitudes. I knew well enough the resolve that is necessary to push on and on through an inhospitable ocean.

It took just one weekend in March to clear up the problem. Brenda showed me a Sunday newspaper colour supplement article about Newport. The glossy photographs depicted paradise on earth. Clapboard houses glistened under fresh paint. Seafood restaurants and ice-cream parlours out-shone each other. Harbours swelled with smart yachts. Well-manicured headlands groaned beneath the weight of nineteenth-century *arriviste* mansions. Within a few seconds my mind was made up: I would not sail to Newport. Heaven is not my kind of place. I have never understood mankind's preoccupation with attaining to that particular state of grace. All that unrelieved perfection would surely bore a man to death, and then what?

That very same day I was once more perusing my charts and saw the trajectory for an ideal voyage. I would make a high latitude Atlantic crossing, yes, but instead of turning south-west to head over the Grand Banks and on towards the heart of advanced civilisation, I would instead turn right, to the north-west. Here I could make my way up the Davis Strait, the narrowing stretch of water between west Greenland and Labrador. In a moment my pulse was raised. *Yes! That's where I should go!* Further north, to the west, lay Baffin Island. *Now you're talking!* My finger moved on, and there it was – the Arctic Circle. Everything fell into place. I could mirror my previous year's voyage into the Arctic Circle to the east of Greenland. There was a pleasing symmetry to this. It felt right. What's more, I could safely make the voyage there and back in one summer. The whole route was well clear of the hurricane zone. Now my mind was buzzing. I peered more closely at the chart. The narrowest section of the Davis Strait lay right on the Arctic Circle. On the western side Baffin Island projected out into the Strait, culminating in a prominent headland, Cape Dyer. I imagined that wind-swept bluff, still locked into the winter ice. *No mansions there, my boy*! My finger traced south, following the tortuous indentations of the Canadian coastline. Here was the history of Arctic exploration writ large: Frobisher Bay, Cumberland Sound, Sunneshine Fiord, Mooneshine Fiord, Queen Elizabeth's Foreland and so on. With spread hand I measured distances. From Plymouth to Cape Dyer was roughly two and a half thousand nautical miles. A quick calculation put it at about forty days' sailing. There and back would take eighty days, give or take. *Mingming* could carry a hundred days' worth of food and water. There was not much margin of error, but we could do it.

My excitement was only slightly tempered by the enormity of the challenge. To spend eighty days, or thereabouts, in the northern reaches of the North Atlantic, at any time of year, was asking for a certain amount of trouble. An endless procession of low pressure systems and their accompanying storms wing their way across this patch of ocean. During the summer months they are generally a little less severe and marginally more short-lived. I was under no illusion, though. Four consecutive summer voyages in high latitudes had taught me that the weather is no respecter of seasons. It was inconceivable that *Mingming* and I would not have to cope with at least one or two severe gales. Our outward route in particular would take us through the most difficult node in the north Atlantic: a large area between north-west Ireland and Greenland where winds and wave heights reach their highest values.

There was too the not inconsiderable question of ice. This would take two forms, each with its own characteristics and dangers. Sea-ice is carried down the east coast of Greenland and around its southern tip, Cape Farvel. In certain conditions this can be pushed far to the south, blocking the path to the west. I had sailed *Mingming* into the east Greenland sea-ice the previous summer and had seen first-hand and close-up the seductive beauty of the floes, their siren glitter concealing an iron and implacable fist. They can swirl around and trap you in a few seconds. The waters off Cape Farvel are a graveyard for ships and fishing boats and yachts. The nasty storms that are generated at that confluence of warm water and cold water, aided and abetted by lying at the juncture between the Arctic high pressure system and the temperate zone, throw an extra ingredient into the cocktail. I would have to keep well clear of Cape Farvel.

The Davis Strait is a main highway for icebergs. They pour down from the frozen wastes of north-west Greenland, borne on the south-going Labrador Current. One thing would work in my favour: this current flows down the west side of the Strait. Warmer water, the last vestiges of the Gulf Stream, makes its way up the east side. This helps to clear the winter sea-ice from the west coast of Greenland and creates its more benign climate. In summer the icebergs are widely scattered. Given their size they are visible from a good distance. The offspring they spawn, though, the growlers and bergy bits that break off and make their own way in life, are a source of unseen danger, particularly in rough weather. The simple fact was that I had no idea what the concentrations of icebergs and their associated detritus would be like. I had no idea whether or not I would be able to navigate with reasonable safety in the more northerly stretches of the Strait. Well, there was only one way to find out.

Within a few hours I had rediscovered the thrill and motivation of a worthwhile voyage. A double Atlantic crossing which would take us to the hinterland of the North-West Passage; here was something suitably outrageous for *Mingming* and me to get our teeth into. This was an undertaking which would test to the limit the experience and methodology I had been patiently accumulating with *Mingming* throughout the previous five years. It was in a sense the next logical step in our development: a protracted voyage through distant and unpredictable waters.

More than anything, though, it would once again take us north. This was my unequivocal orientation. I had already sailed *Mingming* to Iceland and Jan Mayen and into the east Greenland ice. We had skirted the Shetlands and the Faroes and Rockall. We had touched on 72°N. Far from satisfying me, these voyages had set up a yearning for more. I felt that I had as yet scarcely scratched the surface of these remote wastes. I needed to go back, and to keep going back. Something elusive hovered just beyond reach; it seemed that only an increasing familiarity might bring it into some kind of focus. From time to time I had felt at ease in the bleak solitude of my wanderings, almost at home. Perhaps this was an illusion, or a delusion, and a dangerous one at that. Perhaps I was kidding myself, but it seemed that there was more, or at any rate as much, to be learned at this stark interface with an alien and inimical world than in the hothouse of human interaction. Something in the scale and timelessness of the ocean and the life within it and above it seemed truer and more satisfying. It was here that I always felt somehow closer to the essence of life. The coolness and the emptiness of the northern seas enhanced the crispness of this impression, making it sharper, more telling. There was nowhere else I would rather sail.

2

I rang my friend Trevor Leek, the owner of *Jester*. I explained that I was still planning to sail to the North American continent, or as near as would be possible for me to get to it, but with a destination other than Newport in mind. I sketched out the more northerly route I had decided on and offered to withdraw as an official entrant to the Jester Challenge. I would still be at Plymouth with *Mingming* for the start, but would be happy to set off a little later than the main fleet.

The Jester Challenge, unconstrained by rules or dogma, is a delightfully broad church. Trevor was adamant that I should remain as an official entrant. *If the conditions are wrong you might change your mind anyway and decide to head for Newport.* That was certainly a possibility. *But I still feel uncomfortable about it, Trevor. I don't want to be there under false pretences.* Trevor was unmoved. *Don't worry about it. Stay on the list and start with us.*

The entry list for the 2010 Jester Challenge had ballooned to almost a hundred skippers. How many would actually turn up at Plymouth was anybody's guess. To register as a prospective entrant takes no more than a short email. There would undoubtedly be a high proportion of last-minute dropouts. An informal debate amongst the established Jester Challengers attempted to put a number on the actual starters. I thought it might be about sixty. As it turned out that was too optimistic by far.

I remained an official starter for the Jester Challenge. Nonetheless over the next two months I made it clear to everyone I talked to that I was aiming for a different objective. To simplify matters, and to give myself a specific physical goal, I established Cape Dyer, Baffin Island, as the intended target. As a component part of the North American seaboard, and itself on an island, it could, with a small leap of the imagination, be considered a more northerly version of Newport, Rhode Island. It would, however, be somewhat more difficult to approach. If our voyage went to plan, we would be in the vicinity of Baffin Island at the beginning of July. This was early in the summer season from a sea-ice perspective. I was studying daily the satellite-derived Canadian ice charts. At the rate at which clear water was moving slowly north up the Davis Strait it was by no means certain that Cape Dyer would be free of sea-ice when we arrived. Once we left Plymouth I would have no further means of checking. The ice position would be better in August, but by then we would have lost twenty-four hour daylight, and risked worsening weather for the return leg.

The plan had by now taken a firm hold, but I needed a strong mental image to cement my resolve, something suitably fantastic and alluring. I was re-reading Bill Tilman's account of *Mischief's* visit to Cape Dyer in 1962. Ice was of course even more of a problem in those days. After one thwarted attempt he was able to close the coast towards the end of August. The relatively ice-free conditions allowed him to enter Exeter Sound, just to the south of the Cape, and to come to anchor at Totnes Roads. The Devon-born explorer and navigator John Davis had named the sound and the anchorage in 1586. Tilman, in his usual restrained way, indicated his pleasure at using Davis's anchorage by quoting at length the latter's account of his two-day stay there. Here was a prospective double pleasure. What a culmination of the outward voyage that would be, to sail into Exeter Sound and anchor in the same spot as both Davis and Tilman! My imagination took one further leap forward. *How about going ashore?* Davis and his crew had done so to shoot bears, Tilman to climb Mount Raleigh. As yet I had not equipped *Mingming* with any form of tender. Maybe I could think about a compact inflatable. I was in any case about to re-engineer the stowage for my Jordan series drogue. Maybe this would free up some space for a rubber dinghy.

I had found the picture I needed to draw me on. On a glistening summer's day, with the lightest of breezes, we ghost our way up the narrowing reaches of Exeter Sound. The passage is clear except for the occasional unthreatening iceberg. The shoreline is littered with grounded ice. The Sound is locked in an amphitheatre of rock-hewn mountains. To starboard, to the north that is, lies the dominating peak of Mount Raleigh. We nose our way to anchor in a couple of fathoms of crystal-clear water. The silence, timeless and overpowering, is broken only by the flurry of a harp seal surfacing, or the cackle of a distant auk. For half a day I can do nothing but sit in the hatchway and watch and listen. Then I inflate the tender and row myself ashore. I carry the dinghy up the pebbled beach and weight the painter with a rock. *Mingming* sits patiently astern, tiny against a backdrop of rock and ice. I take a stroll. Here is a New World, reached in the tiniest of boats.

Well, it might just happen, but it was pretty damned unlikely. In any case, my wariness of taking *Mingming* too close in to strange coastlines had been reinforced the previous year; entry into a north-west Icelandic bay had caused several hours of extreme anxiety when the conditions had turned against me. No, it was a hopelessly starry-eyed vision, but it served its purpose. It was the sustaining idea which would spur me on through the long hours of preparation, which would compensate for weeks of discomfort, and which would, when the going reached its inevitable nadir, provide a reviving handhold.

I set to work with a new-found will. As ever, the previous year's voyage had suggested improvements that could be made to hone still further *Mingming's* seaworthiness and ease of handling. Having lost my Jordan series drogue off south-west Iceland, I had already spent much of the winter constructing a new one. This involved the patient attachment of eighty-six nylon cloth cones, each a mini-drogue, to the highest quality double braid rope I could find. It was tedious work, mind-numbingly repetitive, but I didn't mind doing it; this was, after all, my ultimate life-saver. Now I had to construct a revised form of stowage for the drogue. To make deployment and, in particular, retrieval and re-stowage quicker and easier, I had decided to store the drogue in the cockpit, rather than down below. I had designed a simple arrangement of removable plywood sides to the redundant cockpit seats, on which the drogue would be stowed. Canvas covers, easily lashed and unlashed, would hold the drogue down.

My kitchen was soon littered with the component parts of this new arrangement: the plywood panels themselves, each one drilled with a series of large holes for lightness and drainage; the timbers that formed the guides into which the panels slotted. Everything soon gleamed with several coats of *Mingming's* trademark Atlantic Grey paint. I hand-sewed the duck-canvas covers, adding a kind of looped bolt-rope that would be used to hold the shock cord lashings. Within a few weekends the whole shebang was constructed and fitted, adding yet another aspect to *Mingming's* single-minded quirkiness.

The idea of rowing ashore and setting foot on Baffin Island still persisted; it had established itself firmly as the guiding objective of this voyage. It was a daft and improbable prospect, but it needed humouring. I ordered a suitable rubber dinghy: not too big, not too heavy, not too expensive. I blew it up and sat in it on the garden lawn. The plastic oars that came with the dinghy were of the poorest quality; I replaced them with a sturdier aluminium pair before setting sail from Plymouth. These toyshop oars were fine, though, for practice. Static on Essex turf, I pulled us along through freezing water. My apple tree solidified to Arctic rock. A narrowing of the eyes transformed my white-painted house to a benign and shiny iceberg. I rowed carefully shorewards, dodging the occasional underwater rock, then jumped out and waded the last few feet to dry land and a triumphant arrival at the ends of the earth.

3

Igor Zaretsky, a man of bold Slavic features and a rumbling *basso profundo* of a voice, lives in Yaroslavl, a provincial town two hundred miles or so to the north-east of Moscow. Igor has three times won All-Russian Championships in his Peterson 25 *Grand.* These championships are sailed on one of the many huge lakes that dot the Russian heartland. Igor wanted to try his hand at ocean sailing, and decided to enter the Jester Challenge.

It is difficult to overstate the many other challenges that Igor had to overcome just to get his yacht to Plymouth. She was loaded onto a road trailer, then pulled by Igor's ageing Soviet-style 4x4 across Russia, Belarus and part of Lithuania, finally arriving at the Russian enclave of Kaliningrad to be launched into the Baltic Sea. This was a journey of nearly a thousand miles, involving a string of difficulties, hold-ups and tense confrontations with border bureaucracies. Igor, helped by his regular crew member Nicolai Ilichev, then had to sail another thousand miles or so, through crowded and challenging waters, to bring *Grand* to Plymouth.

Igor and Nicolai explained all this to me as the Jester Challenge skippers held their Plymouth Gin party aboard Ewen Southby-Tailyour's gaff cutter *Black Velvet.* My Russian was rusty, but gin in moderation is a good lubricant for tongue and brain, and it soon came flowing back.

Crowded aboard *Black Velvet* was the usual eclectic mix

of Jester skippers old and new. Queen Anne's Battery marina was slowly filling up. The new participants were as disparate as their boats. Here was the Swiss sailor and circumnavigator Thomas Jucker, with his voluptuous Lyle Hess cutter *Marta.* Ex-Royal Marine Andy Lane had sailed his mini-Transat *Amadeus* from Bordeaux. Another Russian, Michail Soldatov, had made the voyage from Leningrad in his Albin Vega *Gerda*. Here was yet another circumnavigator, Rory McDougall, with his tiny Wharram catamaran *Cooking Fat.* The South African Gus Davidson had turned up in his self-built twenty-foot Golant Gaffer *Just Right.* It was a constant source of joy and fascination, this unlikely cocktail of design and aspiration and bloody-minded dedication.

Many of the old hands were back too. The effervescent Bill Churchouse was there again aboard his Westerly 22 *Belgean.* So too was John Apps and his UFO 27 *Glayva,* all set to maintain his record as the only finisher in every Jester Challenge. Tony Head and his Twister *Triple Venture* were there, as were Duncan Lougee and his Hustler 31 *Vacquero,* Nigel Stillman and his Kingfisher 30 *Grettal,* and circumnavigator John Margarson, now seriously decked out for ocean racing with his Beneteau Figaro 30 *Fluffy*. The grandfather of the fleet, Roger Fitzgerald, still lean and spry at seventy-three, was back with his Dehler 29 *Ella Trout III.* And of course, there too was Trevor Leek and *Jester*, fresh and shiny in her new livery of dark green.

Twenty-two boats were now in Plymouth ready to start. There was just one latecomer: Alexei Fedoruk and his converted Dragon *Fason.* Alexei was making his way from his hometown of Novgorod, firstly via the inland waterways of north-west Russia, then by sea from St. Petersburg. Late spring ice had delayed his exit from the River Neva locks into the Gulf of Finland.

It was a privilege to be in the company of this raggle-taggle collection of seafarers. In the five years since its inception as a loose idea, the Jester Challenge had somehow developed its own form and persona. Protest, ideology, cult; it was all of these things, and much more besides. Without really trying, without doing very much at all in fact, it had stimulated an enormous following and affection amongst ordinary sailors. At the snootier end of the yachting press there was still some residual hostility towards the presumption, in both meanings of the word, that a skipper could actually be trusted to put to sea without being subject to rules and committees and inspections. But this hostility was waning. The concept had been shown to work. It was clearly here to stay.

I felt a little sad and dislocated to be heading off with a different objective in mind. My voyage would be a longer and more isolated affair with none of the warmth and camaraderie of a Newport welcome. At one point I wondered whether I should change my mind. It was easily done; I had all the appropriate charts aboard; my US visa was still valid. My resolve stayed firm; icebergs exerted a greater attraction than ice-cream parlours.

At ten-thirty on the morning of the start I left Queen Anne's Battery marina under sail. A fair and fresh wind soon had us out to the starting line to the west of Plymouth breakwater. It looked as if for once we would have a decent breeze to get the fleet under way. With a couple of hours of the flood tide still to run, we would need it. An hour before the start the wind died to almost nothing. Light drizzle threatened. *Mingming* drifted back landwards, unable to hold position against the tide. The main body of competitors arrived, intermingled with a mass of spectator yachts, stealing what little wind there was and setting up an awkward slop. We drifted slowly backwards, sometimes following little capricious patches of zephyr from here and there, sometimes deprived of all steerage way. The Brittany ferry arrived, scattering the ghosting fleet. The start time came and went. The tide was due to turn an hour later. The bigger, taller-masted light displacement yachts of the fleet disappeared seawards. The official spectator boat, its upper deck crammed with Jester Challenger friends and relatives, did a close circuit around us, compounding our discomfort. The breeze had headed us almost east. *You're going the wrong way!* yelled John Apps' wife Heather. *America's that way!* It was a good joke, evoking a roar of laughter from the upper deck. I shrugged. *Don't be like that.* My only consolation was that Bill Churchouse and *Belgean* were even further astern.

The spectator boats thinned out. The fleet dispersed seawards. Ewen Southby-Tailyour in *Black Velvet*, starter duties fulfilled, motored past with a final *Good luck!* The tide turned and Bill and I, two old friends enjoying their last moments of proximity, finally headed away from land, pushed on now by a nice little breeze from the south-east. One by one the sails ahead merged into the haze. It was a Sunday afternoon, and the occasional weekender passed the other way, scurrying for home and the working week. Bill and I beat our way past Rame Head in close company. Once clear of the headland we eased sheets and *Mingming* pulled away. I hooked up the self-steering and settled us into our heading for the Lizard.

Freed from steering I wolfed down one of Brenda's home-baked vegetable pasties and followed it up with a banana and a few swigs of water. Now I could relax and sit in the hatchway and watch the receding land, already just a smear of shadow in the silvery murk. It was startling to be so quickly transposed from the rush and roar of a busy city, and from the close press of yachts and fellow men, and to be once more alone with *Mingming's* mutterings as she took up her duties yet again, with the slap and gurgle at her forefoot, that is, and the soft creaking of her blocks, and the grumble of slightly shifting stores as she rolled to the rhythm of each passing swell. For the moment the land was almost gone. *Belgean* was now well astern, no more than a faint imperfection in the sweep of the mist, unseen unless looked for. The world and everything solid, save for the weighty sea that bore us, had evaporated away in just an hour or two. I ducked below for a few moments and wrote up the log, then once more took up my position in the hatchway, heart swelling as we ghosted on through an insubstantial seascape, ocean and sky conjoined in an endless sphere. Dusk came, and then night. The breeze fell away. Up came a near-full moon and by midnight there we lay in glassy immobility, disturbed only by the distant undertone of ships' engines as, just a few miles to our south, the commerce of the world plied its way east and west in unending and inexorable procession.

4

We struggled slowly towards the Lizard, forcing our way west through a mix of light airs and calms. At one point we were pushed in close to Black Head, to the north-east of the reptilian cape, to the land-locked side, that is, and within plain sight of idle ships spread loosely at anchor off the Helford River. A navy helicopter thundered around, its gyrations indecipherable. An oddly-shaped ship, a stubby on-edge carpenter's pencil of a ship, another emissary from our old friend GRIMALDI LINES, passed close by, heading east. Two guillemots dived and chattered almost alongside, their pied markings turned orange by a fiery sunset. I set the light weather jib and towards midnight on our second day, in the faintest of breaths from the north, and helped by the ebb tide and my own efforts at the steering lines, we finally left the Lizard's sweeping light astern.

One down, two to go. It was clear water I was after, and a straight course for the Labrador Sea. The Scilly Isles still barred our way. A merciful and freshening wind, now from the north-east, forced a lowering of the jib, and with the self-steering re-engaged we sped westwards, drawn on by the low loom of the Wolf Rock light fine on our starboard bow. I had settled in to a twenty minute round of cat-napping and watch-keeping, and this was just as well, for before long our course was in a constant tangle with that of a brilliantly illuminated and persistent trawler that was working its way east and west and then back east again right along our track, putting us almost head to head. I kept us well clear with the steering lines, with no adequate means to acknowledge the blinding searchlight that it flashed six times at us in some extemporised code. As a weak dawn relit the world there it was again, the *Kommander Stuart,* come down for a southern interlude from its home port of Leith, and now straining once more west hard under our lee.

On we pressed and were overtaken by yet another newfangled shoebox of a merchant ship, the lettering on its slab-sided and rectangular profile announcing its membership of the WALLENIUS WILHELMSEN line. It puzzled me, this ship, so solidly and strangely rectilinear that it was hard to figure out how anything was loaded or unloaded from it, or how anybody actually steered it, or from where, and impossible to conceive the whereabouts of the crew's accommodation, assuming that it did have a crew and was not controlled remotely by some distant computer, and how, given its extraordinary and uncompromisingly sky-scraping volume, it retained any stability in a big sea.

Three yachts passed us too, no doubt heading back from an excursion to the Scillies, and before long there it was, the last gaggle of islands, fused by our perspective into a single solid mass that belied its devious and insubstantial arrangement. The *Kommander Stuart* made another easterly pass. Thirteen kittiwakes flew north. *Mingming* sped west and by early afternoon the third and final lighthouse, Bishop Rock itself, its unrestrained tumescence somehow at odds with the declining virility of the nation whose proximity it announced, stood tall and clear to the north.

I let us run on another mile or two, then altered course to the north-west. Three hundred degrees magnetic. This would keep us well to the south of Ireland and roughly on track for our long haul to the entrance of the Davis Strait, a run of nearly two thousand nautical miles. There was little need for accuracy at this stage. The first priority was to clear soundings, to escape the shallows of the continental shelf and regain our natural habitat of deep water and long pelagic swells. Once off the Great Sole Bank I intended anyway to push more to the north in search of the more easterly air flows at the polar side of the Atlantic depressions. We would run down our westing between 55°N and 57°N.

Nevertheless this change of course brought the first intimations of freedom. Ahead stretched an imaginary vista of unrelieved ocean; nothing, not one single rock or shoal, now tainted the surface or the under-surface of this great fluid mass, grey sweet mother sea. I was not excited or enervated or overawed or scared or complacent at the prospect of our passage across this alien land. I had been at this long enough to know that what was needed was a dour and persistent application to the task. Our daily position crosses would advance across the spread of my charts with depressing restraint. Whole days would be swallowed up with minimal progress. There was no place here for frothy expectancy or wild notions of a quick and easy voyage. As long as we kept afloat and kept moving, however slowly, and as long as we kept pointing roughly the way we should be pointing, and as long as I could sustain the life and health of my body, then simple logic dictated that we would get where we wanted to go.

As the Bishop Rock lighthouse subsided astern, then, I harboured no delusions about the long and repetitive daily grind that lay ahead. This did not mean that I did not welcome it. The stripped-down austerity of this oceanic life was anything but a trial. It was if anything a liberation, to have life thus reduced to a raw and fundamental series of endlessly repeated tasks: eat, sleep, navigate, watch, write, think. As to the inevitable slowness of our progress across the globe, I had long since concluded that the man who moves quickly has little to gain. The slowcoach sees more, and has more time and inclination to consider what he sees, and may even learn from it. And therein, perhaps, lay the one node of raised expectation that I allowed myself as we sailed out into the Celtic Sea. For more than two months we would weave our patient path across the more remote fastnesses of the North Atlantic. Little by little we would merge into the fabric of that other mode of existence far from land. What surprises did this wilderness hold in store this year? My head seethed with images of bowhead whales and belugas, of auks and orcas and skuas and shearwaters; the hot seed of life that blossoms, infinitely variable and tenacious and uplifting, in the most desultory of corners. It was this, as much as that primary picture of landfall at a distant cape, which drew me on. Each year I knew this life more, and each year I wanted to know it more. Each year it revived me, and thrilled me, and brought me closer to a primal nature now all but lost to the razed and tarmacadamed continents. It was my balm and tonic, addictive, soothing, intriguing, ultimately unfathomable.

For the moment, though, all was desert and disappointment. As we struck far out into the Celtic Sea, in a freshening north-easterly which soon had us reefed down to not much more than a single panel of sail, and which brought with it the first proper rain of the voyage, I noted glumly in my log that all of life had been reduced to the singular: one fulmar, one great skua, one great black-backed gull, one puffin. I may as well have added one man, one boat. Ah well, there was time and distance enough ahead to rediscover some plurality in the world.

5

This will be a long voyage, dear reader, and now I hesitate. How many little wind shifts can I tell you about? How many raisings and lowerings of panels can you stand? How many adjustments of this and that will it take to drive you away from our tale and back to land forever? For the minute by minute minutiae of ship management go on and on and on. There is never any respite, ever, for the ship must be managed, always. The pages of my log record their endless litany of south-south-westerlies and east-north-easterlies and of puffs from all points between, of backings and of veerings, of lovely following breezes and of nasty little headwinds, of calms and of iron-fisted squalls, each bringing its reliefs and its setbacks, and each keeping a resigned skipper stretched on the two-way rack of joy and despondency, for the swirling atmosphere is seldom at rest, and we must somehow force a Euclidean track through every variation of every wind. The vagary of each little breeze forces a response from *Mingming's* mainsail. Up one panel. Down two panels. In a little more. Out a little more. Tension that parrel. Slacken off that line there. Ease sheet. Harden sheet. I am forever playing with the self-steering too, resetting the vane angle to compensate for a gyrating wind and keep our course true. The work is not onerous, often little more than a sleight of hand or a caress or a soft rearrangement, but there is no end to it, and now I face the accretion of all that faithfully annotated detail as, desk-bound once more, I survey the record of it all.

Do I tell it, then, as it really is, or was; or do I apply the censor's pencil and spare you the rude and tiresome bits? Take, for instance, our passage across the Celtic Sea and over the Great Sole Bank and out, at last, into the North Atlantic proper. Here's a morning's worth of log, verbatim:

DAY 5 Thursday 27th May

0115 *The lightest of zephyrs from NNW. We are scarcely progressing at all.*

0400 *Becalmed.*

0600 *A respectable little breeze from SSW gets us trundling in the right direction.*

0625 *A razorbill, just one of course, flies across our stern.*

0800 *I eat breakfast (banana buttie), clean teeth then shave, so feel very regal in the hatch observing the world. A lot of innocuous cloud about, so not sunny. Maybe slightly less chill in the air.*

0840 *Ship 2 nm. off starboard quarter, heading ESE.*

0850 *Ship 2 nm. off starboard quarter, heading ESE, becomes ship 2nm. off starboard beam, heading WNW. These modern ships are so squarely symmetrical it is hard to know which is front and which is back…*

0915 *Wind veered more to WSW, which is a bugger! Can still lay SW Ireland but only by close-hauling. With our current weight progress is slow.*

1000 *Wind veered NW (ugh!) but virtually non-existent. Cannot head NNE so have tacked to go WSW until the breeze sorts itself out.*

1100 *Wind back to SSW but scarcely enough to sail with. I find that the main camcorder is not working with mike – damn.*

Noon Position 50° 25'N 9° 38'W Day's run 49 nm.

No, told thus this is not a riveting tale of derring-do, likely to keep you entranced at every caprice of wind and wave. I will spare you then, dear reader, the worst excesses of an obsessive narrative. For us it will be the light touch, the broad brush and quickly onwards with our tale! But remember that though we may skate merrily along, beneath this glib surface lies a bed of unrelenting activity at the lowest level, the white noise of constant adjustment and readjustment.

It took five days, then, to work our way to the edge of soundings, five days of westerly meandering in a succession of whimsical and insubstantial little winds. High pressure had taken a firm grip on the eastern Atlantic atmosphere. Air moved around in gutless patches, aimlessly. Between each patch the air, and by extension the sea and *Mingming* herself, slumped to immobility. Our daily runs fell to forty miles and less; we were making good less than a knot and a half: three thousand yards an hour, fifty yards a minute, less than a yard a second. We were shuffling our way to Baffin Island; at this rate I would be down to starvation rations long before that distant land hove into view.

I was not in the least disconsolate. Our progress for the moment was slow and indirect, but I knew that over time the balance would be redressed. Twelve thousand miles of voyaging with *Mingming* had produced an average daily run of about sixty-five miles. On a good day we could sail a hundred miles. There was nothing to be concerned about. If anything I was rather pleased at how well *Mingming* had performed, hauling herself to windward with a hundred days' worth of food and water aboard, a substantial burden for her light-boned frame and unaggressive rig. The mild conditions in any case allowed me to settle gently into the round-the-clock routines that by now had become second nature.

I made a silent bet with myself that we would meet a Spanish fishing boat or two as we reached the edge of the continental shelf. Sure enough, at eleven thirty on the morning of the twenty-eighth of May, our sixth day at sea, we passed astern of an Iberian-style trawler straining north along the last line of contour of Europe proper. Another mile or two to the west the sea bed fell away to six or seven hundred feet of depth; just twenty miles further on lay the true pelagic basin, three thousand feet and more below the surface. Within a few minutes a second fishing boat, the *Currana un Celeiro*, bearing a jaunty red hull and the unnecessarily obtuse registration number 3LU3105, came steaming north at a good pace. It crossed our stern and two skippers, myself that is, and a no doubt bemused Pedro or Sancho or whatevero, gazed vacantly into each others' binocular-enhanced eyes.

I had never come this way, or any other way on or off the continental shelf, without this sort of encounter, and it was hard not to impute some responsibility for the poverty of sea life hereabouts to the incessant and largely indiscriminate scourings of these fishermen. They seem to be at it all day, every day, in a non-stop line from Ushant to Rockall. Were there still something a little primitive or homely about what was once considered a noble toil, something that perhaps gave the dwindling fishy shoals at least half a chance and made it an evenly balanced game between hunter and hunted, then it may perhaps seem not so grotesque, but those days are long gone. Offshore fishing is now a branch of industry, requiring the capital of industry, and the return on capital of industry, and driven therefore by an industrial demand for production, production, production, and utilising every electronic and mechanical advance to power that production. The extraction machine steams on, only marginally hindered by the ineffectual controls of ineffectual politicians, and, as has been shown in almost every other major fishery, will steam on until the very last fish is dragged flapping and not screaming from an emptied ocean.

I pushed aside these disturbing thoughts and concentrated instead on the beautiful green and icy hue that had suddenly infused the sea hereabouts. It was a puzzling phenomenon, for the sky was awash with clouds of deep grey; the usual correspondency of colouring between sea and sky had somehow been fractured. I could not deduce the source or cause of this rather ghostly shade of sea water; perhaps it was the result of a bloom of phytoplankton stimulated by the upwelling of the ocean as it pushed into the continental shelf; perhaps it was just a trick of the light.

The wind swung suddenly to the south and blew up hard. The deep grey clouds unleashed a torrent of rain. By evening we were down to just half a panel of sail, enough, with this quartering half-gale, to run gently off to the north-west and away from the last intrusions of the terrestrial world.

6

We ran out into the North Atlantic proper with a half-gale to drive us on and I thought that maybe now we would settle to a consistent wind and long and loping daily runs. This was a vain hope; balmy variability was replaced by a cold and hard-edged round of unsettled weather. The drawn-out calms that soon came sidling along once more brought with them thick folds of misty rain, then more insistent drumming rain that filled my head with thoughts of water.

Water. I had about sixty-five litres aboard, supplemented by five litres of long life milk and a litre and a half of lime juice. At my normal rate of consumption at sea this would last me for about a hundred days, more than enough, on the face of it, for a projected voyage of about eighty days. I knew well enough, though, that there were plenty of circumstances that could prolong this voyage well beyond that length; a dismasting and reliance on some kind of jury rig, for instance. In survival conditions water is much more important than food. No water, no life. Thus far, in all my voyaging, I had never been forced to reduce my already strict ration of water, nor had I bothered to try and supplement my supply from rainwater. With a long and uncertain journey ahead it seemed silly to be drinking from my supply while constant heavy downpours bathed *Mingming* in gallons and gallons of pure and potable liquid.

Eschewing the interview process and the now obligatory

psychometric testing I appointed myself Ship's Collector of Rain. This was a grand title that lent a veneer of importance to my presence aboard *Mingming*. Collecting rain is a skilled and onerous task, key to the well-being of the ship's crew. I soon discovered that it requires a range of specialisations: the ability to assess and analyse rates of precipitation; dexterity in handling bowls and various other containers; a complete understanding of the use of funnels and bottles; a tenacity not given to all. I soon had a selection of rain-catching contraptions lodged around the bridge deck and before long several pages of my note book were filled with sketches for more baroque structures for catching and funnelling the life-giving juice. One even brought the water through the coach roof into a flexible tube with a tap on the end, from which I could drink at will, as from an elongated udder.

My rain-catching abilities improved. The rain came down harder. I was soon creating a healthy swig every fifteen minutes or so and feeling both smug and well-slaked. An afternoon of hard work filled a litre bottle with the purest of water. I concluded that, as an accomplishment, collecting rain is second only to making rain, an art which requires an altogether different order of skill. Having thus been able to supplement my water supply I felt a little easier about being able to last out any eventuality.

By now I was obsessed with all things fluid and my thoughts turned to the greatest fluidity of them all, the ocean on which *Mingming* floated and through which, from time to time, she moved. I thought about the liveliness of this lifeless medium, about its sinuous animal restlessness, and about the incomprehensibility of its composition; two molecules of one gas combined with one molecule of another gas. We were floating on a sea of gas! Things gaseous and things liquid are in effect no more than two sides of the same coin, fluently interchangeable. I thought about those three molecules getting together to transform airy nothingness into something wet and seemingly solid, but then remembered that molecules contain infinitely more space than solid, and that any solidity is in question anyway, the whole lot being no more than electrical charges or quarks or quantums or some such thingies whizzing around, which led to the conjecture that when you get to the heart of it there is precisely nothing there. We were not even floating on a sea of gas, but on a vast ocean of nothingness, or at most rolling around on a bed of infinitesimally detailed electrical activity.

Rain gave way to a thick and damp fog. From time to time I thought I could hear the hum of engines, which unnerved me a little, and persuaded me to break out my little foghorn from its stowage area on a forward shelf. After several anxious false alarms I concluded that I was hearing aeroplanes rather than ships, and that given the modest height of *Mingming's* mast the risk of collision was minimal.

We were reaching that stage towards the end of dirty weather when a slight thinning of the cloud base sometimes allows a brief glimpse, often no more than the vaguest hint, of the sun's pale and filtered orb. This moment of revelation is usually preceded by a sudden lightening as the blanket is momentarily lifted, a lightening that has me scooting to the hatch to search awkwardly for its source, scanning skywards with a contorted neck. I was to learn many times during the course of this voyage that the progression from the first intimations of a clearing sky to the finished article itself could often take days and that, particularly in the sombre atmosphere of the Labrador Sea, the cloud and fog banks could merge so seamlessly that there was never any respite from the overbearing gloom.

On this occasion we were luckier. The weather broke incrementally into a mix of sunshine and fog and light showers. For a while this little meteorological merry-go-round brought a corresponding flourish of bird life. A few gannets appeared. A couple of fulmars attached themselves to our wake. Occasionally a Manx shearwater skittered past on shallow wing beats. A patch of thicker fog came in and we sailed right besides two puffins looking startled and embarrassed, as puffins always do. All in all it was still a meagre tally, but it went a little way towards redeeming a seascape eerily bereft of life.

It was the last day of May, and as evening came the last of the cloud sped off eastwards, leaving us to a sky of limpid blue, a steady breeze fine on the port bow and a long and easy swell. What a release, to be once more in the clear! I sat in the hatchway and watched the sea's skin evolve from grey to green to the deepest indigo as the covers were lifted off the world and the light of endless space flooded once more in.

7

With the wind still well forward of the beam we plugged on and on. Sun turned to mist turned to rain turned to sun as an endless round of short-lived weather poured over the south-west horizon. Nothing was steadfast; neither sky nor wind nor sea. From time to time the wind hauled round to the south and even to the south-east, allowing an easing of the mainsail and a sudden surge in speed. Our daily runs started to aspire to respectability: eighty-five miles, seventy-two miles, eighty-six miles. The line of crosses on my chart probed out into the vast expanse of featureless white. We edged easily northwards; almost too easily as the North Atlantic Current worked on *Mingming*, nudging her away from all things temperate.

On Saturday the fifth of June, our fourteenth day at sea, we reached 55°N and my thoughts turned stolidly westwards. The first phase of our voyage was over. Now was the time to head straight for the coast of Labrador, not much less than two thousand miles to our west. Now was the time to get down to the real business of crossing the great Atlantic Ocean.

I hauled *Mingming* closer to the wind and decided that I needed to get out more. For two weeks I had watched an almost lifeless sea. The emptiness of the ocean had started to get me down. I had not seen a single whale spout. No dolphins had come to play. The bird life so far had been paltry. It seemed that everything living had withdrawn to some other place. I was disappointed, but began to reflect that perhaps the fault was mine. The reason there was absolutely nothing out there was not that there was absolutely nothing out there but that *I was not looking hard enough.* Yes, that was it! I was spending too much time hiding under my blanket, making up for lost sleep I didn't need. Too many hours of potential observation had been wasted making notes for the next Great Work. There may well be nothing out there, but I could only be sure by spending a lot more time looking at this emptiness. I had grown slack as regards my primary purpose of going to sea: to see the sea. I redoubled my resolve. From here on I would spend even more time at the hatch, as much as was possible for every waking hour. If this meant days and days of staring at a barren seascape, so be it. And in any event, what was so bad about that? I had learned over my years of voyaging that the more one looks, the more one sees. I needed to recalibrate my expectations. There is much more to the sea than the creatures that live above and below it. They are the obvious and exciting points of reference, but what about the water itself? Once more my thoughts came back to this great medium, not so much this time to the mystery of its composition, but to the exquisite beauty of its surface. How could I for a second think that there was nothing out there when laid out all around was a magical kaleidoscope of movement and colour?

There had been many times when I had hated every last drop of every single wave from here to the ends of the earth, and no doubt those times would come again, but I resolved for the moment to look with a kinder and more searching eye at the finer detail of the surface of the sea. It took no more than a few seconds' reflection to realise the extent to which I had taken this detail for granted, and grown blind to it. It had become an unseen backdrop to the fleshy, feathery dramas played out above and below. Perhaps I had got it all wrong; the real dramatic content lay at the level and scale of cat's paws and wavelets and foam and bubbles and the interplay of the tiniest of ripples, and at the ever-shifting palette of subtle colouring that accompanied each tiny movement.

Heavy bouts of rain still swept by from time to time, forcing me to raise the folding spray hood and close the hatch, but the second each downpour was over I was back to my observation post, determined now to miss nothing. A pretty little ship, the *Transhawk*, sporting three identical deck cranes and the appropriate lettering TRANSATLANTIC in orangey-gold on her topsides, passed by close to starboard, heading east.

A little later, round about breakfast-time, that is, and just a few hours short of two weeks since leaving Plymouth, a second visitation, so brief and insubstantial as to be almost dreamlike, brought a softer edge to the morning's cold and grey Atlantic pallor. A Leach's petrel came to play around our stern. It is difficult to describe the flight of this extraordinary bird, and the feeling it gives of never quite having been where it just seemed to be, or may possibly have been, and the impression it leaves of something ghost-like, or wraith-like, or, despite its sooty plumage, of not being made of anything truly solid or substantial. This incertitude about where or what it really is derives from a flight that is so quick and elastic, and built around the most supple and rapid changes of direction and altitude, all executed with a fluent grace and a smooth bounciness that seems to imply some underlying *joie de vivre,* that the eye simple cannot track the movement with precision and so gets somehow left behind. To watch a Leach's petrel is always to be looking at something that has just moved on from where you thought it was, leaving no more than a blurred impression.

Although the Leach's petrel shows a little more curiosity

than its slightly smaller and more fluttery cousin the storm petrel, it was rare for one to come so close to *Mingming* during daylight. Often looking aft at night I would sense, rather than see, a twisting and turning against the blacker night that announced a Leach's petrel drawn in by the stern light; there was something bat-like about these silent gyrations in the dark. Now I had one in the full light of day twirling back and forth in our wake, and so close that the rich chocolate brown of its feathering and the slightly lighter barring across its wings, and its white rump and even the fork in its tail were visible in those rare milliseconds when my eye caught up with the movement and produced an almost focused image.

As the day drew on we reaped the first rewards of our northerly trajectory: the wind backed to south-east and then to east-north-east, the first hints that we were moving into the more easterly air flows of these higher latitudes. There was nothing stable or convincing about this change of fortune, though, for the wind was still fickle and sometimes non-existent, but it brought a sudden drop in temperature. I changed out of my cotton sailing trousers into thicker track suit bottoms. My pink woollen blanket was now no longer adequate at night and so for the first time I unrolled my sleeping bag and crawled under it for warmth.

I lay on my pallet, just fifteen inches wide at its narrowest point, its upholstery no more than thin foam now thirty years old, and slept in short stretches of thirty or forty minutes. Between each nap I hauled myself to the hatchway and studied the ocean for any sign of threat. Despite our northerly slant and the shortening nights there was still some density to the blackness of the small hours. *Mingming* ghosted on through the gloom, the brightness and boldness of her navigation lights somehow out of scale with the tiny ship they illuminated. They comforted me though, these beacons of red and green and white, not so much for their protective capacity, which common sense dictated would always be limited, but for the richness and fire-side depth of their glow. It warmed my heart too to think that the emanations from my lanterns were nothing more than sunlight, harnessed and stored and rechanneled and now beaming, by some kind of near-magic, across the midnight waves.

8

As each day passed my diet became more pared and frugal. I had proved by experimentation that I could augment my supply of water if need be, but my store of food was finite. In theory I could always dine on the fruits of the ocean, on anything, that is, from plankton to pilot whales, but I was neither inclined towards nor equipped for that. The blood and guts and scales and the lingering smells of fish caught and butchered on board a small yacht had turned me off fishing at sea many years ago. Besides, it would be a kind of betrayal to start murdering the life I had come to see. I was acutely aware of the double standard I was applying here, for *Mingming's* food barrels were loaded with tins of tuna and salmon and mackerel and pilchards. My justification for this large fish component in my diet – that it was my source of necessary protein, was at best weak and at worst totally hypocritical. On land I eat little fish and no meat. I have not yet managed to adopt a fully vegetarian menu at sea; there is something about the rawness of ocean voyaging that revives the need for flesh.

With such a long and uncertain voyage ahead, and with little or no chance of being able to replenish my supply of food, I became obsessive about making what edible stores I had last as long as possible; every mouthful saved now was a mouthful for later on. My diet was essentially the same as that of previous voyages, but now subjected to a more rigorous rationing. Every evening at six o'clock I prepared a small saucepan of hot food, a three-way mix of tinned fish, tinned vegetables, and rice or pasta or reconstituted mashed potato. My one indulgence was the addition of a splash of sweet chilli sauce to liven up the brew. I ate about half of this straight off, leaving the rest for overnight sustenance if necessary and, more importantly, for the next day's breakfast. This main course was followed by a long-life dessert such as rice pudding or flavoured custard or, from time to time, preserved fruit from a big plastic jar. How much of this I ate depended on the fruit itself. If I had a jar of peaches on the go, for example, then I allowed myself four slices. Prunes were limited to seven only, pineapple squares to ten. Eaten thus, and stored in the cool of the bilge, each jar would last for seven or eight days, with only the slightest hint, towards the end, that the fruit's edible life was running out.

Dinner was rounded off by a portion of Brenda's home-made fruit cake. Two massive and weighty cakes had been cut into full-width slices, each slab then wrapped in foil and packed into large airtight canisters. How easy it would have been to demolish this densely aromatic treat within a few weeks! Each evening I opened the container then in use, unwrapped a slab of cake and breathed in the rich emanations of alcohol and fruit and flour; here was all the warmth of home and kitchen and baking and fun and chatter all compressed and stored in a single concentrate. Resisting every urge to cram my mouth with cake I broke off a tiny portion and ate it slowly and carefully and with a sort of respect for its provenance and for the sustenance, out of all proportion to its negligible size, that it gave to body and spirit. After two or three such mouthfuls, lingered over as if I were savouring a twenty year old single malt whisky, I rewrapped the foil around the slice, resealed the container and returned it to its stowage point under the companionway steps.

I would not eat again properly for twelve hours, until breakfast at six the next morning, that is. The precision of my eating times was deliberate; it gave a structure to the day, and it encouraged my body to settle into a regular rhythm that then allowed for a gradual whittling away at my regime. Were my eating habits haphazard it would have been impossible to monitor and train them. Any pangs of hunger during the long nights were relieved with a few spoonfuls scooped from my pan of food. Occasionally I raided my supply of energy bars – fruit and nuts and cereal coated with yogurt. Like most shop-bought concoctions these were obscenely sweet and cloying and were only eaten as a last resort.

I developed the technique of cooking my evening pan of food with a little more water than on previous voyages. Any extra water added to my main meal came from my daily drinking allowance, and so did not upset my water calculations. The rice and pasta dishes in particular now resembled thick soups. Apart from somehow making the food more appetising, this enabled me to reheat it quickly and evenly, and so have a hot breakfast. As we worked our way north and west, and as each day took us a mite further from the warming influence of the North Atlantic Current, I relished the introduction of a second heated meal into my meagre diet. Having stood for the whole night, allowing the flavours to work and mature and thicken, the morning portion was by far the better. I wolfed down the piping hot spoonfuls of the residual broth, smacking my lips and grunting, and immediately felt more robust and ready for another day's intimacy with a cold ocean.

I found ways of eking out this daily pan of food still further. If the tin of vegetables I had used was a particularly large one, such as ratatouille, I found that I could, with a little self discipline, finish eating breakfast with enough left over to go towards the next night's meal. In this way I could make a larger tin of vegetables, and sometimes a larger tin of fish, last for two days instead of the envisaged one. Each little economy added to the time I could keep the sea, and left me even more relaxed and pleased with myself.

It was during the daytime that I exercised the most stringent control on my eating. The principle here was that a very little, eaten often at a predetermined time, would keep me ticking over. At eight in the morning I allowed myself two squares from the large slabs of fruit and nut chocolate I carried. At ten I was permitted to raid one of my containers of home-made trail mix. This perhaps suggests images of plunging in my hand willy-nilly and bringing out fistfuls of nuts and raisins to cram into the expectant maw. In fact I sat with the container on my knees and daintily, almost prissily, picked out and ate the components of the mix one by one: one Brazil nut, one cashew, one almond, one hazelnut, one walnut, one pecan. That was my nut allocation at each sitting. I had forgotten to buy peanuts. Each nut was sucked and savoured and gently crunched and slowly masticated and finally swallowed as if it were some last rite.

As the weeks passed I became something of a connoisseur of nuts and their *dégustation*. It was soon clear that there is much more to a nut than meets the eye. I first assessed each nut for body and colour, turning it slowly and holding it up to the light to better appreciate its finer points. Brazils and walnuts exhibit the greatest range of visual variations, almonds the least. After a brief assessment of its 'nose', achieved by holding the nut close to a nostril and breathing deeply with a suitably oenological frown, I popped the nut into my mouth and held it in my cheek for a while, allowing the salivary juices to work away at the surface and see what hints of the nuttiness within could be encouraged to float free. Once there was nothing more to be had from this prolonged sucking; once, that is, the surface of the nut had been reduced to an inert blandness, so that I may as well have been sucking a small pebble or a glass marble, and once the lack of progress of the nut towards my stomach was starting to gall me a little, I moved it a fraction inwards so that it was now held between upper and lower molars, ready for the next stage in the process. At this point techniques diverged, depending on the type of nut. Different nuts respond differently to tooth pressure. If held on a vertical axis, for example, and then gently squeezed, an almond can be encouraged to split into two perfect halves. The smoothness of the two interior faces thus exposed can then be appreciated for several minutes by the tip of a probing tongue. The same trick can sometimes be accomplished with a cashew, but more often than not this nut's crescent shape and softer construction lead to an imperfect de-formation. Brazils split aggressively and unpredictably under pressure, producing smaller, hard-edged pebbles. Pecans and walnuts crumble gutlessly but, if the urge to finish them off immediately can be resisted, produce the best finish. I define finish as the propensity of the nut, after several minutes of skilled manoeuvring and pressurising and gentle breaking down within the mouth, to release, in a sudden and unexpected rush, the oils heretofore hidden within its molecular structure. For the second or two before the oils are broken down the mouth fills with sunshine. All that then remains is tasteless fibre, which is quickly swallowed.

Between each nut I picked away at the smaller, more numerous components of the mix: sunflower seeds, raisins, cranberries, tiny cubes of dried apricot. Each morsel was subjected to the same degustatory scrutiny. In effect I was adopting a strategy of slowing down and refining the actual process of eating. By thus concentrating on the minutiae of flavours and textures, the consumption of every mouthful became a sort of drawn out, investigative affair which, over time, distracted me from the question of quantity. In this way I could eat less and still be satisfied.

Lunch, taken at midday as soon as I had written up our position and daily run and made my short report to the Board, was appropriately restrained: a slice and a half of pumpernickel bread topped with butter and thinly sliced cheese, a modestly proportioned home-made flapjack, half an apple. On my previous voyage to Jan Mayen and the East Greenland ice I had run out of apples and was determined this would not happen again; there was nothing I looked forward to more than those few daily mouthfuls of crisp juicy fruit. Prior to leaving Plymouth I had shipped aboard about sixty fresh green apples, a mix of Granny Smiths and Golden Delicious. There was no room for more. To make sure they lasted I halved my normal daily ration. However much I tried, though, I could not impose any discipline on the manner of consuming this daily half-apple. An apple picked at is an apple wasted; the pleasure of an apple is all in a full mouth over-brimming with juice and crunchiness. I ate my daily apple heartily, then, my one indulgence made sweeter by the knowledge that ahead stretched a long afternoon of fasting.

Between midday and dinner time at six I allowed myself just one resuscitative visit to the larder. At four I was permitted to raid the trail mix once more. The rules of engagement were unchanged: one Brazil nut, one cashew, one almond, one hazelnut, one walnut, one pecan, all softened and fleshed out with a few sunflower seeds, raisins, cranberries and tiny cubes of dried apricot.

As six o'clock approached the gnawing in my stomach turned me into something of a clock-watcher. By five-thirty I had usually rummaged in the appropriate food barrel and lined up on the companionway step the components of the meal to come. For half an hour I thought of nothing but the finer points of the imminent feast: of how well, for example, the subtle soda hints of processed peas might set off the oily flesh of smoked mackerel, or of how this time I might just add an extra *soupçon* of chilli sauce to make a really fiery mix of tuna and sweet corn and pasta shells, or of how majestically nuanced was that rare combination of ratatouille and wild Alaskan salmon bound in a bed of tomato and basil rice. Within a short time I was ravenous. At five fifty-five, and not a second before, I lit my little spirit stove and started work. By six on the dot the steaming concoction was ready and the daily round of eating began once more.

9

For nearly three weeks I had been plotting our daily position on Admiralty Chart 4102: Western Approaches to the British Isles. The Sea Lords had given a somewhat liberal interpretation to the term 'approaches'; the chart stretched westwards almost a thousand miles from the coast of Ireland, to slightly beyond 34°W. Sometimes it seemed as if we would never break out of this chart and create some true distance between ourselves and home. Our daily cross was creeping westwards at an average of no more than sixty miles a day, and always there to our east lay the outlines and yellow ochre colouring of the whole of Ireland and most of the British mainland and even a portion of the Brittany and Normandy coastlines. They were a kind of taunt, or reproach, those mustard blotches on the chart, a daily reminder that as yet we had done little more than an extended coastal cruise.

The weather hauled once more to the south-west, blowing up hard and bringing with it thick folds of fog. Sea and sky merged into a thousand tones of grey. Prior to leaving Plymouth I had replaced the rope lines from the self-steering gear to the tiller and now it was only the garish yellow of these lines that gave any relief or contrast to the all-pervading dullness. This new rope was the most expensive pre-stretched line I could find, but the constant work of pulling the tiller one way then the other was still too much for it; the lines became slacker and slacker as they stretched, forcing me to exit the hatch and re-tension the whole set-up. As the voyage progressed I thought more and more about this perennial problem and how I could maintain the correct tension on the steering lines without having to go on deck. This was important; the lines would invariably grow slack after several days of extra hard work in heavy weather, in exactly those conditions, that is, where good steering is critical but where any deck work is the most dangerous.

At just after six in the morning of Friday the eleventh of June, our twentieth day at sea, I was busying myself at the hatch trying to achieve the optimum settings of sail and self-steering. The wind had dropped suddenly, leaving us to a confused sea under the usual mantle of fog. I glanced aft and froze. A patch of fog astern had taken on a darker aspect. I stared at this indistinct shape and as it darkened further and as its edges became less fuzzy and more geometric my worst fears were confirmed. For a second or two this apparition gave a fairytale impression; here was Bluebeard's Castle or maybe Le Mont Saint Michel, soft-edged in the swirling mist, but in no time it was crisply rectangular and devoid of all poetry or romantic nonsense, for here was a ship, a very big ship, bursting its way out of the gloom and straight into the tight circle of our visible world. There was nothing I could do. There was neither the time nor the wind to enable me to take any evasive action. At least the looming black shape was slightly rectangular, with the greater length along the horizontal plane, giving me some hope that I was seeing it from a shallow angle rather than from head on. I had scarcely identified it for what it was when it was on us and past us, just a couple of hundred yards on our starboard beam. I just had time to make out its name, the *Cape Baltic*, as its long hull sped past. Its stern was lost in the fog before I could make out its port of registry. Subsequent research uncovered that the *Cape Baltic* is registered in Singapore, that she is two hundred and eighty nine metres long and forty-five metres wide, that she displaces one hundred and seventy-seven thousand five hundred and thirty-six tons and that she travels at an average speed of fifteen point three knots. I record these statistics here to underline the fact that not only was she was a considerable agglomeration of fast-moving steel, but that at two hundred yards or so from us the ship was less than five times her beam away. I made a quick sketch of her in my log, a rendition easily done, for the seemingly interminable length of her deck was broken by nothing but a series of low hatch covers.

This was the last vessel we would see for thirty-four days. There was something pleasingly appropriate about this; it was only a few hours later that we moved off the Western Approaches chart. With as much ceremony as I could muster in the rapidly deteriorating conditions I folded and stored away this sheet, by now satisfyingly annotated and grubby, not just from three weeks of continuous use on this voyage, but from heavy service three years previously on our passage south from Iceland past Rockall to the Celtic Sea and Plymouth. For the north-west Atlantic I carried a mix of American, Canadian and Danish charts that could take me anywhere from Long Island to Disko Bay. After perusing all of these once more I selected as my next large scale passage chart the Canadian Hydrographic Service Chart 4000: Gulf of Maine to Baffin Bay. Its title alone was enough to inject fresh hope and stimulus into our stuttering project. Now we were getting somewhere! Even the chart itself felt somehow foreign, with its thick soft paper, in white rather than Admiralty cream, and with its coastlines etched in slightly thicker lines, and now representing some features of the land, in particular the icecaps of northern Canada and Greenland,

and with every name and notice repeated in English and French. Although its main purpose was to give an overview of the eastern US and Canadian seaboard, it stretched far enough to the east to encompass Cape Farvel and the full length of the west Greenland coast. For a while I sat with the whole chart spread before me and allowed my eyes once more to range around its full extent. This was the chart that had suggested the shape and possibilities of this voyage, and for which I therefore held a particular affection. It seemed appropriate to revisit it carefully and in its entirety. *Mingming* was now on its eastern margin, literally so, for this and the previous chart did not quite overlap; we had to cross a narrow gap between them, putting us, for a day or so, onto the white surround of the new sheet. In a way this added to the significance of the moment. We were now in uncharted territory, but no more than a few hours from entering, unequivocally, a world that put us into a real navigational relationship with the likes of the Labrador Sea and the Hudson Strait and Cumberland Bay and the Davis Strait itself. I could now measure our distance from southern Greenland with a quick spread of the hand: three hundred and sixty miles.

This transfer to a new chart and all its attendant symbolism, not least that we had now crossed an Atlantic midpoint, was reinvigorating for sure, but only marginally so. Any raised excitement was tempered by a dour knowledge of the realities. We had now entered very dangerous waters. We were now firmly into the epicentre of maximum North Atlantic winds and wave heights. From here on the possibility of meeting stray sea ice or icebergs could not be ruled out. Thus far we had not had to contend with any difficult conditions. I was an old enough hand to know that this could not continue much longer. Even now, as I studied this new chart and ran my finger north-west to the hatched line of the

Arctic Circle and allowed my imagination to run on to the threshold of the North-West Passage, I was aware of a new tone and purpose to the wind lashing the two panels of *Mingming's* sail that were still set. So far our voyage had been something of a relaxed picnic. I sensed that this was about to change. For once I wasn't wrong.

10

Yes, when the storms finally came they came with a vengeance, piling one atop the other like pug-nosed forwards in a rugby maul. They were short-lived, these blows, perhaps twelve hours apiece, but they came one a day for the next three days, howling out of the west and the north-west. Strong winds from dead ahead were nothing new to *Mingming* and me, and with the resigned shrug of old-timers we hunkered down under a single panel of sail, fore-reaching gently into the onslaught of wind and water. There was nothing especially noteworthy about these winds except for their increasing chill which forced me to the next stage of bodily protection as I added thermal long johns and a Guernsey sweater to the mix of layering.

The sea state was a different matter, though; here was a new and distinct entry for the lexicon of waves I had been amassing over the years. A monumental swell had been building from the south-west, independently of the confused weather system in which we now found ourselves. These localised winds now worked on the ambient swell, building it by the hour into something sharper and steeper and more mountainous. The troughs pushed down and down, hollowing out great pits in this incalculable tonnage of shifting water, pits that within a few seconds transformed to cliffs of heart-stopping perpendicularity. I marvelled at this incessant movement and tried to grasp, if just for a second, some concept of the energy required to drive this restlessness, but it was, as ever, beyond me. I could only reduce the calculation to a puny mortal analogy, thinking of the effort required to fill and carry and maybe throw a single bucketful of water, and then considering the composition of one of these advancing monoliths in terms of how many bucketfuls of water might be contained therein but by that point, as I stared at this wild seascape that stretched for a thousand miles east and west, the outlandishness and the impossibility of the whole computation had already overwhelmed me.

What was beyond dispute, and easily comprehended by nothing more demanding than a quick look-see, was that from trough to crest these waves were uniformly bigger than anything *Mingming* and I had thus far encountered. I have always shied away from trying to put precise measurements on wave heights; it is difficult to do this with any hope of real accuracy. There were certainly times, in the sea that was then running, when I felt that the crests were more or less level with *Mingming's* masthead. I could well be wrong; I was, after all, trying to assess the third side of a moving triangle from the least helpful vantage point. If I were to venture a hesitant guess, I would say that these waves were averaging fifteen to twenty feet in amplitude, with the occasional grouping, usually of about three in a row, approaching twenty to twenty-five feet. I had long since drilled into myself the simple fact of physics that for all that it may seem otherwise an ocean wave is not water moving forward but water rising and falling vertically in an infinite series of fluently conjoined columns. It was not always easy to hold this thought in my head as the wave faces reared above us, but time and experience had taught me that they always looked much more threatening than in reality they were, and that any misgivings were principally a product of a rampant imagination combined with a fundamental misconception of the nature of wave movement, and that disciplining myself over and over to think of *Mingming* as occupying no more than a horizontally static patch of water whose only motion was up and down helped defuse the irrational fear that a big sea can create.

Mingming, deliberately kept light and buoyant at bow and stern, ascended and descended the fifteen or twenty or maybe twenty-five feet that constituted the vertical range of each wave with an easy grace. Occasionally a tumbling wave-top hissed past, or gave her a thudding slap on the side. We were close-hauled, clawing as best we could to windward, and so more vulnerable to a breaking wave, but for the moment I was happy enough to take the odd knock; the alternative was to turn tail and run off, losing our hard-earned westing. Having at last got us on to a real foreign-going chart I was loath to be pushed back off it. Somehow we still managed to force our way westwards, but with daily runs now down to thirty, then forty and forty-five miles. Much of that mileage was to north and south as I tried to find the best slant in the shifting winds.

In these conditions my sea-watching was severely curtailed; as a precaution I always sealed the main hatch and the after portlight in the heaviest of weather, transforming *Mingming* into a watertight capsule. I could allow myself no more than a quick horizon scan every twenty or thirty minutes. I was in any case now forced to spend a good part of each day stretched on my bunk, as I had somehow wrenched my lower back. For the best part of a week any movement was slow and painful. I could only reduce the discomfort by lying flat out, stomach uppermost.

With the hatches sealed *Mingming* became an oasis of calm below. Her quietness had in any case been enhanced by the thick foam and carpet with which I had lined her hull. Her sedate rise and fall scarcely registered as I lay there. We were advancing gently, almost surreptitiously, into the oncoming seas, and so were spared the usual slamming of a hard-pressed Bermudan-rigged yacht throwing herself to windward. All in all it was easy enough to forget the extremes of wind and water outside; the only reminders were the occasional lurch, or a bout of drumming of the main halyard on the mast, or a hard slap and a dowsing of the windward deadlights as some green water climbed aboard.

Between each storm the wind fell suddenly, leaving us hobby-horsing in a confused sea. The yard-hauling parrel, the line, that is, that pulls the yard into the mast, and which I had replaced with new, heavier-gauge rope before leaving Plymouth, had chafed badly at its upper end, causing me both concern and disappointment. I had never had this problem before and was at a loss to explain it. For a little while I was also stymied as to what I could do about it. I could not replace or reverse the halyard in these conditions, nor could I leave it as it was. Eventually, when a brief easing of the conditions allowed, I lowered the mainsail and, leaning far out of the hatch, took the offending portion of frayed rope out of service by means of a judiciously placed figure-of-eight knot. It didn't look particularly pretty, but it solved the problem for the time being.

The short-lived ferocity of these three storms did not give rise to any immediate concern; it was clear that *Mingming* could handle these sub-Arctic conditions without too much difficulty. From a wider viewpoint, however, two aspects worried me. Firstly our progress had once more been reduced to well below the average. Despite our high latitude – we were now well into 56°N – winds were still predominantly out of the west. Our objective was still a good thousand miles away. We needed a run of more helpful weather. In the muscular seas that we were now encountering my thoughts turned too to ice. I tried to picture these waves laden with sea ice or bergy bits and of their likely interaction with *Mingming's* modest hull. It was not a pleasant thought. We were still far from any likelihood of serious ice, but I was reminded that the reality, unlike the soft-edged tableaux of my imagination, is cold and hard and unforgiving. If this heavy weather continued unabated I would need to think carefully about how far I could allow us to sail into ice-prone water.

11

And now, dear reader, if you are still with us, despite the cold and the gales and the discomforts that have you aching and shivering in your fireside chair, I must open my heart to you with a confession. Your faithfulness demands that I hide nothing from you, so bend a little closer, and let me whisper softly in your ear: *it was during this stormy period that I felt the first stirrings of an incipient infatuation*. Yes, a sea-going romance, an experience not often given to the solo sailor, unless he or she should fall victim to a sudden excess of *amour-propre*, was in the air. It was not quite love at first sight, but nearly so; it was during the following weeks that this newfound obsession, unexpected, unrequited and therefore pure and innocent and courtly, was to blossom to full-blown adoration.

During the second of those three short gales we were visited by two great shearwaters. They came wheeling in, supremely at ease in the turbulent air, and in a perfectly coordinated display of synchronised aerobatics played follow-my-leader up and down and all around *Mingming*. I had never before seen a great shearwater, but few sea birds are so instantly recognisable. Despite its name, the great shearwater is marginally smaller than its cousin the Cory's shearwater, a bird I knew well from our Azores voyages, but what it lacks in absolute size it makes up for in the beauty of its plumage, and in the athleticism of its flight and, more than anything, in its extraordinary sociability.

I had no idea, as I watched these first two great shearwaters tracing their smooth patterns all about us, sometimes swooping close across *Mingming's* stern with heads turned inquisitively towards us, of the extent to which this bird was to imprint itself into the fabric of our voyage and become one of its defining motifs. Ignorant of the intimacy that was to come, I marvelled at the subtle harmony of the shearwater's coloration: its dark sooty cap and pale throat balanced by a white rump and black tail, its wings and back of the softest chocolate brown flecked with paler striping and patterning, its white under-wing edged with darker feathers, its shapely black bill, long, narrow and, at its outer end, turned downwards to form a sharp hook. The coordinated effect of this arrangement of shades and patterns is one which is subdued in the detail, but striking in the ensemble. In the weeks to come I would never tire of trying to reconcile the softness of the colours with the immediate distinctiveness of the whole. Up close the apparent black of the shearwater's cap, a cap that stretches from the base of its bill to the nape, passing just below the eye and narrowing as it progresses down the back of the neck to eventually merge into the lighter shade of the back, is in fact a deep chocolate brown. The down around the eyes is slightly lighter, a detail that can only ever be seen from very close up, and which gives the bird a hint of a spectacled look. Even the edging of the cap, which from a distance seems to form an absolutely straight line, is in fact quite ragged and uneven. Over time I came to know two birds: the sharply defined bird of distance and the soft-edged and infinitely subtle bird of proximity.

The next day, during the third blow, that is, four great shearwaters soared around us for an hour or so, bound once more in close formation. The weather was too bad for me to sit in the hatchway and follow their spiralling in its entirety;

I tracked their progress as best I could through *Mingming's* tiny portholes. All four birds were identical. The great shearwater, unlike many sea birds, terns and gulls and skuas and gannets, for example, is spared a long period of mucky and indeterminate plumage as it develops to maturity. The sexes too show no obvious differentiation. The great shearwater acquires its beauty from the off, as it were, with no intermediate stages. As I came to know the bird better this instant uniformity seemed appropriate for, as will be seen, its whole existence is one tight-bound social enterprise on a breathtaking scale.

It was two days later, on Tuesday the fifteenth of June, the twenty-fourth day of our voyage, that I started properly to learn something of the great shearwater's extraordinary lifestyle, and that I began to realise that I was witnessing something rarely seen, and that I was therefore somewhat privileged, and that I should be paying serious attention to what was unfolding.

The stormy weather had moved on, leaving us to a failing north-westerly breeze under a clear but slightly hazy sky. Hard use over the previous few days had worn a hole in the canvas of *Mingming's* spray hood; half an hour with needle and palm had it stitched up once again. The canvas had lost its impermeability too, so that in wet weather water dripped through, forcing me to keep the hatch closed. I treated the canvas with a waterproofing spray, but it was inadequate for the job; the next time it rained hard it was only fifteen minutes or so before it started leaking again.

For the moment, though, we were ghosting along in bright sunshine and revelling in the sudden calm. The sea had subsided to a gentle heave. By afternoon we were scarcely moving. A group of thirty or forty birds floated companiably at some distance on our starboard beam, too far away for identification, even with my binoculars. I could only think that they were fulmars, although the tightness and regularity of their spacing seemed unusual; fulmars at rest paddle around in loose and uneven groupings. A little later we passed close by a party of eight similarly arranged birds. They were great shearwaters. As I surveyed the ocean all around, stretching to the horizon in a chequer-work of patches, some glassy, some darkened with the cat's paws of a passing zephyr, I realised that everywhere, in every direction, lay groups of great shearwaters, grounded, as it were, by the calm. A few hundred yards separated each grouping. Some contained seventy or eighty birds. I lost count of these squadrons scattered across every yard of visible seascape.

It is hard to communicate the effect of this sudden and unexpected effusion of life. I had grown accustomed to an almost barren sky and ocean. I still harboured hopes that as we made our way up the Davis Strait, should we get that far, the narrowing seas and enclosing land masses might yield a higher concentration of wildlife. I had not for a second anticipated that here, at this nondescript spot, quite literally in the middle of nowhere, I would stumble across a species living out such a well-ordered lifestyle on such a scale. I still had much to learn about that lifestyle, but as so often before I was immediately struck by two things: first, the supreme adaptation of these birds to their oceanic life; second, and more telling, the complete separation of this life from anything human or even remotely linked to *homo sapiens.* For all that we inhabit the same planet, these birds nonetheless live in a different world. Would, for their sake, that this really were so.

It was not long before the inevitable happened: our course, now to the north-west in the lightest of breezes that had backed to west, had us heading straight for forty or fifty great shearwaters sitting quietly together. We were creeping towards them at an unthreatening pace. I prepared my cameras and held my breath, unsure of what would happen. As we came up to the birds their movement out of our line of direction was almost imperceptible. They paddled gently aside, still holding their tight formation, seemingly unconcerned, and let us pass just a few yards away. Every bird was an exact copy of its neighbour. Every one faced the same way. Their black caps gave them the look of a convention of hanging judges, or would have, were there not such an overall softness about them. They were silent save for a couple of low and guttural croaks. They watched us pass, little *Mingming* and her wide-eyed captain, according us the benefit of the doubt, for there was no lurching away on spread wings, no sudden flight, no hint at all of the slightest alarm or panic. My heart soared at this closeness and at this quiet acceptance and at the indescribable beauty of the birds and of the moment. By then there was no doubt: I was falling in love.

12

As the long northern evening wore on the veil of haze grew thick and yellow and threatening. Despite the near-perfect conditions there was an unmistakable menace in the skeins of high cirrus now fanning out from the western horizon. It looked as if more heavy weather was on the way, but for the moment my attention was elsewhere. The eruption of life above the surface had been matched by one from below. For the first time of the voyage the sea was alive with criss-crossing parties of dolphins and pilot whales. What a transformation! It seemed that everywhere I looked both sea and sky were brimming with hot-bloodedness. What had brought so much life to this seemingly forsaken spot? Was it a chance convergence of random wanderings, our own included, or were we passing through some node in the food chain that defines all habitats? We were not paid much attention; the occasional small band of common dolphins gave us a perfunctory inspection; the pilot whales kept clear.

We ghosted on in a breeze now backing towards the south. As midnight approached, the latent promise of a doom-laden sky moved quickly to fulfilment. Within an hour or two we were down to three panels, and then one panel, and then half a panel. By six the next morning all sail was off; in a rising gale from south-south-east we ran quickly west under the sail bundle alone. Our day of sunny tranquility had been a wondrous and enlightening interlude. Now it was back to the hard grind. This was our fourth storm in not many more days, and as the rain drummed harder on the coach roof, and as *Mingming* was thrown about one way and the other in a manner we had thus far not experienced on this voyage, and as the wind wound itself up into a proper fury, I realised that the first three blows had been a kind of prelude to this, the crowning act of a four-part drama.

It was the configuration of the sea that was the problem. A gale from the south-east, with its attendant wave-trains, was imposing itself over a heavy swell from the south-west; in effect two seas were running at right angles one to the other. Although it was the immediate conditions, the wind and building waves from the south-east, that is, that quickly established the dominant influence on the seascape, the subversive effect of an insistent cross-pulse from the south-west constantly redefined it, breaking the normally easy rhythm of the pelagic wave-set, throwing the seas all skew-whiff, sometimes forcing the tumbling crests sideways, sometimes imposing a sudden and unnatural steepness to a leading face, in short, turning the whole show into a right royal performance.

The barometer, my idle friend whom I had shipped aboard more for company and for old times' sake than from any belief in his usefulness, was roused from his usual torpor and began a descent into his own little atmospherical underworld, finally reaching nine hundred and eighty-four millibars. I did not take this as being an absolute measure; prior to setting sail I had only set the barometer at a rough approximation of the ambient pressure, and in any case he seemed always to operate within a much narrower range than the reality outside, no doubt to save himself work, and with the result that I always assumed that the lows were lower and the highs were higher than the instrument deigned to tell me. Perhaps the canny fellow knew that absolute measurement was less important than the relative speed and direction of movement and so was happy to give me no more than an approximation of these factors, should the mood take him.

There was nothing relative about what was unfolding outside; conditions were fast approaching the extreme end of the spectrum. By nine in the morning I had pulled on sea boots and my full wet weather gear and harness, not for any particular reason other than to be ready to make a quick exit on deck should it be required. The main hatch and after portlight had long since been sealed. I stood in the cabin, face as close as I could keep it to the portlight without misting it up with my breath, and watched and tried to evaluate the movement and height and angles of the waves, and the level of threat they posed, and whether a change of strategy was required, and if so – what?

The principal debate, which raged back and forth for several hours, was whether or not I should launch *Mingming's* Jordan series drogue. There was no doubt that this drogue, a hundred metres or so of the finest double braid line, with eighty-six mini-parachute anchors attached to it, weighted by chain at the after end and set from *Mingming's* stern on a permanently fixed bridle, would neutralise any threat of capsize. I had set the drogue, or at least one similar to it, in survival conditions off south-west Iceland the previous year, and so had experienced firsthand its extraordinary ability to hold *Mingming* stern on to seas of any magnitude, with minimum yaw, and to ride those seas with a supple elasticity.

Despite that I was still reluctant to launch the drogue unless I felt I really had to. I had lost my previous drogue towards the end of that Icelandic storm, because of chafe between the drogue and its bridle. Although I had built a new drogue with a different system of attachment which was in theory chafe-proof, the experience of that loss still weighed on me. We still had thousands of miles of sailing ahead of us; I did not want to risk losing it prematurely, particularly if its deployment was not necessary.

There was too the question of retrieval. As yet I had no idea whether I would be able to haul the drogue back on board in anything but the calmest conditions. I had abandoned the idea of a retrieval line to the after end of the drogue, enabling it to be pulled in backwards and with least resistance, in case it fouled the cones and hampered their operation. A nightmare scenario now played in the back of my mind: *Mingming* adrift for days or weeks with drogue set but unretrievable, waiting for a calm or for me to lose patience and cut it away.

The steepening wave faces forced us skywards into the sometimes alternating, sometimes concurrent brew of rain and fog. Often enough this upwards trajectory took on a lateral component as a cross-sea hit us beam on. *Mingming* shuddered one way then the other, still rising all the while, then began the long descent into the next trough; down, down, for a second or two spared the full blast, into the very pit of the sea. Ah, what a relief it would have been to have stayed down there, safe in the valley from the fury of the surrounding crests! I watched the seascape with two minds, the one revelling in the shape and poetry of the storm, in its power and its fluidity and its sculpted beauty, the other hard at work analysing the mechanics of our interaction with wind and wave, and computing the only odds that mattered: those of our survival.

These odds now had me on the cusp of indecision. It seemed unlikely that we could go much longer without some kind of serious physical threat, yet thus far *Mingming* had shrugged off every assault. Did I wait for some tangible evidence of our vulnerability before launching the drogue, when it may just be too late, or did I disarm the threat right now? The arguments were evenly poised.

At midday our position showed a daily run of nearly ninety miles, much of that achieved with either no wind, or else with no sail set. At one-thirty I climbed out on deck and launched the drogue. It was a simple manoeuvre, given that all that was required was to untie the various lashings and feed the bridle then the line over the stern. It took no more than five minutes. Even as I regained the shelter of the cabin and sealed the hatch behind me I was not convinced that I had made the right decision in deploying it. A short-lived set of particularly steep and colossal waves had raised my pulse somewhat. I suspect too that by then I had been thinking about setting the drogue for so long that I was simply curious to see how well the new stowage system would work, and how effective the drogue would be in such a difficult sea state. The drogue's launch was based as much on a mix of anxiety and curiosity as on rational analysis. There was perhaps nothing too wrong with that, but it left me nonetheless with a nagging doubt and an undercurrent of dissatisfaction; I suspected that I had somehow surrendered a portion the objective guile acquired through so many years of ocean sailing. I will never know whether it was the correct tactic or not, but it was not long before one of my worst fears was realised and our voyage, for the first time, lost its easy equilibrium.

13

Mingming and I were now well beyond anything that could even hint at normality. The terrestrial world may as well have been on another planet, for all the connection that we now had with it. Our universe was no more than a raging sea and a raging sky; here was a pure and glorious mindlessness, dementia on a heroic scale. The logic that drove this world was not the logic of mind but the causality of unrestrained force. Wind and wave are spared the need for thought. They are not driven by an imperative to survive or to adapt or to reproduce or to create works of art or to pay their bills or to make compromises. They are beyond life and the petty obsessions of life. They have no need to care, and they do not care, and it is this freedom from care that gives them their power and their brutality. There is no pleading for intercession with wind and wave. They will do what they will. There is nothing more beautiful than this pure and unregulated action of inanimate nature, and nothing more frightening. It is beautiful because it is untainted by self-awareness or self-interest or even love. It does not know itself and has no need to know itself; it simply is. There are no limits to the possibilities of inanimate nature. Deep down we all know this and are frightened by it. It could well be that the constructs of our lives, with their myriad ruses to give an impression of order and permanence and control, are an attempt to mask this deep-seated fear. We know that there are a million ways in which life as we know it could be sent scuttling to oblivion in a second or two.

Perhaps the lure of the bleak and the stormy is contained within this very fear, or at least by a desire to confront it and to examine it and to test it to its limits. What better place to square up to the fragility and impermanence of life than far out on a deep and frigid ocean? What better metaphor for the shifting, shiftless, shifty nature of our world and our universe than the *moto perpetuo* of wind and wave? Where else can nature be reduced to two such clearly defined and constantly restless elements? Where else can a man be guaranteed to feel so ill at ease, so out of place, so vulnerable, so small, so damned pathetic?

I realised that herein too lay the attraction of making these voyages on more or less the smallest practicable platform. The only interface between the weak but pulsing flesh of my body and these great perturbations of air and water was the thin hull and deck of *Mingming*. In this mindless seascape she was the only fragment that was contrived and rigid. The flatness and hardness of her few square feet of cabin sole were the only dim and fading echoes of the land left far astern. *Mingming* was now all that kept me, or protected me, or perhaps retrained me, from immersion, in every sense of the word, in the timeless and the elemental. She herself was as tiny and as minimised as I knew how to make an ocean-going yacht, and so formed the faintest possible barrier between myself and the heart of a wild nature into which we had now sailed. Being thus as close as I was, I could stroke the tiger, and stare into its eye, and feel its very breath on my cheek, and so know it a little better.

This does not mean that I was without fear. Only a fool, or a child, or a man tired of life would stroke a tiger fearlessly. No, I was afraid all right, but in a dull and deep-seated way. My fear was no more than an undercurrent, a slight tension set far down in my gut, an indistinct and elusive niggling in the furthest reaches of my mind. It is not easy to evaluate one's own fear; irrationality and self-delusion and a certain lack of self-knowledge are more or less guaranteed to impair that process. What was I afraid of, or put differently, what was there to be afraid of? This was the question I asked myself constantly. If I could understand the cause of my fear, then perhaps I could disarm it. If I could banish fear, then I could give myself wholeheartedly to the moment.

I was not afraid of being dead, of that I was certain. Nor was I afraid of dying alone; I have long since accepted that there is no alternative. My only fear around death, and this was a more at the level of apprehension than palpable dread, was the actual process itself: the seconds or minutes or hours during which one knows that the game is up and that there is nothing to be done but to wait for the final closing down of consciousness. That journey from vibrant life to dull extinction can only be taken once, and is therefore unknowable; it cannot be prepared for or visualised or rehearsed. We are told that drowning and hypothermic death, the two principal risks I faced, are gentle affairs. Perhaps at the physical level they are, but I suspected that it was not the bodily suffering of a cold and watery death that irked me, but rather the likely mental torment of those last moments. Would I reach a state of acceptance and serenity, perhaps even of sublime happiness, or would I rage and curse, or would I blubber and moan and void my bowels in a final, cowardly surrender? There was no consolation in the probable brevity of the moment, for surely those seconds would expand and expand and fill a whole lifetime, or become a lifetime in themselves, for by then the past would have no purchase; there would be nothing but the now, and the now has no limit.

These imprecise meanderings provided some comfort, not

so much in their conclusions, but in the palliative effect of my having at least tried to confront my disquiet. By then, though, I had uncovered a more telling aspect of the matter: my real fear was not of dying, but of failing. This fear of failure itself seemed further subdivided. It had its obvious, superficial side: an early bath would provide fuel for the nay-sayers and detractors. *That simple sailor bloke, poor bugger, was too simple by half, ha! ha!* Yes, some good old-fashioned pride was at work here. Unpalatable as it may be to admit, I could not stand the thought becoming an object of controversy or ridicule or, worse still, pity.

More deep-seated than this, though, and of more fundamental importance, was that this voyage, and any future voyages, would be left unfinished, incomplete. As each year had passed and I had added another ocean circuit to my tally, the whole process had taken on a kind of creative imperative of its own. It had not been sought or wilfully imposed, this need to build well-made voyage on well-made voyage. It had simply grown of itself, from the inside out. I was by now starting to discern the shape and texture of this voyaging. It had taken on a life of its own; it was becoming something palpable and, perhaps, in its own small way, meaningful. Without much forethought I had become caught up in kind of aesthetic cycle: build, sail, write. It was supremely satisfying; I had never before felt so fulfilled. Therein lay my most acute fear: my work was not yet finished. I was still too young to die.

14

This brief investigation into the root causes of my fear was soon interrupted by the realities of our physical situation. The series drogue was doing its job, holding us stern on to the advancing crests and defusing their threat, but the ride this time was by no means as supple and elastic as during the previous deployment off south-west Iceland. There, a sizeable but regular sea had brought out all that was best in the drogue as we accelerated then decelerated with a seductive smoothness. The sea we were now encountering was anything but regular, and the insistent cross swell threw in an awkward component to our movement. *Mingming* was effectively locked in beam on to this swell, and so was rolling, sometimes violently, as each pulse came in at right angles to the dominant wave train. The flatter sections under *Mingming's* quarters slammed with each roll, sending a hard-edged shudder throughout her light frame. This lateral movement seemed to rob the drogue of some of its subtlety; we were certainly not being brought up sharply each time its deceleratory force came into play, but the action was less forgiving and therefore less reassuring than previously. *Mingming* seemed not to be making any forward movement through the water, and I wondered whether dispensing with some of the cones on the drogue might soften its performance a little. A consultation of my hand-held GPS showed that we were advancing north-westwards at one and a half knots, progress I put down mainly to a mix of surface drift and current.

I made myself as comfortable as I could on the cabin sole, wedged between the galley and my bunk, my legs draped over the two food barrels lashed at the forward end of the sole. As low down and as centrally placed as I was, I was now at the pivot point of the rolling and so was spared the worst of its violence. As each wave from astern tried to power *Mingming* forward, the drogue and its bridle and its attaching chain-plates and, it seemed, every component part of *Mingming's* entire hull groaned and creaked as the pressure came on and the whole caboodle, a hundred metres long from *Mingming's* bow to the chain weighing down the after end of the drogue, stretched and stretched under the strain. If I were lucky there was a brief moment of weightlessness as my own fleshy hull, unrestrained in its forward movement, lifted gently off the cabin sole before settling down again as *Mingming* and her attachments sagged back on the after face of the now disappearing crest. This fore-and-aft push and pull interacted uncomfortably and unpredictably with the sideways rolling, leading, overall, to a dismayingly anarchic motion, the gist of which I could never quite master.

For four hours we were thrown one way then the other in riotous disorder before the wind suddenly dropped. Within a few minutes it fell to little more than a Force 5 or so, a relative calm given what had preceded it. The barometer was still falling. I tried to figure out the implications. Were we now at the centre of the depression? Was the wind going to wind itself up again, swooping in from another quarter? Or was the lull a signal that the blow was over? I had no way of knowing. What I did know was that the drogue now had us tethered to the ocean, locking us into an inflexible vice. With the drogue deployed I had no control whatsoever over *Mingming*, no choice of tactics for whatever was to come next. All freedom of movement had been surrendered. This passivity was fine in survival conditions, but now that the wind had eased a little it became somehow alarming. I wanted to sail again, to liberate *Mingming* and once more feel her coursing lightly and freely over the waves. The restraint of the drogue now induced a kind of claustrophobia; this leaden immobility and helplessness were suddenly hateful.

For a short while I hesitated, daunted by what I knew I had to do. There was still a massive and confused sea running. It was quite possible that I may have to deploy the drogue again before too long, but for the moment I needed to regain control of *Mingming*. I had no idea whether I had the strength to retrieve the drogue in these conditions, but this lull offered perhaps my only opportunity of trying. Yes, I baulked alright before hauling myself on deck and setting to work, and with good reason. I knew well enough that the job would be hard and dangerous and that it may turn out to be impossible. I ran through it all again, trying to work out if there was any rationale for leaving things as they were, but there was no escaping the simple imperative: the drogue had to come in.

I hauled myself on deck once more, sealed the main hatch behind me and, always keeping my harness attached to two strong-points, worked my way aft to the port quarter. I kneeled down awkwardly on the after deck and stretched out my right hand to grab hold of the bridle. It was bar taut, inflexible as steel. The strain on the line was probably a ton or more. I waited, and for a few seconds, as we came off the back of a crest, there it was: a brief slackness in the line that, if I were quick, might allow me to take in a foot or two of its length. I knew well enough that I would not have the strength to hold the line and the tiny amount I had taken in once the strain came on again. The rope would be ripped out of my hands in a second. If I could take up a little slack I would then have to take a turn around the mooring cleat close to my right knee, allowing me to hold on to my gain. At the next moment of slackness I would have to un-cleat the line, take in the next foot or so of slack, and then re-cleat it before the strain came on again.

It sounds simple in the telling, for this is exactly how I retrieved the drogue, inch by painful inch, but the reality of the hour that followed, once I had started work, is one of many-layered tribulation. I had to be very quick in this take-off-turn, take-in-slack, take-another-turn sequence, very quick indeed, both to make any progress and to keep my fingers from being crushed. Any slack in the line tautened again with vicious speed and absolutely unyielding force; to have a finger trapped between line and cleat would have seen it pulverised in a fraction of a second. I therefore had to haul in whatever length of line I could, using brute force, with two hands, then take a turn around the cleat with a kind of lightning delicacy, always, always keeping my fingers light and nimble and away from any danger zone where they might be trapped. As my strength waned, and as my fingers grew colder and less responsive, and as the blood started to flow from all the inevitable scrapings and scratchings to my skin, it became harder to maintain this fleetness of hand movement. The rhythm of the slackening and tightening of the line was irregular and unpredictable. Sometimes I was seduced by a great loop of slack that suddenly hung down astern of us. *Wow! Look at that! I can maybe get in six or seven feet in one go!* I soon learned that this was where I had to be at my most alert, and where I had to resist the temptation to keep hauling in the drogue without taking that vital turn. Several times I was caught out with two hands still gripping the line, and no holding turn made, and now no possibility of making a holding turn, as the strain came on. Now I had a real problem. If I released the line I would lose all of the drogue I had managed to haul inboard, and would have to start all over again. If I held on tight I risked being pulled over the stern. By now I was lying flat out on the deck, gripping as best as I could with my stomach, my feet hooked over the aft end of the cockpit well. The drogue was of course still doing its job, holding *Mingming* stern on to the monstrous growlers bearing down on us. From time to time a breaking crest washed over me; within a short time seawater had penetrated the collar of my jacket and seeped inside, soaking me to the skin. My over-trousers had long since given up any pretence of being waterproof. Cold, wet and bleeding I sometimes held on to that drogue as if it were my final life-line, straining and groaning, almost tearful, determined not to let all my work be undone, for as I hauled in more and more of the line I knew damn well that I would not have the strength to repeat the exercise. From time to time I had no choice but to let it run through my hands, burning my palms, but still keeping a grip so that I could retrieve what I had lost the second the line slackened again. It seemed to take an age just to get as far as the swivel between the bridle and the drogue-line proper. This was an awkward moment, for now I did not just have rope to deal with, but three hard eye-splices and three half-inch shackles and a huge half-inch swivel, all forming a heavy bundle that of course was not given to being wound around a small mooring cleat. The shackles were all wired with stainless steel wire, the ends of which cut deep into my fingers as I negotiated the bundle over the stern and onto the deck. Then I had to retrieve the twenty-five metres or so of the drogue lead, the length of line preceding the cones themselves. The braking force of the drogue, its designed resistance to forward motion, was still at its maximum. It took another lifetime of shoulder-wrenching work before the first cone broke the surface and gave me some hope that if I stuck to the task I may just succeed.

Yes, it gave me a little hope, to have my numb fingers

around the first of the drogue cones and the tapes that attached it to the line. I now had a chunkier bundle to hold on to, less slippery, marginally less prone to escape my grip. This advantage was more than outweighed, though, by the increased difficulties of taking and releasing a turn around the cleat. The extra overall diameter of the drogue made it harder to pass the line around the small arms of the cleat. The tapes were forever snagging on these arms. The whole process required even more dexterity from hands now burned and shredded and stiff with cold. From time to time I took a turn then allowed myself a minute or two of rest, cradling my head in the crook of my left arm, closing my eyes, allowing the tense and aching muscles of my neck and arms and shoulders a short reprieve. *Mingming* rode to the waves; the waves broke over my supine body; my body shivered with sweat and sea water. I could easily have slept in this hot embrace with a cold maternal sea, but it was not yet the time. Rousing myself I took up the work again. Haul in, take a turn, wait, release the turn and haul. One by one the eighty six cones were dragged back on board. It was only after the first forty or fifty were retrieved and flaked down in the cockpit that I started to feel the first intimations of a declining resistance. Now I could just about hold on to the line once the strain came on; I only needed to take a turn to give myself a rest. More cones came aboard and then, at long, long last, I started to haul in the line hand over hand. This was not a quick and fluent hauling. My shoulder muscles were drained of all but the faintest residue of strength. Groaning and clenching my teeth I dragged the last few cones aboard and then the long tail of the drogue, cone-less and unresisting save for the final length of heavy chain that was soon scraping over the transom into my relieved fingers.

I put a few lashings on the bridle and drogue, to make sure that a rogue sea could not carry the line overboard and enable it to deploy itself unbidden, reset the self-steering pendulum and climbed below. From the safety of the hatch I unlashed the sail bundle, raised a couple of panels of sail and settled us on an approximate course.

I closed the hatch and for fifteen minutes sat motionless on my bunk. For the moment I had neither the will nor the strength to pull off my gear and start drying myself. I would have to strip off completely and change every stitch of clothing. I stared at my hands, now almost unrecognisable. My palms were red-raw. Every finger was swollen and indented with the deep wrinkles of water immersion. Blood ran from a criss-cross of scratches. Worse, three or four knuckles now lacked any skin. Raw flesh oozed blood. Never mind. We were free of the drogue. *Mingming* was sailing once more. Little else mattered.

15

I sat motionless on my bunk and for a little while revived myself with numbers. There was comfort to be found in the strange accretion of statistical trivia. We had now been at sea for six hundred and seven hours, which is thirty-six thousand four hundred and twenty minutes, which is two million one hundred and eighty-five thousand and two hundred seconds. Had I had it in me to savour every millisecond of our voyage I would already have experienced more than twenty-one billion brief nodes of pleasure. Twenty-one billion! Since leaving Plymouth I had drawn breath more than four hundred and thirty-seven thousand times, and until now had not thought about a single one of them. I felt a surge of affection for my bruised and bleeding flesh; here it was, just getting on with the business of keeping itself going, without, as far as I could tell, the slightest reference to myself.

I examined those hands of mine, palms up then palms down, squinting at them in the murky light of the cabin. The red patches were swelling to coin-sized blisters. The ugly wounds to my knuckles recalled the torn finality of road-kill, or would have, were we not still conjoined by all the highways and byways of bodily connection that were now setting up a fine old traffic in throbbing pain. They would need nursing back to wholeness, these hands of mine. I looked more closely. Here still were the residues of past assaults on their integrity: the scar where I had almost sliced off my fingertip in the Tasman Sea; the faint insignia of a south of France car accident; the calcified knuckle of a soccer injury. Here I was, just a few days from my sixty-third birthday, and still this flesh kept coming back and rebuilding itself and reforming itself into hands that were indisputably mine and no one else's.

Using those very same hands and a boathook I retrieved the waterproof bags of clothing stowed out of reach at the after end of the starboard quarter berth. Helped by the labels that listed each bag's contents I extracted a fresh set of clothing: two pairs of thick socks, underpants, thermal long-johns, thermal vest, polo shirt, thin sweater, thick sweater, track suit bottoms, track suit top. I pulled off my sodden layers, protecting my hands as best I could by means of a dainty fingertip grip on each item, then dried myself and slowly dressed again.

Now a little warmer and more comfortable I could attend to the final job. I delved into the bilge locker under my stove and brought out the two plastic containers that housed an assortment of first aid and basic medical stores. With a sail needle I lanced all the blisters and squeezed out any fluid, then set about dressing the knuckle wounds. One by one each patch of gaping flesh was liberally treated with antiseptic cream, then covered with a sterile plaster, then bandaged with gauze. Later I learned to keep this final bandage dry and in place with a further binding of gaffer tape. The treatment and re-dressing of these wounds became a regular ritual for weeks to come; it was vital to keep them clean and sterile and clear of any risk of infection.

I cooked my evening meal as best I could, ate it slowly, then stretched out under my sleeping bag. My body had not known such hard use since my attempt to row *Mingming* out of a north-west Icelandic bay the year before. I lay there, drained and aching, and let my thoughts drift. *Mingming* was still running easily west in a wind that had neither veered nor strengthened. The decision to retrieve the drogue had been the right one, but it was clear that I would have to rethink the question of retrieval. Now was not yet the time. I thought instead about this series of storms that we had been through and their impact on the shape and rhythm of our voyage. It had been a necessary rite of passage, to keep forcing ourselves west through the worst of weather. For the moment I was unsure of our ultimate destination, unsure, that is, whether once in a position to head north up the Davis Strait I would be bold enough to do just that, or whether I might be deterred by the prospect of more heavy weather combined with ice. For now the only imperative was to keep on sailing west; without a good slug of westing nothing could be achieved. The storms too had erected a kind of barrier astern; they had dispelled any illusion that we might have a smooth run back the other way. At some point that gauntlet would have to be run again. It was now evident that we had pushed through to the far side of something, that any easy connection with home had now been severed. Normally I would revel in this distance and this dissolution of any sense of temporal or geographical tie to the world left behind; they were, after all, the prerequisites for the kind of uncompromising solitude that I was seeking. Emptied as I then was, I felt adrift rather than centred, provisionally aimless, for once unsure of myself and uncertain why we were there, rolling on and on in a race to the west. I wrote in my log that I was now sailing on west out of nothing but habit. We had been doing it for weeks; there was nothing else to do; why do anything else? I may as well have queried whether in the final analysis it makes a jot of difference which way a man sails. North, south, east, west; the final destination is one and the same, and not a pretty one at that.

At eleven in the evening a change in *Mingming's* motion

brought me to the hatch. The tiller was flopping about as aimlessly as my thoughts. The self-steering lines were still in place, leading correctly from the tiller to the attachment ring-bolt on the self-steering gear. There was just one problem: the ring-bolt itself was no longer attached to anything. As far as I could make out in the half-light the bolt had sheared. *Damn!* I had no doubt I could conjure up a repair, but I was not yet ready for another trip to the after deck, or for midnight shenanigans with my newly-bandaged hands. I lashed the tiller to allow *Mingming* to lie-to and drift gently to the north-west, then stretched out once more on my bunk. Sleep came for a few hours, but it was a fitful affair. My hands throbbed; every last muscle of my body ached; my lower back complained incessantly. At three-fifteen the next morning, as a weak light started to filter through the fog once more rolling in, I hauled myself on deck, pockets loaded with tools and spares, and fixed the errant bolt. It had not sheared, but somehow unthreaded itself from its restraining nut. It would cause me more trouble, this bolt, but for the moment I soon had it back in place and operational.

The configuration of wind and sea had now reversed itself: a wind from south-west vied with a south-easterly swell. Close-hauled under three panels *Mingming* pressed gamely on whilst I, I took once more to my bunk and fell into a deep and reviving sleep.

16

By noon on Friday the eighteenth of June, our twenty-seventh day at sea, we had reached 56° 30'N 43° 38'W. In broad terms this meant that we had moved a little further north and a lot further west. One aspect of our precise location gave rise to a small rush of pleasure: we were now due south of Cape Farvel. It wasn't much, this change in our longitudinal status, no more than a small handhold that would keep our ascent to the Davis Strait on track, but any handhold was better than none; I had, after all, been scrabbling along for a little while in a less than determinate way. Not only were we now due south of Greenland's southern tip, and therefore on the threshold of the first objective of the voyage – to put ourselves to the west of that ice-laden landmass, we were now just a hundred and eighty miles off the coast.

No, it wasn't much, to have our coordinates thus redefined. It changed nothing in the world. The fog came in as thickly, the winds blew as chill, my fingers throbbed and my back ached and I still allowed myself just one cashew, one almond, one walnut. The great whales kept away and the great shearwaters kept us company and incalculable molecules of water kept us, somehow, afloat. Nothing was different and yet everything had changed because our relationship to it all was no longer what it just had been. For weeks Greenland had lain ahead, distant and nebulous and only possibly attainable. Now it was right there! We were almost jostling each other, shoulder to shoulder! If I kept on and held true to the first principles of this voyage as envisaged on an early spring day I would soon be looking back at Cape Farvel, way back there over the starboard quarter. Yes, if I just kept going, Greenland would soon be *behind* us!

It spurred me on, this thought, and brought me back to the chart. We were four or five days behind schedule, this laggardliness caused by no more than a five mile drop in our anticipated daily average. Whilst it was unlikely that we could ever recapture all of that lost time, I could certainly make inroads into it by taking a shorter route towards Cape Dyer. I revised my original intention of sailing well to the west, almost to the middle of the Davis Strait, before turning north, and decided instead to cut the corner. I would try as best I could to follow the perimeter of the circle I had drawn with a radius of a hundred and eighty miles around Cape Farvel. We could then creep a little closer than planned up the Greenland coast. I drew a second circle, this time of a hundred miles radius, around the next major cape up that coast, Cape Desolation. A line of tangent grazing these two circles laid a perfect course for Cape Dyer, now just seven hundred miles to our north-west.

Yes, it revived my spirits, to have now a line on my chart heading straight to that not-so-distant headland. Just seven hundred miles to Baffin Island! The coast of Labrador was now little more than five hundred miles due west. The names sprinkled sparingly down that barren seaboard were cold and hard and somehow uninviting: Cape White Handkerchief, White Bear Island, Cape Harrigan, Cape Makkovik. The weather too took an increasingly chill turn. Heavy rain penetrated *Mingming's* spray hood and then the seals of the main hatch. Bouts of fog came more often and more thickly. I pulled on a third pair of socks. There was no rhythm to the winds; they came and went haphazardly from all quarters, sometimes leaving us to our own devices and a maddening slop, sometimes driving us happily to the north-west, more often than not blasting sharply from dead ahead and forcing us inside the line, closer to the coast, closer to danger. My back complained at the cold and the hard usage. A party of thirty or so pilot whales, unmoved by fog and rain, shepherded us though the night and I took to singing. I stood in the hatchway and sang to the world. I filled my lungs and for hour after hour sang every song I knew with all the force I could muster. I sang rugby songs and folk songs and sea shanties and songs in French and songs in German and songs in Russian. I sang to the fulmars and I sang to the great shearwaters and I raised my voice to a grand *fortissimo* as a lone puffin circled us then sped off then came back to circle us once more. I sang to the fog and to the sky and to the waves and to the jet planes passing unseen above, drowning their dull drone with an

I don't want to join the aaaaarmy!
I don't want to go to waaaaaar!
I'd rather hang arooooound Picadilly undergroooooound,
Living off the earnings of a high-born laaaady!

The more I sang the more I wanted to sing. Oh, it felt good, to impose myself on this uncaring seascape, to shout at it and to rail at it, to bring out a lifetime of memory and hot-blooded association and sing it straight into the face of an insensible nature. Yes, my life was in those songs. I sang my life. I sang my very heart out. I opened my heart to the waves. I spread my arms wide and threw back my head and sang and sang and sang. And there, out of the deep recesses of an aging brain, it was again:

In South Australia I was boooorn!

Heeeeeave Away! Haaaaaul Away!
South Australia round Cape Hoooorn!
Bound for South Austraaaaalia!

I had not sung those words for forty years. I remembered my shipmates. I remembered how we had clung together and yelled those self-same words to ward off the fear of a cold and imminent death. I remembered that icy water and trembled now as I blasted those long and comforting vowels into the silent mist. Yes, I trembled and my eyes moistened, for I was still here, after all, still searching these waves, still singing at them, still somehow going strong. Adrift in a sea of silver I asserted my life, my being alive, to the unhearing elements.

On and on I sang, and as I sang I felt a growing heat and defiance and courage. My chest swelled. My blood pumped harder. I was no longer tip-toeing through this alien world, no longer skulking along with head down. I had declared myself brazenly, with the loudest voice I could drag from the depths of my lungs. *Here is my flesh! Here is my blood! Here is my one voice!* What more can a man do than shout to the sky that he is alive?

I announced my life to the Labrador Sea and to the winds that swept it. The sea and the winds said nothing in reply. They did not hear. They did not care.

I felt nonetheless a little braver and set my heart firmly on sailing on to the far north. The Arctic Circle was now little more than a hand's span away on my chart. Surely we could force our way across those last few hundred miles. I thought that it was only ice that could stop us. I was wrong. I sang to the world, but I did not charm it. No, I did not subdue the elements with my song, or earn free passage, or any kind of privilege. The sea and the winds make no exceptions; that I was soon to learn.

17

I am now tempted, faithful reader, to rush forward with our tale, to race on pell-mell to those few seconds that signified the end of our outward voyaging. We are now so close to that moment, and it is all that I can think of. The picture that I must soon paint stretches wall to wall in my mind's eye, dominating that inner scene, pushing aside the plodding minutiae of the days that preceded it. It would be so easy to leap on to that defining tableau, but I must not rush; I must hold back, not better to enjoy this imminent climax, for there is not much of the ecstatic to be found therein, but to stay faithful to the rhythm of our voyage.

Let us pause, then, and take stock. We had now crossed the worst waters of the North Atlantic. We had skirted around the southern tip of Greenland. We were now comfortably to the west of the Greenland coast and into the southern reaches of the Davis Strait. We had been at sea for more than a month and sailed well over two thousand miles. But still, but still, as we forced a passage to the north, every mile came grudgingly. There was simply no bounty to be had. Our daily runs subsided once more to paltry levels as the winds fell away, leaving us languishing in an ocean drained of all colour. Thirty-three miles in twenty-four hours, much of that due to the north-going current, slumped, on my birthday, to a mere twenty-four miles. One mile an hour! Poor *Mingming* could scarcely raise a single bubble from an inert sea. The mists came in and held us tight, mocking our immobility. Three long-tailed skuas, marauding elegantly, swooped and bounced around us in tight formation. I opened my birthday cards and the little packages of welcome treats: chocolaty, chewy things, and Fortnum and Mason lemon biscuits, light as air, sharply evanescent. I read every word on all of the packaging, then re-read them and read them once again, and resolved to ration out every mouthful and prolong the future pleasures. Later that day the murk evaporated and we lay there in a world transformed to the crispest of blues above and below. For a while there was just the slightest hint of warmth from a sun now unveiled and ranging with lazy ease across the northern skyline. I sat in the hatchway, caught up in the beauty of the moment, but knowing that we really must be getting on. This sub-Arctic brilliance was all very well, and this near-stasis on a softly heaving swell was not without its metaphysical charm, but I could not contain my frustration. Even the extraordinary bi-partite scene that developed after midnight was not enough to soothe my impatience; a full moon pushed up low on the port quarter, a huge brilliant blinding orb, round and rotund and searingly white, while ahead, a sun now hidden, but only just, behind the northern ends of the globe infused the night sky with a half-circle of orangey fireside glow. I had never before felt so intensely a sense of orbits and planetary interactions as that aroused by this strange and short-lived arrangement of sun and moon and earth, now aligned as neatly as in a life-sized orrery, and rendered vivid by this startling interplay of black and white and golden red. Yes, it was a breathless moment, but we needed to be getting on; time, or at any rate its sneaky counterpart, the illusion of time, was running out.

Another year of my life had dropped astern, never to be retrieved, and so it was scarcely surprising, this sudden sensitivity to the passage of each minute and each hour and each day. For a moment or two I wished I could escape the tyranny of the clock and exist in a timeless and beneficent now, in the endless present inhabited by the sea birds and the whales and the fishes, where thought is no more than instinct, and awareness of self an unnecessary conceit, but there was no avoiding the trap: to lose time one must also lose oneself. To live outside of time may be a fine thing, but it presupposes the absence of mind, and is therefore a state that can never be known or appreciated. I sat in the hatchway, sixty-three years now behind me, intensely mindful of moon and sun and earth, fully conscious of stars and galaxies and unthinkable intergalactic distances, painfully aware of my own smallness in this grand arrangement, sad at the finiteness of my own span of time, but happy without measure that all this was known to me. Yes, I had not a shred of doubt; this knowledge and awareness and attendant joy and despair were a fair enough exchange for the constant ticking of an implacable timepiece.

18

It crept up gently, the final storm of our outward passage. At seven the next morning, under an unblemished sky, the faintest of zephyrs stirred *Mingming* from her torpor. It was scarcely perceptible, this movement of air, but it was something rather than nothing, and it came from the south-south-west and so had the makings of a fair wind. I sat in the hatchway and willed the breeze on, and by seven-thirty there was no doubt about it: *Mingming* was once more under way. Finely patterned ripples, no more than the tiniest of undulations, emanated out from bow and quarter. From time to time the interaction of hull and sea and air created a bubble or two, incontrovertible signs of forward movement, and my favoured measure of velocity. I hung over the side of the hatch and watched the increasing flow of frothy spheres alongside and listened out for the true sound of sailing and meaningful advance: the slap and gurgle at the bow. By eight we were holding course to the north-west, over-riding a swell from that same quarter. Impatient to be getting on, I thought about going forward to un-gasket the light-weather jib. The jibs had lain trussed up on the foredeck since the Western Approaches and I wanted if possible to leave them thus and complete the voyage without them; their occasional usefulness was in equal measure to their capacity to disturb the harmonious simplicity of our sailing. I held off and was soon justified in so doing; within a short time we were prancing along under full mainsail with a perfect beam wind.

Oh, if only that tableau had lasted! If only we could have held that pose and loped on and on in that happy conjunction of wind and sky and sea and sail! If only, if only! By eleven I was forced to lower a panel of the mainsail to keep *Mingming* balanced in a breeze that already hinted of what was to come, not so much by its strength but by its moaning consistency. Yes, within an hour or two our lovely little zephyr had become a nasty moaner. I had met moaners before: off the Dogger Bank and off Iceland and off the Faroes. A moaner is just that – a wind that by dint of absolute regularity of air flow sets up a low and moaning vibration. It rings in the rigging and in the hull and in your head, and it presages nothing good. Within a short time we had lost the sun as high cloud fanned out from the north-west horizon. By two in the afternoon we were down to three panels and the moaning had raised itself a semitone or two. By three we were down to two panels. At three-thirty the wind backed suddenly to south-south-east, an ideal quarter for us to run off to the north-west. By four we had just one panel set and I stared balefully to the west; massing on that horizon was an agglomeration of the blackest cloud I could ever remember seeing. At first I thought it must be caused by a provisional trick of the light, for here was night-time transported *en masse* into the very heart of day. It had no texture, this blackness; it was the infinite black of a starless night. I stared into the deep core of this blackness and thought *bloody hell!* By six-thirty those ebony skies were on us, releasing floods of solid rain. By seven-thirty all sail was off and the bundle lashed down. By nine the moaner was starting to reinvent itself as a screamer, its ambient regularity interposed with high-pitched and withering gusts, and by midnight we were racing along under bare poles, driven on by a full sub-Arctic gale.

Black cloud had long since fused into black night and so we ran on into the very heart of darkness. *Mingming* skipped easily through the building seas; with the wind fine on the port quarter she was at her happiest. I squeezed myself into my sleeping bag and dozed on and off. There was little else to do. The self-steering was set and the hatch and portlight sealed. Doubly cocooned I saw out the brief night.

I had grown accustomed to the rhythm of short-lived blows. A slight lifting of the barometer, combined at first light with a hint of blue sky to the west, deceived me comprehensively. *This'll soon be over.* I convinced myself that the gusts, the strength and duration of which were easily measurable by the length and intensity of each bout of rattling of the main halyard against the mast, were growing less severe and less regular. I watched the waves bearing down from astern and soon had myself believing that the crests were not rolling forward so aggressively. In short, I saw and heard what I wanted to see and hear.

After one major false start the skies did in fact clear, but by mid morning I was no longer deluding myself. I started to suspect the reality: that we were in for a long blow, and that it was going to get worse before the day was out.

Yes, those great masses of coal-black cloud sped off to the east, leaving us to a sky of the most pellucid icy blue and the hard-edged light of a piercing sun, and it was then that the wind really got going. There was nothing now above or below to impede that blast; the field was absolutely clear for it to do its worst. It came in fresh and uninhibited and well-puffed out with a magnificent *joie-de-vivre,* this new wind. It thudded down with a malignant, open-armed, hail-fellow-well-met gaiety, coursing along in screaming toothy gusts that shook the heart out of poor old *Mingming.* It took hold of her mast in both its meaty palms and fair rattled it out of its partners, setting *Mingming* all a-shiver to the very ends of her keels. I had never known a wind like it. Here was a wind that by its sheer force of character made itself known to the deepest recesses of *Mingming's* interior; every last can and bolt and knife and fork and match and plate jumped and quivered as those gusts came in. *Mingming* became a great Aeolian harp, a sounding board, a tight-stretched drum, cymbal, maracas, castanets, bassoon and wailing violin as that wind bashed out its demonic improvisation on her cringing structure. Nor did this wind tire of its little game; it went on and on and on, relentlessly. No, this was not a scurrying, localised fellow, quickly come and gone. This perturbation of the atmosphere was built on a grand scale. Centre-stage under the brilliant spotlight of an incandescent sun, our wind swelled with self-importance and settled in for the mother of all performances.

That day, Friday the twenty-fifth of June, our thirty-fourth day at sea, was not without its compensations. Our noon-to-noon run, during which sixteen hours or so had been spent under bare poles, was up to eighty-five miles, all of it in the right direction. More importantly we had, at last, crossed 60°N. By midday we were little more than three hundred and thirty miles from the Arctic Circle.

We were racing towards Cape Dyer, but two things troubled me. Firstly there was the growing possibility of meeting ice; not sea ice, but a stray berg. The thought of being borne down onto the windward side of an ice-mountain, in these conditions, was enough to unsettle a man's bowels. Therein lay the second, more immediate, problem: I desperately needed to use the toilet bucket but was unsure whether I could complete the whole manoeuvre without a nasty mishap. I could retrieve the bucket from its stowage spot in the cockpit well; a line was permanently attached to its handle for that. A well-timed second or two should suffice to dunk it over the side for some water. Having once more sealed the hatch, I could probably wedge myself in securely enough to relieve myself, although this was not guaranteed; *Mingming's* motion was becoming more wild and unpredictable by the minute. It was the final part of the process that worried me: the lifting of a well-loaded bucket above head height to work it through the narrow hatch. This was a two-handed job. Any sudden lurch or roll could have an unpleasant outcome. For an hour or two I resisted my bodily demands, but in the end it was no good: I had to get on with it. I had by now been through this process in *Mingming* well over two hundred times, and all of that practice and experience was brought to bear. This was truly an Olympic test in the sport of pelagic toilet procedures. I had never before applied so much grit and concentration to the task. Sheer necessity, combined with terror at the prospect of anointing myself with my own effluent, brought out the very best in my waning athletic skills. In a performance of rare artistry that would have had any panel of even the most curmudgeonly judges reaching for their 10/10 placards and that would have brought roars of approval from an enthralled spectatorship, I handled that bucket like a true master, with deft and well-drilled movements, maintaining always the most exquisite balance and body outline, with unmatched aesthetic poise and easy grace, and, having finished the basic task at hand, worked it unerringly upwards and back through the hatch. It was only then that, to use the vernacular, the wheels came off. Hampered somewhat by the sail bundle lashed along the leeward cabin top, and perhaps prematurely self-congratulatory at my medal-winning performance, I completely mistimed the final fling overboard and deposited the whole lot roundly on *Mingming's* side deck. *Tough,* I thought, throwing the bucket back into the cockpit and sealing myself once more below as rapidly as I could. Sea water climbing regularly aboard would soon scour the deck clean.

Throughout the afternoon, an afternoon elongated well into the evening as the sun described its shallow halo around the frozen pate of the earth, I studied the unfolding storm in all its detail. Peering through *Mingming's* tiny portholes I watched the interplay of air and sea, and learned to read the language of the patterning stamped on the wave faces by the press of wind. They came and went in a second, these filigrees, setting up a momentary relief of extraordinary and regular complexity across swathes of ocean, only to be replaced by a new variant before the first had scarcely registered. In essence they were no more than brief arrangements of cat's paws, these patterns, but cat's paws magnified by the strength of the gusts into huge scalloped dinner plates, or a kind of overlay of giant fish scales, heavily rutted and deeply imprinted into the water surface, but scudding in a flash across the surface as each gust whooshed past.

It was the brilliant light that, this time, made all the difference, for every least component of this vibrant sculpting was illuminated in startling clarity, pitting the surface with a million miniature peaks and shadowed troughs. The sea was an accretion of wave on wave on wave; there was a whole hierarchy here, and for once I concentrated on the most humble end of this hierarchy, the tiniest and most short-lived waves that briefly graced the turbulence on waves that themselves were no more than undulations on waves that rose and fell on the backs of what might be called the real waves, the great mountains rising and falling all around. It was easy to overlook these tiny scurrying wavelets, no more than inch-high curved ridges, that came and went with every squall, but a moment's reflection suggested that it was these waves that were at the generative end of the spectrum. This was where it all started. The cumbersome monster waves were the result, not the cause. The grand perturbation of the sea surface started at the level of the cat's paw. I watched the surface patterning with a greater respect, knowing too that it was here that I would read the first signs of an eventual relenting of the sea state.

For the moment there was no sign of the least let-up. On the contrary, as the day wore on, the pitting of the surface grew deeper and more angular, an impression exacerbated by the lower angle of the sunlight, and the gusts set up a furious non-stop shaking of the mast and everything associated with it.

I did not once consider setting the series drogue. *Mingming* ran on steadily, light and free, seemingly unthreatened by what was now a glorious following sea. My hands anyway were still far from healed and unfit for heavy work except in case of the direst need.

Since 59°N we had left behind the last of the great shearwaters. Our fulmar escort had dwindled to a token bodyguard. I stared out of the portholes and caught a brief glimpse of a guillemot, fat and somehow incongruous, whirring past. For no apparent reason I pulled out my little radio from its stowage spot on a forward shelf. I had not used it for the whole of the voyage so far. I switched it on and scrolled through every frequency on every wave-length. I extended the aerial and turned and twisted the radio as I went. I held it close to my ear. I turned the volume right up. My sole reward was the endless sizzling of white noise. Not a single syllable of human speech came through the airwaves. I realised that I was searching not for comfort but for something to replace, if only for a few seconds, the incessant clattering of the mast and the halyards. I wanted a momentary distraction from the screaming of the wind. Nothing doing. I lay down on my bunk, hunkering down against the leeward side of the hull. Sleep was impossible. I closed my eyes and listened to my ship and to the wind and to the hiss-hiss-hiss of the sea.

19

Just after midnight I took to the air. Over the years I have engaged in many a short flight across *Mingming's* cabin, and now all that practice brought me to the pinnacle of aeronautic excellence. Without recourse to mechanical propulsion or the least aerodynamic styling I lifted myself off my bunk, on which I had been laying face downwards, performed a perfectly executed one hundred and eighty degree roll, held my inverted position, arms and legs all akimbo, then flew with precision across the few feet that separated bunk from chart table. It was a fine piece of levitation, caused by a rogue wave that had caught *Mingming* on the wrong quarter, gybing her on to the other tack and putting me on the uphill side of the hull before rolling *Mingming* on to her beam ends and flipping me neatly off my bunk.

Only half awake, I was well into my flight path before I could fully appreciate the sensation of floating free. What a wonderful feeling it was, to be momentarily released from the tyranny of mass and gravity, and to arc like a bird across *Mingming's* air space! To be rid of this pudding flesh and bone! To fly through the air! I could have zoomed out through the hatch, arms outstretched, and swooped and wheeled and sheared the wave-tops like a bird of the ocean! Instead I crashed to earth, so to speak, spread-eagling myself awkwardly across the angular protrusions of the lee-side joinery. For a moment I lay across this mountainous terrain, emitting a pained *aaaargh* at the wrenching of my already tender back, and then, as *Mingming* righted herself, slid down in disarray onto the cabin sole. I slowly re-gathered the component parts of body and limbs into a workable arrangement and pulled myself to a sitting position on my bunk. *Mingming's* cabin had achieved its usual post-knockdown anarchy, and for a moment or two I half-heartedly pushed bags and blankets and coils of rope and food containers back towards their usual haunts, all the while collecting my thoughts.

The priority was to get *Mingming* back on track. She was laying beam on to the seas, all her settings arse-about and ineffective. I would have to disconnect the self steering and gybe her back onto the correct tack using the steering lines. I opened the hatch and stretched out my right arm to grab a steering line. A loud and hollow *crack*, a *crack* that was echoed by a sudden discomfort under my right armpit as two ends of fractured and displaced bone regained their rightful alignment, a *crack* that administered the last rights over any hope of reaching Cape Dyer, Baffin Island, in short the mother of all bloody *cracks,* stopped me in mid-movement. *Oh no!* Somehow, during that heavy landing, I had broken a rib.

I held that unlikely pose, arm half-extended as I stood in the open hatch and leaned out into the unrelenting gale. In those few moments our voyage was redefined. It was no longer about reaching the Arctic Circle to the west of Greenland, nor about fanciful runs ashore in icy coves. I had never broken a rib before and had no idea of the extent to which it may or may not impede me, but I knew immediately that I could not continue on north; to sail on into the ice while physically hampered was a risk too far. From here on there was only one imperative: to bring myself and *Mingming* safely back to Plymouth.

I completed the manoeuvre, now using my right arm with a tentative respect, and settled *Mingming* back on course. For the moment there was no choice but to keep running to the north-west. As soon as the gale eased we would have to turn for home.

I sat down on my bunk, transformed by that single *crack* from able-bodied seaman to invalid, and slowly reset all my mental levers. My right rib-cage ached dully, raising questions. Will it get worse? *No idea.* Will I have to endure weeks of extreme pain? *Don't ask me.* How difficult will it be to raise and lower the mainsail? *Haven't a clue.* Will I be able to pull myself in and out of the hatch? *Search me.* Will I be able to sleep? *Don't know.*

I realised that as of that very moment I was starting a new kind of voyage; that I was going to have to devise a different system for handling myself and *Mingming.* One thing was clear: *Mingming's* ease of management was really going to be put to the test. What was to an extent a conceptual conceit – simple sailing, that is – was now going to face a stark physical examination. With a damaged body I was going to have to sail *Mingming* over two thousand miles across the higher latitudes of the North Atlantic. There was nothing in the least theoretical about that little prospect.

The short night turned to day and the wind screamed on and on. The halyards clattered incessantly against a mast that itself juddered and jarred with each mighty gust. After thirty-six hours the noise and constant vibration had penetrated to the very marrow of my bones; I could feel the quivering and oscillation of every last cell of my broken flesh.

At seven I looked forward and groaned. The sail bag that held *Mingming's* two jibs had partially escaped its lashings and found its way over the side. Each time *Mingming* pitched forward the bag was dunking itself into the sea, filling itself with water and threatening to carry away. Those damn jibs!

That damn sail bag! They caused me nothing but trouble! Well, there was nothing for it. Many of the questions I had been asking myself were about to be answered. I was going to have to try and go forward to retrieve and re-lash the bag. It was hard to imagine a sterner test. The seas had built to a boiling cauldron, streaked and monumental; out there it was icy cold too. I had little doubt that if I could haul myself to the foredeck and back, I could sail *Mingming* back to Plymouth.

Well, I made that little journey: fifteen feet there, fifteen feet back. It was painful, yes, especially the difficult moments of stretch and balance as I exited and re-entered the hatch. It was slow too, as I shuffled and crawled a few inches at a time, every movement planned and deliberate. My fingers were soon frozen, but none of the discomforts bothered me. What mattered was that I could still reach, under the worst conditions imaginable, the far ends of my ship. I could still find the means to haul the water-filled bag back on board and re-do its lashings.

I settled in below and slowly pulled off my sea boots and wet weather gear. As long as I kept my right arm close in to my side the pain was little more than a dull undercurrent. What the fracture did not like was any stretching out of my right arm. I rearranged the stowage of my navigational equipment, pencils and dividers and the like, kept on a shelf above the chart table, so that I could reach them with my left hand. Using a new repertoire of movements I made a drink of hot bouillon. My matches, once struck, were hard to keep alight, and I realised that two days of confinement in a sealed cabin had depleted the oxygen level.

As midday approached there was no doubt about it: the storm was coming off. Lengthening patches of golden silence interposed into the wailing and clanking. Fewer gusts set *Mingming* shuddering. I was wary nonetheless: wary of disappointment, wary of making premature manoeuvres that would have to be undone.

My mental orientation had reversed. I was now thinking about the best route home and how to exploit the likely winds and currents. Our following wind was now a head wind; as soon as it was possible I would have to harden up and face it. I waited, and listened to the easing of the wind, and hugged my arms tight around myself.

20

At noon, local time, on Saturday the twenty-sixth of June, after thirty-four days at sea, we reached the limit of our outward trajectory: 60° 42'N 53° 29'W. We were one hundred and sixty five miles due west of Cape Desolation and just under four hundred miles short of Cape Dyer, Baffin Island. The wind was slowly easing. I opened the hatch and, mainly using my left hand, unlashed the sail bundle and raised the first panel of the mainsail. Cold rain was falling, and I suspected that we were crossing into the Labrador Current, the south-going stream that could, if I were prepared to run the heightened risk of ice bergs, help us quickly back to lower latitudes. It was not my intention to retrace our outward track. The priority now was to head south, or at most south-south-east, and to get us to 50°N, the latitude of Scilly Isles. Here, with luck, we should pick up a mix of westerly winds and a predominantly east-going current. We could then run down our easting more or less straight across the Atlantic, avoiding the stormy node to the immediate south-east of Greenland. For the moment all we could do was fore-reach slowly to the south-west and wait for conditions to change.

At four that afternoon I had my first lesson in the reality of a broken rib: without thinking I sneezed. *Aaaaaargh!* My right side exploded. The top of my head blew off. Within a second or two I had broken into a cold sweat. I came close to vomiting and thought that I was going to pass out. For several minutes I sat with my head in my hands and nursed myself back to normality. *Bloody hell!* I was shocked at the severity of the whole thing. A new commandment wrote itself in large letters at the back of my head: THOU SHALT NOT SNEEZE! But how could I avoid sneezing in the constantly damp and chilly ambience of the Labrador Sea? I didn't know, but I determined then and there to find out.

At five-thirty I raised another panel of sail. This time my movements were even more hesitant and considered: my right side was still smarting from the after-effects of the sneeze. Nevertheless I now had two panels up. Another panel or two would give enough of a jury rig to bring us home. I made some quick calculations. Notionally I had a maximum of forty-five days in which to get back to Plymouth. To achieve that I needed to average only forty-four miles a day. I had enough time, and enough food and water, to make the voyage home within my allotted time.

I felt a little easier; in fact I perked up considerably. On the face of it this lift in my spirits made little sense. Our voyage had been turned on its head. My original goal was now beyond reach. We were adrift, as it were, in less than hospitable waters; the entrance to the Hudson Strait lay just a few hundred miles to our west. I was injured and, from time to time, in severe pain. Ahead lay well over two thousand miles of sailing. Yet here was a situation that could only bring a smile to my face. Now I had something to bite on to, something to get my blood tingling. Our voyage thus far had been a humdrum, nondescript affair, neither quite one thing nor the other. Yes, we had experienced the usual run of calms and storms and little alarums and emergencies, but nothing outside the norm. For over a month I had pressed on to the north-west with admirable diligence and scant reward. It may seem a little perverse, but for the first time I felt a deep-seated, visceral engagement with the voyage. Thus far I had been skating along on the surface, perhaps too habituated to *Mingming's* ease of management and to her almost faultless sea-keeping. Together, over our five voyages, we had covered about fourteen thousand ocean miles. Perhaps I had grown too comfortable.

Here now was a new and unexpected challenge, something to wake me from the slight air of torpor that had started to infuse itself into the proceedings. Here was something that would require a different level of management of self and ship. From here on I could take nothing for granted; much would have to be reinvented. The return leg of any voyage is usually the less interesting, but my injury had introduced an edge of uncertainty that was sure to keep me alert and involved all the way to Plymouth. My disappointment at having to abandon our bid for Baffin Island was soon eclipsed by the prospect of the technical and physical challenges that lay ahead. I had no doubt that it would be a long and difficult haul, but I looked forward to it with relish. *Mingming* had never let me down; it was now up to me to show that I was worthy of her.

I had scarcely slept for two days. I stretched out on my bunk and rolled gently onto my left side. A bit of adjustment soon established the least painful position. I pulled my unzipped sleeping bag over my shoulders and, for once dispensing with a regular horizon scan, slept for five hours straight.

21

It seemed for a while as if we would never escape the Labrador Sea. For ten days we described a slow and lazy loop that gradually had us facing properly homewards. Daylight came and went, suggesting that somewhere there was still a sun, and that the heavenly bodies were still spinning and orbiting across the great void, but all of that was lost to us. Day after day we were wrapped in a miasma of choking mist and fog. The horizons could only be guessed at. The world had lost all delineation; there was nothing, simply nothing, but the encircling grey.

Our curving trajectory, forced on us by unhelpful winds, took us further to the west, and to this dull and stifling seascape was added an overlay of biting cold. In the cabin I shivered. My breath provoked short-lived clouds of condensation. I pulled my favourite pink blanket, my McCallum Craigie Ltd. (of Glasgow) Lan-Air-Cel woollen blanket, an almost antique relic of my mother's linen cupboard, tight around my knees. I sipped mugfuls of boiling bouillon. I rubbed my hands to keep up the circulation. I broke out my last line of defence against the cold, my heavy snow-boarding jacket, and pulled it on over the burgeoning layers. My spells in the hatchway allowed no escape route for the meagre cabin heat; my layering had brought me to such rotundity that I comprehensively stoppered the hatch opening.

I tried to make sense of the weather, and could not. Within a span of daylight winds came in at half a gale, from two or sometimes three directions, with calms between. It was fierce, and anarchic, and without logic. The constant shifts set up ugly seas that made mincemeat of us in the quieter patches. One calm lasted for twenty-four hours; our daily run of ten miles was all down to drift and current.

And all the while there was nothing, simply nothing, but the encircling grey. As each day passed I felt more dislocated. All sense of place had evaporated into the insubstantial murk. There was nothing to grasp on to. Only *Mingming* herself lent any solidity to this contracted universe. I searched for the least sign of the sun, for the merest hint of a sphere, for something beyond this indeterminate mist, for anything that would place us firmly back into relation with a wider cosmology, but there was no relenting of this ethereal gloom.

The bleakness of the place aspired to the sublime. I had never known such emptiness, such narrow-eyed coldness, such magnificent brazen featurelessness. There was nothing to puncture the integrity of this stupefying barrenness; for day after day it rolled on, grandly indifferent, lord unto itself.

Yes, it earned itself some grudging admiration, the Labrador Sea, as we struggled back south and tried to build some momentum for the return passage. This momentum was slow to come, and so I occupied myself with my expanding duties as Ship's Medical Officer. My hands still required regular re-bandaging; the raw flesh of my skinned knuckles was slow to heal. Unwilling to allow any chance of infection of these open wounds I still kept them well smeared with antiseptic cream; I experimented too with more robust forms of bandaging. This was simple doctoring; more subtle was the management of my fractured rib. I started a separate medical log in which I recorded its daily progress. This varied according to how much physical work I had to do, how solicitous I was of the injury, and how well I could control coughs and sneezes. I referred regularly to my medical notes with many a sagacious nod and tut-tut, and lacked only a white coat, stethoscope and patrician air to complete the picture.

This new-found persona attracted immediate approval and popularity on board, thanks to his insistence that I take a cure of complete rest. He was right too; it soon became clear that the less physical activity I engaged in, the less my rib complained. What a happy conjunction of natural sloth and medical necessity! The more loafing around the better! Bone idleness is good for bones! That spud-eared clodhopper of a foredeck hand, that skulking shifty fellow, who so far on this voyage had been little more than a sullen shadow of his former self, now piped up at every opportunity, a brazen grin from ear to ear. *Doctor says can't do that, sir. No good for the busted rib is that. Better take it easy's what I'd say, sir.*

The Ship's Quack also prescribed bodily warmth at all times. His logic was faultless on that one too. Changes in body temperature induced sneezing. Sneezing induced extreme pain, which was not nice, and slowed down the healing process. I was better off to stay below, out of the nasty cold air, and keep myself well wrapped in my pink blanket. Who was I to argue with the wisdom of Hippocrates?

I did my best, then, to remain inactive and to keep myself warm, but the ship still needed managing and I refused to abandon totally my vigil at the hatchway. In the calmer periods I was now managing to raise four panels of the mainsail, using my left hand for the hauling and my right hand just to hold the halyard while my left hand reached forward for the next heave. With eighty percent of the mainsail accessible we were now back to almost full cruising trim.

The ring-bolt on the self steering arm worked itself loose once more, and so I pulled myself out of the hatch for a second time and negotiated my way aft to fix it. I re-tightened the bolt, wired it heavily with monel wire to discourage it from moving again, and bound it with gaffer tape for good measure. Clumsy cold fingers dropped a washer into the sea, and the wire-ends cut into my fingertips, turning them bright red with my warm blood. Dried patches of that self-same fluid still disfigure that day's page in my log book. My side ached for half a day in protest at this hard work, but I didn't care; I was grateful that I was still able to carry out these basic tasks. That cabbage-growing cabin boy never missed a chance, though. *Better have a good lie down now, sir. You don't want to be overdoin' it.*

From time to time the temperature dropped suddenly. Whether it was the air, or the sea, or a combination of both that drove these fluctuations I could never quite determine. I suspected that we were moving south somewhere along the line of demarcation between the warmer north-going current and the cold south-going Labrador Current. That would certainly explain the volatility of wind and temperature, and the persistency of the overbearing gloom.

22

Adrift in the fastnesses of the Labrador Sea I took comfort in birds and in photography, for as we wound our circuitous route back to 59°N we once again began to meet increasing numbers of great shearwaters. Apart from a few resident fulmars and a brief and breathtaking encounter with a pair of fin whales that let off two whooshing spouts, rolled their long backs forward in a momentarily endless rotation and then were gone, it was only the great shearwaters that brought some relief to the frigid lifelessness of the place. Already infatuated, I now felt a growing complicity with these birds. A reading of my sea bird guide had revealed that they too were here on the briefest of visits. They, like me, had scarcely arrived and would soon be gone. But whereas my voyage was a modest geographical displacement that had begun and would end at the upper end of the northern hemisphere, these shearwaters were engaged in a heroic annual migration from the depths of the southern Atlantic. They were in fact over-wintering up here in the north.

The more I thought about it, the more extraordinary it seemed. The entire global population of great shearwaters breeds and nests *en masse* on a couple of remote islands in the Tristan da Cunha group. As the southern winter approaches the adult birds, perhaps four or five million of them, take to the air and begin their annual circuit of virtually the whole of the Atlantic Ocean. From about 40°S they fly, as we have seen, to almost 60°N, generally favouring the western Atlantic as they head north and the eastern Atlantic as they return south. This adds up to a round trip of well over twelve thousand nautical miles. A meandering route and a weaving flight pattern no doubt brings this up to closer to twenty thousand miles of voyaging before the birds return once again to their long burrows to restart the cycle.

It was hard to reconcile the tightness and uniformity of the shearwaters' social structure with the expansiveness of their migration, or to think of any parallel example. I began to understand, nonetheless, the basis of their close-knit gregariousness, and looked on them with an even kinder and more admiring eye. I tried to fathom how a single species could evolve such a singular life-style. How far back does it go? How did it start? How has it developed? How do they know what to do? The questions piled up, but the time frames involved, and the subtleties of the myriad interacting processes of evolution, were altogether beyond imagination, let alone comprehension.

The greater picture was beyond my ken, but I was struck by the unforced ease of the shearwaters as they live out this monumental cycle. To them it is nothing. They just do what they have to do, in a continuous and unthinking present. For them there is nothing but the sea and the air. No latitude or longitude. No north or south. Just an endless ocean over which they wheel in a subconscious dance driven by some inner apprehension of sun and moon and stars and maybe some response to the most subtle of electro-magnetic charges thrown out by the globe over which they range. Distance is a meaningless concept. They spread their wings and fly this way and that, knowing where to shape their course, but not knowing that they know. They fly and fly, and sometimes rest, and sometimes feed, and after six or seven months of nothing but sea and air, half a year of one of the most far-ranging circuits of any living creature, there again is the land, not by magic, but by the force of millennia of imprinted knowledge; there once more are the slopes of their natal islands, there is the peaty earth into which they will burrow and lay and incubate and raise a single chick which, should it survive to adulthood, will form yet another tiny link in the transmission of this simple but prodigious round.

My own stuttering trajectory across the ocean, lumpen and over-burdened and laughably heavy-going by comparison, had nevertheless coincided with this timeless journey, effortlessly fleet and light as air, of the great shearwaters. I decided that, injured or not, I would do my best to record this crossing of the ways. I was poorly equipped to cope with the technical difficulties of bird photography at sea, the difficulties of capturing, from a randomly moving platform, a good image of a small object following a quick and unpredictable flight path, but for the first time in all my voyaging I felt motivated to learn how to do it.

Fortunately my main camera, a single lens reflex camera near the top of the amateur range, combined the best features of digital technology with a good old-fashioned view-finder. The digital aspect allowed me to view the images immediately and both discard the duds and measure how well I was progressing. The view-finder enabled me to follow precisely the flight path of the bird I was photographing in a way which is now impossible with the usual viewing screen on the back of a digital camera. I lacked a good telephoto lens; the variable lens that came with the camera went up to a focal length of only fifty-five millimetres, far short of what is ideally required. Nevertheless I decided to experiment with it and see what I could achieve.

I soon settled into a routine which added an extra element of interest to my hours of observation from the hatchway.

My camera was always there, either in my hands, or around my neck, or out of its case and waterproof wrappings on my bunk, all prepared for instant action. Constant readiness was absolutely essential; the opportunities to capture a good image generally lasted only a second or two, or even less. I gradually learned to cope with this unpredictability. The key was to develop total fluency with the use of the camera, to learn to switch it on and make the right settings and bring the subject into view and adjust the focus in a quick and correct sequence. Along with that was the need to learn how to follow a fast and weaving flight with fluid movements from the waist. Then there was the problem of the timing of the actual shot. Here I quickly learned one of the disadvantages of a digital camera: in terms of wildlife photography there is a huge gap between the pressing of the shutter button and the opening of the shutter itself. Sometimes this delay seemed to be up to about half a second as the computer chip did its work making all the internal adjustments. Many a bird was lost behind the mainsail before the shutter clicked.

I persevered, because as each day passed my skill improved. The photographs were not especially good. Most were discarded immediately. Even the ones I kept were, at first, only at the margins of what might be thought acceptable. However there was no question that they were getting better. To an extent it was a numbers game. The more I photographed, the greater the chance of a lucky image. The better my basic skills, the more likely it was that a fortuitous combination of light and proximity and timing might just produce something worthwhile.

This new pastime brought me still closer to the shearwaters. I now watched them from an altogether different and more penetrating perspective. The constant tracking of their individual movements, the perpetual second-guessing of their likely flight paths, slowly nudged me towards a better and more intuitive understanding of the mechanics of their aerial mastery. I knew more precisely when they were likely to bank and glide; I could better judge that moment when wariness would overcame curiosity, forcing them to wheel once more away. I became more responsive to the subtle shifts of light on their plumage, and to the timing of their wing beats, and to the infinite variations in their visual interaction with the ever-shifting backdrop of sea and sky.

As we worked our way south-east through a cold cocktail of calm and half-gale and headwind, and as our progress took us slowly back into the heart of the great shearwaters' wintering grounds, so that the flocks, both water-borne and air-borne, were a constant presence, my search for the best images I could produce became an overriding passion. I decided to expand the quest and catalogue every species that came our way. Before long I had added Manx shearwaters and sooty shearwaters and a Sabine's gull and arctic skuas and long-tailed skuas to my library of images. My right side ached from the hours spent swivelling in the hatchway. The Ship's Doctor prescribed rest. The Cabin Boy nodded furiously in agreement, but I stuck to my post, knowing that I may never have such an opportunity again. A little discomfort was not going to keep me from learning and recording all I could about these glorious pelagic wanderers.

In the way these things work, it was not until several weeks later, when we had almost made our southing and wound our way back to mid-Atlantic, that I reaped the real and unexpected harvest of all this preparatory self-education. By that time my camera handling had become slick and assured and second nature. Hours and hours of practice were to reach their culmination in just a few short seconds.

23

At one in the afternoon of Thursday the eight of July, our forty-seventh day at sea, I sneezed for the second time since breaking my rib. For thirteen days I had managed to keep myself from sneezing, but for once my repertoire of nose-pinching and upper lip-squeezing and head-slapping and yelled commands to myself not on any account to sneeze, a regular performance that started as soon as I felt any suspicious tickling of the nostrils, failed to work. Bodily necessity took over and I wracked my rib-cage with an explosive expiration. It wasn't pleasant, but I could feel that something had changed. The two ends of fractured bone no longer moved apart, then clashed together, with total freedom; soft tissue, the beginnings of the re-knitting of the bone, restrained the movement and slightly moderated the pain. I was heartened to have the first palpable evidence that the healing process was under way. There was no doubt, though, that the sneeze had put back progress; for a day or so my side complained bitterly as it recovered from this sudden wrench.

There were consolations. For several days the wind had held in the north-west, pushing up daily runs to seventy, then eighty, then ninety-four and finally, for the first time on this voyage, one hundred miles. We were scooting along to the south-east, with 53°N just a few miles ahead. There were occasional intimations of something more warm and temperate and summery in the air. The sun deigned to reappear. In a calm patch I spread socks and blankets on the bridge deck to air and dry. A guillemot zipped by, all alone and doing God knows what over four hundred miles from the nearest land. I pulled out my kiddies' sea-side fishing net and tried to catch one of the great shearwater feathers that floated by from time to time, a hoped-for token to take home and treasure, but without success. Most days brought a flurry of whale spouts, invariably at distance. We were nearing the seamounts of the mid-Atlantic Ridge, and I hoped this might improve our chances of a more intimate whale encounter. I spent a morning replenishing my now empty food barrels from supplies secreted in *Mingming's* darkest and most inaccessible corners. I wrote a comic poem or two and once more practised my singing at the hatch. I cleaned the stove, and shaved without fail every two days, and wrote down every variation in the wind, and noted every raising and lowering of panels of the mainsail. I made copious and erudite medical notes, along the lines of:

Day 16 11.7.10 Was sore last night but a little quieter today.

The numbering of the days for this particular log started from the day of the fracture.

I tried too to remain equanimous in the face of an annoying leak. Every time we were on starboard tack and heeled to port, water appeared from somewhere and accumulated on the lee side of the cabin sole. In heavy weather I was forever sponging this up and squeezing it out into a bowl and throwing it overboard. I could never determine exactly where it came from; my best guess was through a bolt hole under the port rubbing strake. There was never a huge amount, never more than a litre or so, but it was a constant irritation. It sometimes forced me to keep sea boots on when I preferred stockinged feet. From time to time it caught me unaware and soaked my socks. It brought a sour note to the dry haven of *Mingming's* cabin. *Wet water! At sea! Outrageous!* I puffed in indignation and carried on sponging.

From time to time the wind wound itself up to half a gale and more. These were heavy blows, and the seascapes they created fulfilled every expectation. The waves were as chiselled and as monumental as anything we had seen, and in the less oblique light of these lower latitudes the foaming crests and the great swathes of turbulence that each one left as its forward momentum dissipated now had us sailing through the most startling kaleidoscope of watery textures and tints. The myriad refractive tricks and interplays of restless liquid suffused with an infinity of tiny bubbles and foam and momentarily trapped air turned the sea white-green and emerald-green and sometimes, and best of all, a translucent icy-green; yes, these patches of enervated ocean recalled nothing so much as the ice-floes of eastern Greenland, somehow melted but without the loss of their ghostly, glowing coloration. They were not small, these parcels of aerated water left by each breaking crest. We sailed through Olympian pools of cool green, set square into a grey-blue sea. The delineation between the untrammelled ocean and these acreages of residual turbulence were as clear cut as if pegged out by some kind of pelagic surveyor armed with staff and theodolite. I hung out of the hatchway and stared down into this ice-water, trying to plumb its depth, to see if I could determine how deep-seated it was. Logic said that it could only be superficial, that it was no more than a surface perturbation, but my eyes saw it differently. Looking down into the heart of this exquisite and unworldly green, this soft and insubstantial and hypnotic green, I saw no bottom, no end.

It was only strong winds and an energetic sea that could

produce these effects, but by now we were so inured to heavy weather that it had almost become the norm. Besides, these were mainly following winds, and the current was now firmly in our favour; I was starting to feel that lifting of spirits of the homeward bounder. We were now almost at 52°N, and had made nearly twenty degrees of easting since our outward point, and so were once more back onto my 'Western Approaches to the British Isles' chart. Our point of re-entry onto that increasingly tattered and grubby compilation was about two hundred and fifty miles south of our exit point.

I folded away 'Gulf of Maine to Baffin Bay' and thought for a while about Baffin Island and Cape Dyer and bowhead whales and icebergs big as houses. Those dreams were, for the moment, dead. I wasn't bothered. Aspiration is a means, not an end. What mattered were the voyage and the voyaging, and the accretion of experience, and the thousands of hours of disciplined observation: the studied accumulation of minutiae that make one, perhaps, a little wiser. I said a silent farewell to the Davis Strait and to the Labrador Sea and turned my thoughts to the east and to home.

24

It was a nondescript day. The breeze was unremarkable, just a steady draught from the north-west, enough to keep us moving. Grey cloud, static and uniform, neither high nor low, fused the horizons north to south and east to west. We rolled gently on through a sea that had settled to a repetitive stretch of waves so diminutive and effete that they produced little more than a tired ruffling of the surface. It was a day strangely drained of the usual vigour of the north Atlantic; not an unpleasant day, but a day whose only feature was its overweening blandness.

At ten in the morning I took my usual snack: one cashew, one almond, one Brazil nut and so on. The stillness and torpor of the day could well have induced me, meal over, to stretch out on my bunk and follow doctor's orders. I had thus far spent a fruitless morning at the hatch in contemplation of nothing more riveting than a thousand tones of unrelieved grey. A little nap and a resting of my rib was a not unattractive prospect. I could have slept, but engrained habit brought me back immediately to the hatch. I was there to see the sea. It was not for me to apply a filter of selectivity to the task. Who was I to say that one particular day or hour was more worthy than the next? How was I to know whether this minute would be more rewarding than that minute? What, in any case, was wrong with unrelieved grey and overweening blandness? Did the dull have anything less to teach than the sensational?

I settled once more in the hatchway and noticed immediately that a bird was coming in from the port beam, low over the water. It was still some way off, but its size, and the brilliant white of its body, and its dark, almost black, upper wings and back, suggested that it might be a great black-backed gull. I was surprised; although I had often seen these gulls well offshore I had never encountered one in mid-ocean. The habits built up over the previous few weeks now took over. Without a moment's thought I ducked below and grabbed my camera. Within two or three seconds I had the camera switched on and set and trained on the approaching bird. The view-finder had now reduced it back to a black and white spot heading purposefully towards the port quarter. I followed its track in, waiting for the moment when it would be close enough to take a series of shots.

It came in quickly, surprising quickly, and as it neared *Mingming's* stern it lifted away from the surface to a height of nine or ten feet. It passed directly astern, just a few yards off, and it was only at that moment, as for the first time I had a near and clear view, and as I was about to take the first shot, that I realised what it was I was photographing.

It is hard to describe that moment. The day crackled alive with a ten-thousand volt charge. A sudden tide of warmth rushed through my body. I was gripped by a profound joy, for as I pressed the shutter for the first time I knew that I was photographing a black-browed albatross. It crossed our stern and then turned slightly to its right to head once more directly to windward, dropping effortlessly back to wave height. I took three shots in quick succession, by which time it was almost lost in my view-finder. Then suddenly it arced skywards, up, up and banked to its right, presenting itself for one final tableau, pure white body intersected in perfect cruciform by those great dark wings, eight feet from tip to tip. For a second it seemed to hang there and consider the world and where it might go, and I hoped that it might swing right round and come in for a second pass, but it wheeled away to windward and on those colossal and unmoving wings glided back to sea-level and was gone.

Fifty-two days at sea had finally reaped their priceless reward. The albatross is not a bird of the northern hemisphere; its territory is the wide ocean of the deep south. From time to time a few wander across the equator. Even fewer make their way to higher northern latitudes. A couple of black-browed albatrosses have attached themselves, in past years, to gannet colonies of the Shetlands and the Faroes. The sightings of albatrosses in the northern Atlantic can be counted on two hands. A man could cross this stretch of ocean a thousand times and still have little chance of encountering the king of all sea birds.

Yes, all the odds were stacked against *Mingming's* track crossing that of an albatross. Yet what were the additional odds, not only that I should happen to be on watch at the time, but that I should be ready and able to take four photographs in the thirty seconds or so between the first sighting of the approaching bird and its disappearance over the north-west horizon? Not only that, the albatross had passed so close that the first shot I took had part of *Mingming's* stern rail in the same frame. All in all it was a stupendous confluence of the most unimaginable good fortune, far and away enough to justify the profound ecstasy that I now felt.

Perhaps you think that this is all somewhat absurd. *What's the fuss? It's only a bird!* Yes, that's true! How could a few pounds of flesh and bone and feathers create such a reaction? How could I feel so privileged that a mere bird had altered its flight path and looked with its inquisitive eye, for just a second or two, at *Mingming* and her ancient skipper? Why would I happily go once more through storm and injury and months at sea for one such moment? The answer is clear: for a seaman in particular, no other bird combines such physical magnificence with the power of embedded myth. To look at an albatross is not just to see a bird; it is to feel too the weight of centuries of sea lore. The albatross is symbol as much as flesh. It speaks simultaneously of mastery of the ocean and of the guilt of man. It lifts us with its power, yet hangs around our neck, weighing us down with the knowledge of our own follies. Somehow, we have all shot that albatross with our crossbow; we have all done a hellish thing. Every one of us is but a step away from a long grey beard and a glittering eye.

No other bird can engender such a complex reaction. The albatross exudes innocence and reproach in equal measure. It shows us what we might have aspired to and reminds us how we have failed. And in this uncomfortable new century, as we continue to kill them, it symbolises, in eloquent silence, our collective madness.

I was profoundly affected by the unlikelihood of the encounter and by all the imagery aroused by this ocean wanderer, but that was all at the level of generality. For a second I had looked too into the soft eye of this single bird as it traversed *Mingming's* stern, and had felt both affinity and sadness. Its change of course to pass close by was the brief nod of a wordless traveller. We were both making our own journeys, in our own way. For my part, at least, there was a hint of the communion of the road, of the brotherhood of the sea; neither of us had passed by unacknowledged. It was warming to the core, to know that an albatross had looked at *Mingming* and me, but as it soared on to the north-west, unhurried, stately, I sensed too the awful loneliness of the bird. It was lost. Now thousands of miles from its native waters, in the wrong hemisphere, with seasons and weather and day and night and magnetic fields all at odds with its genetic memory, it may never find its way back to home and a mate. It seemed condemned, save for the greatest stroke of luck, to range around these northern seas in a fruitless quest for the familiar. It may never again meet another of its kind. There was something heart-wrenching about its final ascent. It rose high into the sky the better to see, as much as the better to fly. It was seeking, but I feared that it would never find.

25

By noon the next day, the fourteenth of July, we had sailed over three thousand miles, measured by our noon-to-noon runs. At 51°27'N 31°51'W we were exactly mid-Atlantic. Plymouth lay a thousand miles to the east. A quarter of our voyage still remained, but as we neared 50°N, and as the temperatures grew increasingly milder, and as we began to feel the push of more favourable winds and currents, it nevertheless felt as if we were closer to home. That impression was bolstered early the next morning when a moderate-sized ship, the *Sea Trout*, its black hull set off by a jaunty yellow funnel, passed us half a mile to port, heading west. It was the first vessel we had seen for well over a month, and was followed the next afternoon by another ship of similar size and design, this one sporting a hull of the most fetching and unlikely teal-blue and heading the other way. All this traffic was puzzling, until I checked my North Atlantic Passage Chart and realised that we were crossing the great circle route between the Lizard and Cape Race, Newfoundland. These were the only two ships we would see until reaching soundings.

There may have been only a thousand miles or so left to sail, but I was growing increasingly concerned about the state of *Mingming's* mainsail. Vertical splits were starting to appear in the leech, the after end of the sail. I had long since noticed that when the sail was bundled it was the rear sections of each panel that were most vulnerable to wind and to sunlight. Ultra violet rays degraded the cloth, after which the wind took over, lightly flogging the loose folds in the sail and eventually causing these tears. None was longer than three or four inches, but I knew it would not take much for one to extend itself to the full vertical width of a panel.

For the first time since breaking my rib I could not carry out a routine task. I had once repaired a two-foot long split in the leech by simply leaning out of the hatchway and getting to work with needle and palm. Even when fully fit, though, this was very hard work; on that occasion the strain of sewing heavy cloth at arms' length while being thrown around in a post-storm seaway had reduced me to a heavy sweat and extreme nausea. I knew without even trying that I would not be capable of mending the sail properly.

This is not to say that my broken rib was not making progress; far from it. The Ships' Doctor could not be faulted on the quality and detail of his daily note-taking, and on the positive results of his ministrations, and although he was bemused at the amount of time I was spending at the hatchway trying to photograph, of all things, *birds*, he grudgingly acknowledged that it was at least keeping the patient happy. Nearly three weeks had passed since the fracture, during which time I has sneezed just four times. The third sneeze, on the eighteenth day, had been remarkably less painful than the preceding ones, and had evoked a rush of satisfaction that was comprehensively destroyed when I sneezed again a little more than an hour later. *Aaaaaaargh!* Two wrenches in such short succession were more than the knitting bone could cope with, and set back the healing some days. Fortunately I was well supplied with tins of wild Alaskan salmon, tins which contained a good measure of bony matter. I shovelled down this extra calcium with relish, imagining it heading straight for the scene of destruction and speeding up the repair. My tins of pilchards, too, were well-laced with fishy skeletons, but whereas there was something mildly pleasing about the thought of my rib being rebuilt out of matter from a sleek ocean-going salmon, I was more ambivalent at the prospect of being re-ossified by a pilchard.

The two top panels of the mainsail, my storm canvas, had been replaced a year or so previously, and so were exempt from the general deterioration. This was just as well, for as we reached 50°N and began our final run due east, the weather once more found its true Atlantic fury, scotching any chance of making repairs. Every day, day after day, it blew hard out of the south and the south-west and sometimes the north-west. *Mingming* raced east, mostly under just one panel of sail, rolling gently on and on. I had now consumed two months' worth of food and water, and for the first time sensed a lightening and a quickening in *Mingming's* pace. Our daily runs pushed higher and higher. For the second time on this voyage we clocked up a hundred mile non-to-noon position; over an eleven day period we averaged more than eighty miles per day. Great shearwaters, attracted by the smooth slick in our wake, hovered close to *Mingming's* stern and lunge-dived for food. I took a final series of photographs before we left them astern. Their course would soon take them once more to the south and their distant homeland.

For just one morning the breeze relented, leaving us motionless beneath a mottled sky. Still anxious about the tears in the mainsail, I took advantage of the calm to make temporary repairs: as best I could I pressed strips of gaffer tape to each side of every split I could reach. It was an unsightly, slovenly piece of work, but it did the job, containing the damage for the rest of the voyage.

Seduced by the unexpected stillness I leaned out of the hatchway and watched the sea. For two months I had been studying the infinite complexity of the interplays between wind and water. Now the wind was gone, but there was no let-up in the endless subtlety and restlessness of the shapes and colours and swirling movement of the sea's surface. Unruffled by passing air, the sea became a kind of mirror of the sky, fusing the blues and greys and browns into a fluidly distorted doppelgänger. I stared for long minutes at the tiniest of patches, just a few feet square, and saw them as the most exquisitely executed paintings, but paintings in constant metamorphosis, paintings made with live, mobile pigments, paintings that flashed and sparkled, paintings that spoke of the mystery of light and matter and movement and energy. I photographed patches of sea, with a vague intention of reproducing them and hanging life-size squares of ocean on the walls of my study, as a reminder, but knowing too that it would take more than mere pixels to collect and package and recreate these infinitely nuanced interactions between sun and cloud and air and water.

The meteorological pattern that had repeated itself over and over throughout our sixty days at sea began its cycle yet again; long fingers of wispy high cirrus, innocuous at first, delicately feathered, fanned out from the western horizon and slowly took control, transmuting to thick haze and then heavy cloud and finally fulfilling their initial promise of rain and, of course, a hatful of wind. *Mingming* picked up her skirts and romped off once more, driving eastwards and rarely deviating more than ten or twenty miles from our line of latitude. I felt indecently smug at having chosen such a successful trajectory for our passage home, while acknowledging deep down that as much as anything it was a matter of pure luck; the weather could just as easily have turned easterly, driven by summer high pressure over northern Europe. As it was, this confused system of fronts and depressions, bringing with it a messy, multi-layered sky and a merry-go-round of mist and rain and occasional squalls, this edgy weather, always threatening a little more than it actually delivered, but invariably bringing with it wind out of the west, was exactly what we needed.

In the heavier blows I lay on my bunk and listened to the wind, and finally found the sense and form and pitch of its endless soughing:

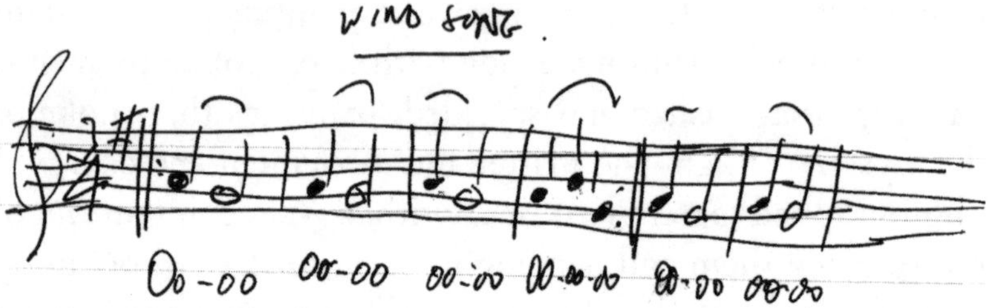

Our above-average daily runs continued day after day, and I filled pages of my notebook with versified comic invention. I tried to work out why it is that the last stages of every voyage bring a surge of off-beat creativity. It is always in the last week or so that serious thought gets pushed aside by a flood of silly doggerel. Is it caused by a lifting of the spirit at the imminent prospect of a successful voyage? Is it an attempt to counterbalance the weight of weeks of heavy observation and ponderous introspection with something a little more frivolous? Or is it that that same observation and introspection have by then so refined one's sense of the absurd, and that months of solitude have stripped the world so bare, that there is now no residual capacity for constructive thought?

The days grow longer o'er the springtime hills
And bluer sky and sunshine leave no doubt
That fast approacheth all the yachtsman's ills;
It will 'fore long be time for fitting out.

No longer can those duties be delayed
Which were ignored throughout the winter months.
Yes, soon will all the heavy debts be paid
That mounted from a year of negligence.

The anti-foul lies thick upon the hull
Encrusted like a carapace of steel.
Even the sharpest blade will soon be dull
That tries to scrape this armour from the keel.

The brightwork is, alas, no longer bright
But hangs in tatters, peeling and opaque.
No quick fix can ever put this right,
Of pig's ear handiwork a silk purse make.

Look how the topsides now have lost their sheen!
And how those bumps and scrapes are showing through!
What labour will it now take to redeem
The fruits of many berthings gone askew?

Whilst down below what pleasures now await,
Lurking amidst the stale and fetid air?
Old food and mould and rusty cans create
An atmosphere of squalid disrepair.

The batteries are flat, the engine stiff.
(How can a man forget to change the oil?)
Clogged filters, bent impellors give a whiff
Of many future hours of greasy toil.

And so the yachtsman trudges to the yard,
Beneath the weight of tools and paint pots bent.
He knows the next few weekends will be hard,
But soon he'll be afloat – so he's content.

26

Just after noon on Sunday the twenty-fifth of July, our sixty-fourth day at sea, we crossed onto soundings. In the vertical plane just six or seven hundred feet now separated us from the outer lip of the continental shelf. The earth's crust was rising to meet us, but it would take another hundred and fifty miles, two days sailing with these fair winds, for the sea bed to thrust itself sufficiently skywards to become land proper. We still had a little way to go horizontally, but the proximity of solid earth beneath *Mingming's* keels could be sensed in every way: in the changing rhythm of the waves, in the thickening and dulling of the colour and texture of the water, but more than anything in the sudden proliferation of life. Parties of gannets, from dazzling white adults to raggedy piebald immatures, crossed this way and that on their various missions. After so many weeks in the company of the great shearwaters, and after our encounter with the lone albatross, there was now something disappointingly parochial and unadventurous about these boobies. Every wave trough flickered with the twist and turn of a storm petrel: at one point we passed a flock of twenty or so bobbing together in tight formation on the surface. We nearly ran down a massive ocean sunfish. A pair of basking sharks basked. Dolphins swished in from time to time.

The workings of nature were winding themselves up, but so too were the workings of man. With an inevitability that now verged on the humdrum, our arrival at the perimeter of the Great Sole Bank brought several close contacts with the Spanish fishing fleet. I was an old hand at this ritual and had already put myself on a regime of short catnaps and very careful three hundred and sixty degree visual assessments. This was doubly necessary given the arrival of a restless fog that had visibility expanding and contracting as if driven by some giant bellows. I kept track of the positions and movements of these fishing boats as best I could, threading through them with the occasional bout of hand steering.

Then the real ships arrived. They were all there: container ships, giant shoe-boxes, bulk carriers, and later a small and extravagantly lit cruise liner with a real old-fashioned funnel, or at least a facsimile of one, and later still a dirty little coaster *sans* salt-caked smoke stack. I did not see all the ships that hove by one way and the other as we made our way in; now and again nothing more than a cloud of noxious fumes, an unmistakable cocktail of diesel exhaust and stale cooking smells, signalled the passage of a ship somewhere to windward.

I now needed all my wits about me, and with the nights darkening and lengthening, I needed too the bright rays of my navigation lights. For five voyages my little system of solar panel, gel battery and LED lights had worked faultlessly. In even the remotest of seas I had always, always, switched on those lights when night arrived; it had become an article of faith, and a source of comfort, that *Mingming* should always announce herself to the midnight world with her trio of white and red and green illumination. Now, for the first time, and perhaps when I needed them most, my lights, or at least the battery that powered them, gave up the ghost. The weeks of fog and mist and overcast weather had deprived the solar panel of the direct sunlight it needed to work at full capacity. I cursed myself for having grown too complacent and for not having done more to conserve the battery for this critical last leg.

It was unnerving, as we crossed the Celtic Sea through a rash of fishing boats and converging shipping lanes, to be sailing unlit. It was also un-seamanlike. Several times I was forced into the old expedient of shining a torch on the mainsail to announce our presence. One fishing boat directed its searchlight on us long and hard. I could feel the derision and accusation in that powerful beam. *Look at that idiot, would you! Not even carrying bloody lights!* I skulked along, guiltily, and feeling somehow naked.

At three the next afternoon, exactly sixty-two days since taking our departure from it, the Bishop Rock lighthouse rose high on the port bow, to be followed soon after by the fringing reefs of the Isles of Scilly. A happy conjunction of bright sunshine and low tide showed to best effect the toothy awfulness of those lines of rocks. The island of St Mary's was soon abeam and then well astern, and with the flood spring tide now under us we raced eastwards into a night of one moon and a million stars. Other lights soon joined the party: Wolf Rock, the Lizard, lines of ships to seaward, fishing boats, first intimations of the glow of civilisation in the bays of Cornwall; lights everywhere and on everything save *Mingming's* dark and scurrying form.

Dawn came and I felt a little easier, or would have, were not the breeze starting to fail. A kind of symmetry was imposing itself on our voyage. We had forced our way seawards through the inconsistent waftings of a high pressure system; now, after two months of mainly turbulent weather, we were back to a round of little zephyrs from here and there. Off the Lizard the wind, for a while, dropped away entirely and we lay mouldering. Big ships passed inshore and to seaward, lines of them trundling east and west, squeezing us between the tracks of their relentless progress. I was grateful for a faint but adequate breeze that came in from the north-west. Hand-steering with the tiller lines I worked our way landwards to the east of the Lizard with a zig-zag course that kept us as far as I could manage from the advancing steel prows of those sea-borne juggernauts.

One of these prows was not advancing. A large red ship, whose name and provenance I never discovered, was simply drifting on the tide, engines down. At first I thought this was maybe some temporary expedient, but three or four hours later, by which time we had weathered the Lizard and were waiting for the turn of the tide to whisk us eastwards, it was still there, gyrating idly to the currents. After lunch I took a short nap. Surveying the world after my sleep I was shocked to find this self-same ship laying silently just a couple of hundred yards ahead of us, stretched transversely across our course. I prepared to take evasive action, but then the strangest thing happened: the gathering flood tide took hold of it and pushed it rapidly away from us. Within half an hour it was hull down on the eastern horizon. At that point I noticed that a second ship, this one well inshore of us, and which I had thought was anchored off the Fal, was also drifting eastwards.

It beggared belief. Here were ships drifting back and forth between the Lizard and Start Point, six hours one way, six hours the other, not fully under control, and within a smidgeon of one of the world's busiest shipping lanes. I assumed it was a new variant in the management of idle ships. Perhaps the ship-owners made some saving in insurance or other fees as against anchoring while waiting for work.

The afternoon stretched to evening as we made our final run in to Plymouth. Once more the breeze was failing. As ever, I was heading first for Cawsand Bay, to anchor for the night and come in to Plymouth proper on the morning tide. As we closed Rame Head our progress slowed almost to nothing. I watched the transit created by the western end of that conical headland against the woods and fields and occasional houses on the hills set further back on the Devon coastline. For whole minutes we seemed to hang immobile, a fixed point on an imaginary line. We were moving through the water, but the tide was now turning against us; it was a kind of stalemate. I feared the worst, but for the moment I was content to sit in the hatchway and observe the land and its curves and its solidity and its grainy softness in the waning summer's evening. From time to time a more muscular patch of air pushed us forwards once more. The detail of the land fused to an indeterminate blackness and my gauge was now the distant line of lights falling one by one behind Rame Head's looming shoulder.

For three or four hours we edged in towards Penlee Point, opening up first the lights of Plymouth Sound and then the lights of Cawsand itself, but it was no good. After well over four thousand miles of sailing our anchorage, just a few hundred yards away, could not be reached. The wind gave up entirely; the ebb tide strengthened. I turned *Mingming's* head away from the land and let her drift seawards. I lashed a torch to a grab rail to light up the mainsail, then slept for three hours. Under a brilliant moon and a sky alive with shooting stars we moved once more away from the line of hills that now lay in one flat dimension against the different darkness of eternal space.

I had not expected any wind, but at three that morning it came in fresh and frolicking from the north-west. The tide turned too, and as a crisp midweek dawn relit the world we loped easily landwards through a near-deserted Plymouth Sound. By eight thirty, just a few hours short of sixty-seven days since casting off, we were once more moored at Queen Anne's Battery marina. The Ship's Doctor declared the Skipper fit to go ashore under his own steam. The Skipper declared himself satisfied with his voyage. As for that snivelling Cabin Boy, he was most unhappy that he'd have to wait at least three hours before downing a well-earned glass of beer.

Running out into the Atlantic.

A meagre snack of nuts and dried fruit.

Ingredients for a typical evening meal.

A great shearwater flies close…

… and lunge-dives…

… scoots on the surface…

… and feeds in Mingming's *wake.*

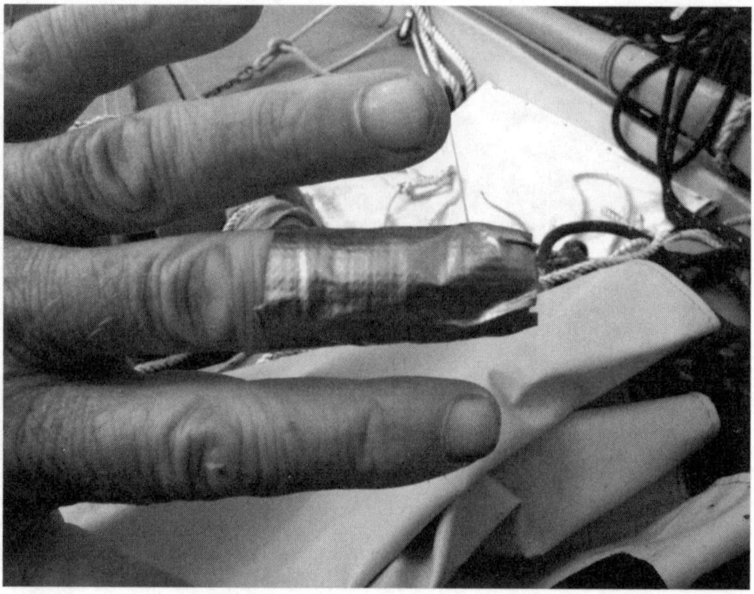

One of my damaged fingers bandaged with gaffer tape.

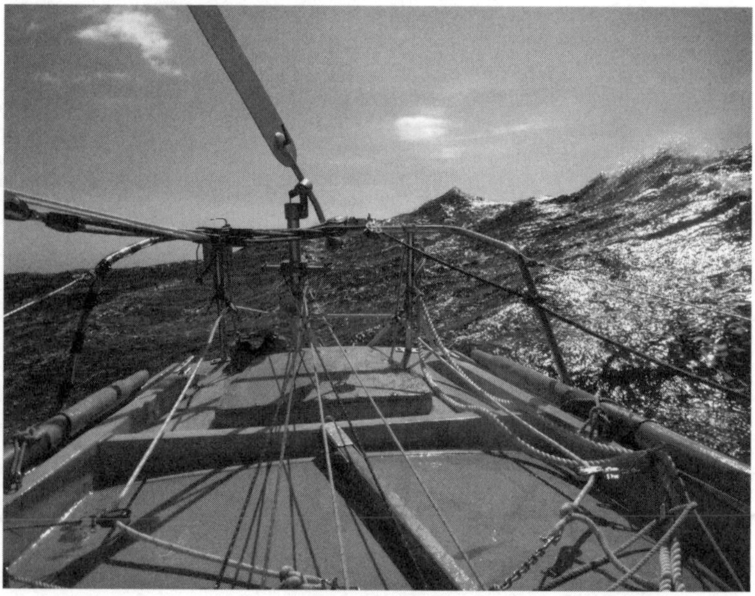

Running up the Davis Strait in a south-easterly gale.

Mingming *reaches her most westerly longitude.*

Drying socks in the Labrador Sea.

We meet a black-browed albatross.

Heavy weather mid-Atlantic.

Mingming *back at Queen Anne's Battery marina, Plymouth, after her 4100 mile voyage.*

PART TWO

MOUNTAINS

1

To the north-west of Spitsbergen a tongue of warm water, the last dying filament of the Gulf Stream, pushes north into the pack-ice of the Arctic Ocean. It probes sensuously, advancing and retreating with the changing seasons. Sometimes it searches deep into the frozen wastes; often as not it is held to a wide but shallow strip, the merest indentation, its probing arrested by the swirling power of the millions of square miles of ice that is the polar cap.

I had been studying this tongue of water for several years, watching, via the ice maps, the rough-edged patterns it makes as it moves in and out throughout the yearly cycle. Every day I had followed the geometry of its progress and retreat, and tried to grasp some sense of the mechanics of its restless gyrations. I wanted to understand, as best I could, the shifting relationship between ice-edge and open water at this uneasy meeting-place of the last of the tropical with the first of the polar. For this stretch of ocean holds a particular significance: it is, for most of the year, the open sea closest to the North Pole. If a man wanted to sail, in the month of July, as close as he could to the top of the world, this is where he would go.

The end of open water at the end of the earth; the prospect was too enticing to ignore. I had been sailing north year after year, drawn on by the pristine indifference of all that was cold and bleak and empty. Each year my voyages had pushed a little higher and a little wider. Each year I had learned a little more in my search for that elusive interface between the improbable and the impossible. Now, as I studied that tongue of water, I knew that for *Mingming* and I to sail into it was no longer beyond the limits of our possibility.

During the early summer months the base of that tongue lies along the line of latitude 80°North. *Eighty degrees north*; there was something solid and wholesome about those five syllables. *Eighty degrees north;* as the winter drew on those three words chimed ever louder in my mind. The more I studied the ice-maps and the longer I considered possible routes and distances, the more feasible it became as a target. *Eighty degrees north;* the phrase became a kind of *leitmotif*, weaving itself into the fabric of my daily life.

To sail *Mingming* to the most northerly stretch of open water would the logical culmination of our many thousands of miles of high latitude voyaging. Whilst our previous journeys had not in any way been a conscious preparation for such a venture, it was clearly the next step in our progression. Added to the draw of that unlikely latitude were two other attractions. I could, on the way, revisit the island of Jan Mayen and perhaps catch a sight of the elusive volcano Mount Beerenberg. More importantly, I could make a pass along the north-west coast of Spitsbergen.

The ubiquitous cruise ships have robbed Spitsbergen of its aura of almost unreachable otherworldliness; these days anyone with a few thousand pounds to spare can book themselves an Arctic voyage with the click of a computer mouse. I pushed that from my mind and thought about that distant land as if I were a sailor of fifty or a hundred or even two hundred years ago. The prospect of sailing there in my tiny engineless yacht was more akin to the precarious voyages of the early Arctic fishery than to the three-day jaunts of retirees from Stoke Poges. To take *Mingming* to Spitsbergen would bring us into the ambit of a string of islands that rings the polar sea, islands whose names still resound like frozen hammer-blows in the mythology of the Far North: Franz Josef Land, Ellesmere Island, Novaya Zemlya, Severnaya Zemlya. I might just, if I were lucky, get a sense of how it once felt to sail on and on into the final stretches of a cold and poorly charted wilderness.

On my own charts it seemed, at first, a long way, but that was as much as anything a misapprehension encouraged by the Mercator projection: the further north one goes the wider the degrees of latitude. The islands of Svalbard, of which Spitsbergen is the most westerly, balloon, on a Mercator projection, to a disproportionate volume. The northern reaches of the Greenland Sea expand to oceanic dimensions. Nor do the distortions of a flat paper chart give any sense of the spherical. It was only when I looked at my globe of the world that my stomach gave a slight lurch; 80°North was the last line of latitude marked and was less than the width of my little fingertip from the pin holding the top end of the sphere. Despite the symmetry of the globe the polar area seemed somehow tucked away around a sharper corner; hidden, by some trick of the eye, from the regular expanse of our normal and more temperate world. I knew, of course, that our target lay ten degrees of latitude, six hundred nautical miles, from the North Pole itself, and six hundred miles is not, on a global scale, a very great distance. Nevertheless it was a sobering and serious reminder, looking at the globe, of just how close to the extremes of the earth we would be heading.

Once I had measured the distances carefully I was surprised, nonetheless, at the relative proximity of north-west Spitsbergen. To sail there from northern Scotland is only marginally further than a run from Plymouth to the Azores. A slight deviation to the west to take in Jan Mayen brings the distance up to about fifteen hundred nautical miles.

This gave me some comfort; it was considerably less than our voyage to the west of Greenland. Mistakenly, as it turned out, I thought that we would therefore have lots of time to spare, that our voyage would be leisurely, and that there may well be opportunities for some further exploration in the Svalbard region.

I would, if all went well, be sailing close to Spitsbergen. I quickly determined that I would not, however, cross the twelve mile limit into Norwegian national waters; that would bring immediate entanglement with a raft of rules and regulations related to private travel around Svalbard, none of which bore any relationship to *Mingming* and our kind of voyaging. Such bureaucratic interference was the antithesis of the unbridled freedom to which I had become addicted. I would stay offshore, where in any case I always felt more comfortable, and where *Mingming* was designed to be.

Eighty degrees north. As the winter progressed I accustomed myself to the outlandishness of the idea. The more I thought about it, and the more I analysed the potential dangers, the more I realised that, despite the overtones of extreme adventure, a voyage so far north, if properly planned and executed, was in essence little different from any of the voyages we had so far made. The weather, for example, was likely to be less boisterous than that encountered crossing the North Atlantic to the Labrador Sea; we would be well north of the depressions and subject to the lighter winds of the Arctic High. It would probably be somewhat colder, but *Mingming* was well insulated and designed to be sailed without too much exposure to wind and water. The biggest potential threat was from sea ice. However my long and continuous studies of the ice maps had enabled me to identify a narrow vector in which the probability of meeting any serious concentrations of ice was very small.

This area lay between 5°East and 10°East, on latitude

80°North. This gave a line of approach about fifty miles wide. There were, as far as I could determine, just two aspects of the approach that would require extreme caution. The first was that there would be three or four weeks from my last assessment of the ice maps to our arrival on site, as it were. Although the likelihood was that the ice would have retreated further, this could not be guaranteed. In any case, the maps do not necessarily show very low concentrations of ice. These can move quickly and are no less hazardous than the more solid pack-ice. The second danger was the possibility of embayment. There would be ice to our west and north, and land and ice to the east. The sole escape route was to the south. These twin threats meant that once within range of the target I would have to advance slowly and carefully, and be fully prepared to turn tail if necessary.

If we did not reach 80°North I would not be overly disappointed. It was only a focal point to give some impetus and direction to our voyage. The priority, as always, was to execute a safe and well-made passage.

There was, however, another aspect to my intended route that, as I traced the curve from Jan Mayen to Spitsbergen, gave rise to a slight quickening of the pulse: we would be sailing in waters where virtually no vessels, be they merchant ships or fishing boats or yachts or cruise ships, ever go. On my charts the soundings lay along widely separated lines of transect. The further north my finger ranged, the wider the gaps between the charted depths. Huge swathes of the Greenland Sea, thousands of square miles of it, lay white and unplumbed.

I drew a line between Longyearben on Spitsbergen and Scoresby Sound on the east Greenland coast, the most northerly possible sea-route that may have any hint of commercial significance. I could not imagine that there would be much traffic between these two Arctic outposts, but one thing was sure: to the north of this line the ocean would be totally devoid of human incursion.

That was where I wanted to go: to the seas that lay between the last link of man-made commerce and the great expanse of polar pack-ice; to that raw pelagic wilderness where man rarely wanders. I wanted to know what was there. Would we sail for days through seas and skies empty of all life, or would this forgotten corner teem? How would it feel, to push slowly along through such a frigid backwater? Would I experience alienation or absorption? Would the thousands of hours I had now spent trying to fashion some kind of rapport with these out-of-the-way seascapes finally deliver their reward: a sense of belonging, or some hint of easy familiarity, or the evaporation of all that is so strange and unknowable about these far wild places? Or would that hard-edged wildness frighten and repel? I expected little there that would bring comfort or repose or anything that smacked of ease or homeliness. But could I nonetheless feel finally at home?

I had once described sailing the seas just to the north of Iceland as navigation way beyond the back of beyond. Now we would be heading for an altogether different level of what might be called the beyond. If we could make it to 80°North we would reach, in navigational terms, the most distant edge of the very back of beyond. For there the water ends; there is nowhere further to sail.

2

Our last voyage in the north-east Atlantic, to Jan Mayen and into the east Greenland ice, had begun and ended at Whitehills, a quiet fishing village on the south coast of the Moray Firth. I had made lasting friendships during our brief transits in and out of the harbour, and looked forward to using Whitehills as the launch pad for another northern trajectory. A small harbour, on a modest and human scale, it was perfectly in keeping with the diminutive *Mingming*. With just forty permanent berths for a selection of undemonstrative yachts, the harbour's inner basin neither overwhelmed nor shamed *Mingming's* Lilliputian proportions and quirky looks. We had felt immediately at home.

At five in the morning on Sunday 19th June I left Burnham-on-Crouch by road, with *Mingming* in tow. The winter months had seen the usual round of maintenance and repairs and innovations, though nothing of major significance. I had spent many hours hand-sewing new patches onto *Mingming's* mainsail, particularly along the heavily-split leech. I had bolstered the chafe protection on the yard with the addition of yet more leather strips nailed in place with copper tacks. Under the supervision of my engineer friend Simon Dunn, the Windpilot self-steering gear had been stripped down, cleaned and re-lubricated. Following the experience of retrieving the Jordan series drogue while there was still a big sea running, I had reverted to the idea of using a floating retrieval line attached to the outboard end of the drogue. I had chosen a soft, easily-handled nylon braid for the line and added an extra cleat to the bridge deck. This cleat was within easy reach of the main hatchway in the hope that, should I feel so inclined, I might be able to haul most of the drogue aboard from the safety and shelter of the cabin.

In essence, though, *Mingming* was little changed from the previous year. She was a little older, a little more tired, a little more patched up, but so too was her skipper. Two geriatric sea-goers, we wove our way north through the turbulence and push-and-pull of the motorway tides and at eight that evening hove to a halt in front of the harbour office at Whitehills. I took a short walk to stretch my legs and ease my stiff back. I peered over the massively thick wall of the harbour and considered for a while the smooth evening sea that lay open to the northern horizon. In a day or two we would be ready to sail; all that was needed was a fair wind to enable us to cover the first two hundred miles quickly, taking us clear of the Shetlands and the oil rigs and the last of the commercial traffic.

I strolled down into the yacht basin and found that my old friend Martin Wibner was there aboard his classic wooden sloop *Calloo*. We drank a beer together and swapped a few yarns. Martin had been forced to postpone a planned voyage to Norway; for several weeks the weather charts had been a mass of solid red as gale after gale had swept through. I made my way back to *Mingming* and the harbour office. Jimmy Forbes, local farmer, harbour Commissioner and a staunch supporter of *Mingming's* voyages was there, as was the new harbourmaster, Bertie Milne.

Bertie, a soft-spoken man whose helpfulness knows no limits is, like his predecessor David Findlay, another ex-fishing skipper. Over the next few days he told me about his tough life at sea: the long hours and the lack of sleep with its associated dangers when handling heavy machinery. Those winches and wires can rip a man's arm off in a flash. Bertie explained how he had to drill himself to think through every move, to rehearse exactly why he was pulling this lever or that, what it did, what the consequences would be. A false move, encouraged by a tired brain, could have disastrous consequences. Bertie's life supervising his village harbour is now a little less stressful, the hours more congenial. Bertie spoke proudly too about Whitehills, itself home to many of Scotland's top fishermen. He was only sorry that they now had to work out of other ports.

Jimmy had been liaising with Macduff Shipyards, who were due to send a mobile crane the next morning to lift *Mingming* in. I turned in early, knowing I would have to be up at first light to start preparing *Mingming* for launch. By ten the next morning *Mingming* was afloat with her mast stepped, and I was ready to start the long job of transferring aboard all the stores and equipment loaded on my truck. Slowly and steadily I prepared *Mingming* for sea. Food barrels were stowed and lashed. Water containers were washed out and refilled and fixed securely in place. I rigged the mainsail and the foresails and set up all the control lines to the hatch: halyards, parrels, topping lifts, downhauls and so on. I attached *Mingming's* ensign to the uppermost span of the mainsheet, and seized her radar reflector to its halyard. With some misgiving about the ultimate usefulness of the task I screwed my barometer into position in the cabin. I set up the control lines to the self-steering gear and flaked down the Jordan series drogue into its stowage bins on the cockpit seats. Gradually I brought some order to the cabin as spare food and tools and clothes and navigational gear and all the other necessary bits and pieces from foghorn to binoculars to rigging knives to alarms and torches and matches and harnesses and so on and so forth were made ship-shape and sea-ready.

The weather deteriorated. As I worked the wind set in from the north-east, bringing with it bouts of persistent rain. It was clear that we would not get away immediately, but I was not too concerned about that; I needed a couple of days rest.

On the morning of Thursday the twenty-third the sky finally cleared and the wind backed to north-west. It was my birthday, and time to go. Before setting sail I drove behind Jimmy up to his farm, where my truck and trailer would be stored during the voyage. Jimmy showed me his Highland cattle, long-haired, thick-fringed and living a life of lowland ease. He showed me too his wife's exquisite St Kilda sheep. One was as black as polished ebony, fine-lined, with curling horns and a tight frizzy coat. Jimmy is the third generation of his family to farm this land, but his heart, I think, yearns for the West Coast, for the higher, wilder places.

We were due to leave harbour at about five in the afternoon, at high water. James Lovie, another harbour Commissioner, was to tow us out with his creel boat *Moray Pearl*. Not long before five I was delighted to have a final visitor: Jim Abel, ex-fishing skipper and relief harbourmaster at the time of our last visit to Whitehills. Jim is a quiet, kind man who knows a thing or two about hardship at sea, and who has given up the fishing to tend his pigeons. I tried to explain to Jim the principle of a servo-pendulum self-steering gear; that the pendulum is not a rudder that steers the boat by virtue of turning, but that when it turns, the pressure on the side facing the flow of water then forces the pendulum to swing, creating a powerful lever, and it is this lever which, through its links to the tiller, applies the necessary course corrections. I am not sure whether Jim grasped the full mechanics of it immediately, but it is a slippery concept, one that had taken me a good year or two to absorb, despite, in my twenties, having built one of them.

By now my tow had arrived and nomenclature was getting tricky, for there was James helming his creel boat, with Jimmy managing the tow rope, and Jim casting off the shore lines. *OK James, go ahead slowly. Take up some slack, Jimmy. Cast off the stern line, Jim.* I somehow negotiated those verbal shallows without creating offence or confusion, and *Mingming* moved slowly through the tight turns of the inner basin, across the outer basin and, with a final ninety degree flourish to starboard, into the narrow channel that leads seawards. Here we met a healthy swell left over from the previous few days of north-easterly wind. *Moray Pearl* and *Mingming* rolled their way past the end of the harbour wall with its tiny white lighthouse, out beyond the hidden rocks to port and to starboard, out into clear and less turbulent water. I went forward and shouted to Jimmy to let go the towrope, pulled it quickly aboard, and returned to the cockpit to start hauling up the mainsail.

It would have been nice if *Mingming* could have put on a lively display for James and Jimmy as I settled her on her course slightly east of north; if she could have bent to the wind and surged off with foaming bow and curling wake. How I wanted them to see her at her best, dipping with light ease to the prancing billows! As it was we wallowed, the failing evening breeze combining with the awkward swell and *Mingming's* laden state to rob us of any chance of a showpiece departure; we had steerage way, but only just. *Moray Pearl* made a final circuit around us. James and Jimmy smiled politely, wondering perhaps how we would ever make it out of sight of land, let alone to the Arctic Circle and far beyond. With a final wave and a shout of *see you in a couple of months* they headed back to harbour, leaving *Mingming* to claw slowly seawards.

Nothing much changed. Nothing much improved. In the lightest of zephyrs that came and went we pulled painfully away from the land. A small ship carrying eight or nine massive empty cable drums on its deck, the *Elektron II* of Oslo, passed close across our bows, heading east. It was followed not long after by a Royal Navy patrol boat, the *Charger,* its bridge packed with waving university cadets. I waved back and gritted my teeth as we rolled in leaden immobility to the passing wake. *Mingming's* mainsail slatted joyously from side to side, finding its voice after ten months of enforced silence. I was yet to learn that calms and a raucous mainsail would be a dominant theme of this voyage.

The Banffshire hills astern narrowed imperceptibly as we drifted eastwards and northwards on the ebbing tide. I sketched the coastline in my log book, tracing the dip and curve of the contours to east and west of Whitehills and its defining headland, Knock Head. I counted and marked the arrays of wind turbines topping the skyline, all this in the hope of a quick and accurate landfall and final approach, should we return.

Ah yes, the return. That was, of course, yet to come. My sketch, it turned out, was to be of no use or import, for we were to race into the land on a black night with the most vicious of storms hot on our heels. I was not, at that final moment, concerned with the delineation of hilltops or numbers of turbines or the subtlety of shading in some distant declivity. But I run a little ahead of our tale; there are still three thousand miles of ocean to cross and a capful of adventures to relate before we once more close that line of hills and its rock-girdled and implacable foreshore.

3

For the third time in four years we settled in to the task of clearing the final headlands and islands of the kingdom. Whether we passed to the east or to the west of the Shetlands was of little consequence; all that mattered was to head north. It could have been frustrating, in those first hours, to be ghosting through a patchwork of uncertain wind that once or twice deserted us completely. I was not bothered; frustration and uncertainty had been our constant companions since our first tentative voyage together. I had grown, if not to love them, then at least to accept them without reserve and to savour the piquancy they brought to our wanderings across the ocean. In weaker moments I sometimes envied the Euclidean precision and the constancy of speed of the ships that crossed our path; the *Hamburg Star* of Monrovia, for example, that thundered by as we entered the Fair Isle Channel, laying down a wake devoid of a millimetre of deviation and progressing east with the mechanical certitude of a Swiss railway engine. Yes, I sometimes hankered after that kind of easy trajectory, but never for long. It was, after all, the aleatoric nature of our progress, the never-knowing, the unexpected and unplanned twists and turns, the stops and starts, the constant and unpredictable mix of euphoria and dismay, that invested every voyage with its interest and its character. I knew well enough that to travel to a preordained and dependable timetable, however superficially attractive, would soon rob any voyage of its most delightful elements.

As if to prove the point the wind suddenly swung to the south-west and blew up hard. With just one panel of sail set we now raced easily north through an onslaught of murk and driving rain. Fair Isle, already to our east, was soon lost in the swirling moisture. Somewhere ahead lay Foula, the westernmost of the Shetland Isles. Two years previously she had risen stark and black against the liquid gold of a sub-Arctic dawn. Now she was veiled, invisible, and would remain so as we surged past her western approach.

We were now clear of land; were we to hold a course due north from here our progress to the Pole would be arrested only by the Arctic pack-ice. I could not yet relax, however, as ahead, directly in our track, lay those monstrous expressions of man's artifice, the steel islands of the Clair oil field, great anchored quadrupeds that sucked the substratum dry and belched flame and oil and despoiliation. They breed on the water like infernal mosquitoes, these oil rigs. I had tried unsuccessfully to determine their current number and positions, and so was reliant on visual contact alone for traversing the field. I knew the precise position of the original Clair rig. I had marked an approximate position for a further rig encountered two years previously. That was all I had to go on.

For pretty much the whole of that Sunday, then, I sat in the hatchway, sheltered by *Mingming's* spray hood from rain that from time to time lashed down in blinding torrents, and conned our way through the unseen rigs. I sat there glowing with a mild smugness, for scarcely a drop of water now penetrated the well-worn cloth of the spray hood. Over the winter I had glued another layer to the top section, the roof, as it were, to double its thickness. I had then worked a thick coat of lanolin into the whole of the spray hood. This was a hard and messy job that left my hands smelling of sheep and farm. Now, as the Clair rig itself insinuated itself into the monolithic grey to starboard, sometimes losing itself as a heavier squall passed over, sometimes looming tall in an unworldly and threatening silhouette, my nostrils were once more wound about with fleecy odours that spoke distantly of the high tops and pattering flocks and the baa-ing of ewe and lamb.

The wind backed to south-east and on we sped to the north, eating up the minutes of latitude and leaving all man-made danger astern. A final fishing boat, blue-hulled beneath a white superstructure, crossed our track ahead, heading south-west in a rare flaring of brief and chalky sunshine. Squadrons of gannets patrolled left and right in interlacing flight paths. The rain closed in once more but failed to dampen my elation; we had traversed well over ninety miles in one span of night and day, hurled forward by wind and current.

Another short-lived night came and went, taking with it the last of the cloud and leaving us to a new-minted sky of the purest blue and a rollicking following sea. The land was gone, so too the artefacts of man's restless striving. As if to underline this transition and put the seal, as it were, on our exodus from all that was even-keeled and terrafirmaceous, pelagic nature joined us in a sudden explosion of exuberance and power and movement. A vast pod of pilot whales, thirty or forty of them, attached itself to our roistering wake and hurtled along with us. *Mingming* was flying, borne lightly on the foaming crests. The whales flew too, launching their great domed heads heavenwards as they broke the propulsive surface of each advancing wave. One huge male, infected perhaps by an excess of exhilaration, or driven maybe by nothing more than a look-at-me assertion of his strength, took himself out of the sea and in one imperious leap joined the birds of the sky, airborne from nose to the tips of his fluke, and for a breathless second or two arced through the ether before returning to his rightful medium with a thumping plash. Outriders of common dolphins, small and slick by comparison to their more meaty cousins, cut the surface this way and that. The waters boiled with streaking fins and the close-packed brows of the whales and the suds of *Mingming's* wake and the curling wave-tops scoured white by the freshness of the breeze.

The ferment below was matched aloft; the army of leaping whales had pulled in every kind of avian camp follower keen to transact its own particular line of commerce. Gannets stuttered and stalled and plunged seawards. Great skuas attacked the gannets, relieving them of their hard-earned breakfast. Stormy petrels skittered about at the lowest of altitudes and picked off the tiniest of leavings left floating. Fulmars and Manx shearwaters swooped and banked on rigid wings, sometimes pouncing in a raucous pack to fight over some presumed delicacy and churn the water still further with lunge and squabble.

I sat happily at *Mingming's* hatch, the unwitting centrepiece of this great effusion. The previous ten months ashore dissolved away, merging our new voyage into a seamless unity with the last; with *Mingming* refreshed and restocked we had leaped with an unbroken wake from English Channel to Norwegian Sea. I still carried the strong images of our crossing to the west of Greenland and our running of that endless gamut of storms and big seas, and it was now that I realised how much that crossing had recalibrated my sense of what might constitute an oceanic normality. It had redefined too my assessment of *Mingming's* abilities. We were now plunging north in a boisterous sea, a sea that not long ago, while not causing any particular anxiety, may have put me on edge, or seemed potentially threatening. It was now a sea that for all its muscularity verged on the effete. This heightened scale of assessment brought with it a new sense of relaxation; it was as if we had finally come of age. We had completed all our rites of passage and now, with so many thousands of sea miles in our meandering wake, could settle to our business as wind-hardened and salt-stained hands. Despite this, I was by no means complacent. My new-found ease was underpinned by the sure knowledge that the final say will always go to the sea itself.

4

Eighty-two miles. Ninety-three miles. Eighty-nine miles. With a breeze now holding firm in the ideal quadrant between south and west-south-west, and with the North Atlantic current compensating for the occasional periods of near-calm, our daily runs settled to an almost metronomic consistency. We were racing to the Arctic Circle. Despite long spells of sunshine there was a creeping chill to the wind, especially when it hauled more to the west, bringing with it intimations of the Icelandic glaciers it had only recently traversed.

I resisted all temptations to pile on extra clothing. My thermal underwear and all the other paraphernalia of high latitude sailing, woolly hats and thick sweaters and fur-lined boots and, should I be reduced to unspeakable wimpishness, gloves, all remained well-wrapped in their waterproof holders. It seemed sensible, given the latitudes I was aiming for, to give my body plenty of time to acclimatise. My only concession to the falling temperature was to pull on a second pair of socks and to replace my cotton polo top with a long-sleeved fleece-type shirt.

We were not yet into the Arctic, but the days were already starting to acquire that clear and crystalline brilliance associated with cold and high places. This impression was fortified by my daily application of sun block to nose and cheeks. By chance the tube I had brought along was one used many times when skiing. It was heavily laced with a particularly astringent and enticing citrous perfume, an unforgettable and evocative odour that immediately called up remembered images of jagged peaks and sparkling snowfields and skies so blue they were almost black. I sat in the hatchway and breathed in this heady aroma and somehow created a perfect conjunction of sea and mountain. I closed my eyes and made a swishing descent of the Cîme de Caron, the imagined ski sounds merging with the swirl of water along the hull and the soft hiss of tumbling waves. The creak of the yard against the mast could for all the world have been the squeaking of skis on dry powder. It seemed at first an unlikely juxtaposition, this sea surface with the topmost Alpine peaks, but they are, after all, the two geographical extremes that sandwich the temperate middle ground on which we live. It is, in the main, only the ocean and the most inaccessible of mountain ranges that have evaded the compass of man's encroachment. Only here, in the hidden heights and the reaches of the furthest seas, is there any residue of wilderness.

It gave me a double lift to be thus scudding north at the level of the ocean with, somehow, a parallel sense of high crag and mountain glacier. This first leg of our voyage was in any event a kind of climb, not only up the ladder of increasing latitude, but towards the permanent light of the Arctic summer, and was therefore invested with much of the mountaineer's imperative to press on upwards to the highest limit.

These lofty musings were soon offset by the lowliest of physical realities: I was developing a tooth-ache. A dull pain was jabbing now and again in the region of my left upper molars. This was more than a little worrying; only a few months earlier I had undergone root canal work on the opposite side. Was nature now about to redress the balance, infecting me to port as well as to starboard? I had managed to persuade my dentist to prescribe a course of antibiotics, just in case the original infection flared up again, so I was not totally without a medicinal defence. I was mildly alarmed, though, at the thought of some nasty and incurable tooth problem.

At that point I remembered that tucked away in my box of medical stuff was a kind of do-it-yourself dental kit. It was about time it was looked at properly. This was clearly a job for the Ship's Doctor who, still glowing from his rib-healing triumphs, was keen to venture into new fields of medical endeavour. With the expanded title of Ship's Doctor *and* Dentist already forming in his insufferably smug brain, he elbowed all-comers aside and pulled out the dental kit with a surgical flourish. One by one its contents were examined and laid out on the chart table. The mere opening of the pack had already flooded the cabin with the strong smell of oil of cloves, the defining odour of dentistry itself, which immediately lent an air of legitimacy to the madcap idea of self-propagated tooth surgery. This was reinforced by the first item to come out of the pack: a pair of surgical gloves in a *sterile* wrapping. This was followed by miniscule tubes loaded with all kinds of cements and compounds, weird little plastic clamps, various plugs and yes, one of those round inspection mirrors that every dentist uses with such aplomb. The Ship's Doctor *and* Dentist seized on this with a practised air, keen to demonstrate its use. He opened his mouth wide and stuck the mirror in. Only then did it dawn on him that it is impossible to view a mirror stuck in one's own mouth. Undaunted, he pulled out a little hand mirror and held it in front of his face to reflect the first mirror's image back to his overly triumphant eyes. By that time the dental mirror had fogged over. He wiped it clean and by the clever manipulation of both mirrors finally arrived at a clear view of the inside of his mouth. Every detail of tooth and gum and tongue was displayed in disgusting clarity. It all seemed to belong to some other slimy and unwholesome creature. Never mind; this dentistry lark was going to be easy.

At that point two further thoughts occurred. The first was that with both hands holding mirrors there were no more hands available for the manipulation of the surgical instruments. The second and even more telling realisation was that in any case there were no surgical instruments to manipulate. The creators of the do-it-yourself dental pack had evidently forgotten to include a nice selection of those shiny stainless steel probes and knives and scrapers and pliers that line up on any self-respecting dentist's tray. The only tool was a disappointingly dull plastic probe, rather like the end of a small screwdriver, which was set at the other end of the handle of the dentist's mirror. It was clear that the pack was not designed to support the surgical extraction of a triple-rooted molar, or even a bit of routine drilling and root canal work.

The Ship's Doctor *and* Dentist carefully put away all the limited instruments of his potential trade, disappointed that he would not be able, should the need arise, to make an incision or two. The Skipper suggested he stick to sailoring. The Ship's Boy, strangely quiet during this whole interlude, smiled a lob-sided smile of relief.

5

At ten in the morning of Thursday the thirtieth of June, just less than a week after leaving Whitehills, we crossed the Arctic Circle and our voyage entered a new phase. The strong and consistent breeze that had driven us so easily north hauled round to the north-west, giving us our first headwind and a taste of the many weeks of mainly light and contrary and unpredictable gyrations that would characterise so much of this journey. This was the year in which we were to make an intimate acquaintance with the high atmospheric pressure that installs itself over the Arctic regions during the summer months, pressure that creates dense swathes of stable and immobile air, pressure that robs a sailor of his motive force and leaves him languishing on a mirrored ocean. The first of the succession of calms that would stretch almost end to end throughout two months of voyaging was still a day or so away and so, still flushed with the rush and fizz of a perfect week of downwind gambolling, and still thereby lulled to imaginings of some kind of charmed and effortless progress around our prescribed circuit, I took this unhelpful shift of wind as no more than a temporary setback. At first I welcomed it, noting in the Ship's Log that we were now back to honest sailing; the free ride which we had so far garnered from a quartering breeze was starting to make me feel a little uneasy.

At fifteen minutes to midnight I checked aloft and

discovered trouble. The stitching of two vertical seams on the third panel down was simultaneously failing. It seemed extraordinary that two lines of sewing, one near the leech and the other close to the mast, should give up the ghost at the very same moment after thirty-one years of faultless service. It suggested, nonetheless, a consistency of effort over that long period and so many thousands of ocean miles, and perhaps too some kind of equality in the different kind of chafe that each seam had suffered. The thread of the after seam had, I think, been rubbed away by contact with the topping lifts; the forward seam had suffered from chafing against the mast lift, the line from the masthead that supports the boom. I had not picked up on the wear to these seams when overhauling and re-stitching the sail over the winter. Now they were both gaping, each one opened up a foot or more down its length and, it seemed, popping another few stitches in every gust. It would not be long before both seams would be unravelled from batten to batten.

In the half-light of the low Arctic midnight, and with a bucking sea below, I lowered the sail to the damaged panel and tried to sew up the after seam. It was hopeless. To be able to pass the stitches in the right place I had to keep the panel drawing, but as each new stitch pulled the two sides of the seam together, pressure elsewhere unravelled more stitches above and below. I was making things worse. It was already clear, too, that it would be even more difficult, if not impossible, to sew up the seam alongside the mast; it was almost inaccessible at sea.

I abandoned my attempt to sew up the after seam, lowered the sail to just two panels, thereby taking the damaged panel out of service, and retired below for an hour or two's sleep. By two-thirty the next morning I was not only refreshed; the head sea had eased in a failing breeze. I hauled myself on deck, armed with a selection of short lines, and set about lashing together the battens above and below the damaged panel. It was the simplest solution; rather than exacerbating the problem by trying to sew up the seams I would just take that panel permanently out of service and sail the rest of the voyage with a reduced mainsail. In 2007 I had sailed well over two thousand miles after the fracturing of two battens had required a similar expedient. It was yet another example of the flexibility of the junk rig; so much of it can be broken down into smaller, more manageable parts. The panel I had dispensed with made up about a sixth part of the area of the mainsail. Its loss would of course impact on our speed, but only in light weather when a full sail was required. I was never able to determine the exact extent of this impact during the many weeks of gutless winds that we would soon experience.

With five lashings from luff to leech clamping together the two battens and the abandoned panel, I once more raised the mainsail. *Mingming* settled back to her work, pushing on north in a breeze that was backing to the west and therefore becoming, once more, a benign wind, or would have been, had it not been too a wind that was inexorably failing. We were approaching 68°North and the night-time chill now had me shivering even in my sleeping bag. I finally relented, first stripping off and then encapsulating my flesh from ankles to neck to wrists in a second skin of thermal underwear, the old-fashioned woolly kind: grandfatherly, creamy, comforting.

The new and cosy feeling brought on by this additional layer of protection was given a further boost when I discovered, in a rucksack pocket, a packet of mint sweets, left over from the long drive to northern Scotland. Aboard a ship on which every consumable item and its specific role in the grand plan of bodily maintenance has been weighed and planned and predetermined with an almost obsessive precision, and on which every mouthful of every voyage is a known quantity and therefore devoid of any element of chance or the unexpected, it was scarcely surprising that these stowaways, especially ones so obviously self-indulgent as boiled sweets, twenty-three of them in total, should cause such a reaction of delight. They immediately presented me with a problem, however: how were they to be allocated? I could not allow myself to gobble them up any-old-how; that was contrary to my years of disciplined eating at sea. I could not allow a free-for-all. Were I to allow any hint of randomness into my consumption schedule it might spread to other areas, destabilising my regime, causing eating anarchy. I needed a plan, and one that took on board, as it were, the rarity value of the sweets, and which awarded them as treats or reward. After half an hour of thought and calculation I had worked out what to do. Twenty-three sweets would fulfil the following reward system: one sweet for every degree of latitude crossed on our northern trajectory to 80°North, one sweet for every two degrees of latitude crossed on the return leg, with a single sweet left once we were back at Whitehills.

Yes, it seems silly. They were only sweets. Why not just eat them? Well, I could have done just that, but it was surprising, as the weeks passed, how much this seemingly infantile game of sweets for latitude became a permanent theme of the voyage. As much as anything those sweets as reward became the symbol of our progress, or, as happened many times, our lack of progress. Those twenty-three globs of mint- and honey-infused sugar, each one individually wrapped to give it a status beyond its inherent worth, famously British but on closer examination manufactured somewhere in Turkey, became the milestones, or more precisely the sixty-mile stones, and later the one hundred and twenty-mile stones, along our path, occasionally rushing by, more often than not lying tantalisingly ahead at the brow of the next watery hill, out of reach, unattainable.

That very afternoon, for example, we crossed 68°North. I now had legitimate cause to unwrap the first of the sweets and savour this new input to my diet. I did not eat it immediately, preferring to save it until after my evening meal. The moment itself was invested with a certain degree of ceremony; trumpets could well have sounded offstage. I doubt I have more enjoyed the slow and considered sucking of a sweet, its gradual reduction from gobstopper to aftertaste. I needed something positive to lift the evening, in any case. Outside the wind was nearly gone; the horizon too. Our world was now bound about in folds of dense summer fog.

6

It was not a persistent fog. Over the next four or five days, as we hauled ourselves inch by inch towards the South Cape of Jan Mayen, it made itself the third part of a revolving threesome of fog and drizzle and sunshine. They came and went and came again, one after the other, round and round, these three, each elbowing the others aside in a constant fight for the centre stage. Each was a class act, well-honed in its own particular delivery. The fog, when it rolled in, was good and thick and smothering; the drizzle was uncompromising in its solidity and its all-pervasive wetness; the sunshine threw in interludes of blinding brilliance.

It might have been fun, this procession of quick-change weather, but underlying it was sobering reality; the wind was declining in direct proportion to our proximity to Jan Mayen. Every day there was a little less. Every day the periods of immobility lengthened. Our daily runs fell away. In one scarcely credible twenty-four hour period we covered just fourteen nautical miles. We had all but stopped.

Yes, for long periods there was no gurgle at the forefoot, no froth or bubble, not the slightest perturbation of the ocean surface that might indicate the passage of a solid body through that fluid medium. From time to time the silkiest of ripples may have rolled outwards from the bow, an almost imperceptible ruffling quickly gone, but this was no more than the sign of our gentle pitching to the swell, the product of our own inertia on the ocean's restless heave.

We had all but stopped, and my heart swelled at our stasis. What a joy it was, thus to cock a snoop at the rush and hurry of the world. What a treat it was, thus to be rid of that incessant press for forward motion, to be relieved, for a few precious hours, of all that scrabbling and scrambling. The rain fell heavily on a windless sea and I took comfort from the beauty of the myriad circular waves generated at the point of impact of water on water. These perfect circles, emanating eccentrically, rarely attained the diameter of, say, a beer mat, before their limited energy caused them to be subsumed once more into the general flatness. The occasional bigger drops created whole dinner plates, with secondary and tertiary waves rolling out and gone in a second. As the rain came on more thickly the density of these quick-fire circles brought them into constant overlap, creating a mosaic of rapidly shifting patterns as the wave forms intermingled and diffused in newer, more complex arrangements. I photographed these circles, and in frozen close-up they looked for all the world like moon craters, as well they should, the both taking as their causation the effect of matter hitting like matter, and both being subject, although on a different scale and density, to the same Newtonian laws.

Only one treacherous thought darkened the lightness of my heart: should the weather continue with such a preponderance of mist and heaviness, what chance then of a clear view of the great monolith, the seven-thousand foot Mount Beerenberg? This was the driving impetus behind this second visit to the island: to see the volcano exposed from tip to toe. It dawned on me that I had assumed that virtue would reap its own reward, that by making so much effort to revisit the island I would accrue credit and grace and that the clouds would thereby withdraw and that I would have my wish. It was only as I stared out through the streaks of vertical rain that I rumbled the absurdity of this expectation. It was plain daft. Much as we like to delude ourselves otherwise, the world is not like that. Meteorology is not driven by spirit or intent or perseverance. My chances of seeing Mount Beerenberg in its entirety would be a function of statistics and chance. Realistically neither was in my favour, given, during the summer months, the low ratio of clear days to overcast days in those parts. Even worse, a generally clear atmosphere was no guarantee of an uncovered Mount Beerenberg; its icy slopes create its own micro climate, cooling the air around it and thereby manufacturing its own almost permanent mantle of cloud.

With time at a standstill as we lay amongst the crowds of chattering fulmars drawn in to our dwindling wake, fulmars whose intermittent bickering was the only punctuation to the ceaseless heave and groan of *Mingming's* gentle rolling, I let my mind wander on beyond Jan Mayen, beyond our previous northerly limit of 72°North, and thought about that ocean territory where man seldom goes. Although to sail towards Spitsbergen from Jan Mayen requires an almost north-easterly course, I was drawn to the idea of continuing directly north from Jan Mayen, for a while at least. This would take us towards the ice edge, and even further off a track that is virtually unused anyway. It would also put us more firmly into the south-going and therefore adverse East Greenland Current, and was therefore not an ideal trajectory. For the moment, though, it held sway, this thought of an indirect approach to the north-west of Spitsbergen, and it was driven by my examination of the topography of the Greenland Sea.

I had discovered that to the north of Jan Mayen, in 73° 30' North, and therefore at a distance of about a hundred and fifty nautical miles from the island, the flattish contours of the seabed are broken by a sudden eruption. A mountain rises from a depth of about three thousand metres and comes within a mere hundred and twenty-three metres of piercing the surface of the Greenland Sea. Its lines of contour suggested an almost perfect cone, which in turn gave it the look of an ancient volcano. In my notebook I drew a sketch of its north-south cross-section, as near to scale as I could manage.

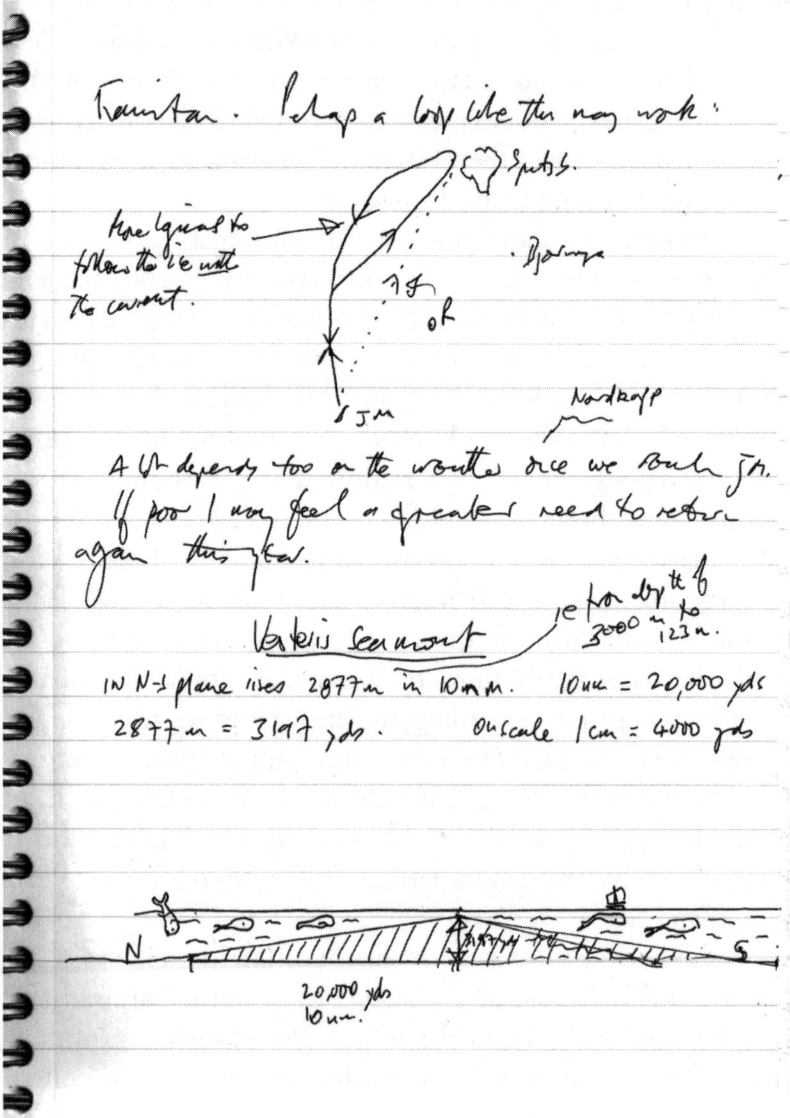

Sure enough, here was a conical profile, smooth-sided and regular, rising from the underwater plains and almost kissing the sky. I conceived the idea of sailing, if conditions allowed, to its topmost point. Surely this single patch of shallow water, topping an almost-island in the vertical, with its inevitable harvest of nutrients pushed by the currents up the encircling slopes, must be the focal point of an oceanic feeding chain. Perhaps this was where the humpback whales I had seen trundling north two years previously had been heading. Perhaps in the summer months, when the ice has receded, this is a location for convocations and colloquies of all manner of great creatures. What better place for life to disport itself, in such a corner of the world, out of sight, out of mind?

In a succession of little winds so devoid of energy that they could scarcely impose the slightest ruffle or pattern on the surface of an inert sea, we ghosted slowly towards Jan Mayen, while I thought about those two hidden mountains: Beerenberg, thrown into the sky but wrapped in its veil of cloud; Vesteris, inferior in every sense, brooding unseen beneath the waves.

7

Our noon position on Monday the fourth of July, our twelfth day at sea, put us just sixty-five miles south of the South Cape of Jan Mayen. In the persistent calms, some spanning seventeen or eighteen hours of each noon to noon period, and thereby stealing huge tranches of our potential sailing time, it was only the North Atlantic Current that enabled us to maintain some forward momentum. Static in the water we still crept north, or more precisely north-north-west, borne on that unimaginable mass of convected fluid.

After nearly two weeks at sea it was not only the ocean-going rhythms which had once more integrated themselves into the structure and pattern of life; I had by then been subsumed into the delicious solitude of the lone sailor, an expansive, all-embracing solitude that becomes, of itself, the very best of company. Added to that companionship were the constant visitations from pelagic society. Since our encounter with the pod of pilot whales we had not crossed paths with any cetaceans, but the birds kept coming: now an Arctic tern bouncing in on elastic wings, swooping at a floating fulmar, inspecting the cockpit then bouncing off; now a Leach's petrel; now a meaty Pomarine skua; now a kittiwake hovering close, looking for a landing spot; and now, as we closed Jan Mayen, the first Brünnich's guillemot of the voyage, whirring hell-for-leather on its own singular mission.

All of this, enframed by a broad sea and a broader sky, had once more become the world as it is; I needed and wanted neither more nor less. Coming to the hatch after lunch it was a rude shock, then, to look astern and make out, low on the horizon, the silhouette of a tall triangular sail. Here was another yacht advancing into our patch of quietly sleeping ocean. *Mingming* was barely making way; the sea was patterned abstemiously with the darker rufflings of occasional cats' paws, the world infused with post-prandial torpor. I grabbed the binoculars and studied the interloper. It seemed, at first, to be coming up on us from directly astern, steadily narrowing the distance between us. After a while two things became clear: the yacht was evidently motor-sailing under mainsail alone, hence its unnaturally rapid progress; it was on a parallel course to ours, but would pass us somewhat to starboard.

The gentle equilibrium of the day had now been broken. I wanted to ignore the yacht; I could not ignore the yacht. I wanted it to disappear over the horizon; I wanted it to pass as close as possible. I wanted to look the other way; I could not keep my binoculars off it. I wanted to retain some philosophic poise; had the yacht been closer, I would happily have given myself over to inane grinning and waving.

The yacht passed well to starboard, so far in fact that I could scarcely discern the hum of its engine, despite the pervasive calm. With the binoculars I could just make out the shape of its hull and coach roof and the solidity of the mast; everything inclined to the traditional rather than the modern. I saw no movement aboard or anything that hinted at human form, but given the distance that was scarcely surprising. After yet more internal debate I assembled my handheld VHF radio and called up the yacht. No answer came, nor any answer to the several calls which I put out as our companion drew level, still far on our starboard beam, then moved on forward and tipped inch by inch over the edge of the world and into whatever was the void beyond.

This whole interlude, no more than an hour or so long, served up, in the ensuing reflection, a further round of turmoil, for the yacht, scooting past in such a determined and unimpeded fashion, had inadvertently held up a giant mirror to *Mingming* and her lackadaisical progress. For a moment or two I had observed *Mingming* from the outside, as it were; through other eyes. I did not think we had in fact been seen; we would have been no more than a blemish on the horizon and, who knows, the yacht may have been on auto-pilot, with a watch keeper only making the occasional sortie to check for dangers bigger than our wisp of a cockleshell. Observed or not, we had been left mouldering. This other yacht, had it fuel and will enough, could be at Jan Mayen by early morning. We might yet take days.

For a moment or two I almost envied that yacht its ability to ride roughshod over the stillness of an ocean calm. It seduced me for a second or two, the fast passage of that yacht, and had me wishing that I too had a great contraption under the bonnet that I could fire up at will to send us hurtling forwards willy-nilly; yes, it seduced me for a second or two until through the still air I fancied I heard the faint exhalations of whales.

Something was out there, somewhere. I held my breath and listened. It came again, a perturbation of the air, insubstantial, ethereal as gossamer, then another. They were hard to place, these soft sighs caressing the languid day; they seemed to come out of the sky rather than the sea. I finally made a connection as a whaleback rolled forward some way off the starboard quarter. Soon afterwards more brief crescents of black cut the surface further towards the horizon. The quick and random circlings gave the impression of a pod out foraging. It took a while to put a name to them, but at one point they came in closer, and the nature of their ungainly roll forward, somewhat stiff and heavy shouldered, and their bulbous brows, and their intermediate size, pointed to northern bottle-nosed whales. For an hour or two we shared the same patch of blue, and I was now glad that I had not had the means to power off over the horizon, and that *Mingming's* progress was always gentle and unhurried, and that we thus came to know the ocean better, and all its various creatures.

8

On we crept towards Jan Mayen, with short-lived and inconsequential little zephyrs from here and there pushing us north between the long interludes of total calm. The rain had gone, leaving the sky to a two-way struggle between fog and sun. The fog, in the main, had the upper hand, coming in more thickly and trying to establish a permanent grip on the atmosphere thereabouts.

I debated long and hard about whether to set the light weather jib. A rough calculation suggested that I had now completed about seventy-two days of ocean sailing since the last time I had flown a jib; I had almost squeezed the need for a headsail out of the system, and felt better for it. Whatever small benefit it gave in terms of extra speed was counterbalanced by the loss of equilibrium of the rig, and by the upset to my own equilibrium brought on by the need to exit the hatch, and by nagging fears for the well-being of the mast. In this endless light weather I finally relented, and crawled forward to ungasket a headsail. I set the nylon multi-purpose genoa. As anticipated, it increased our speed marginally, but at the same time pulled the head off ten or fifteen degrees, a misbalance that could not be corrected by any amount of adjustment to the helm or the self-steering gear. Inevitably the wind soon picked up anyway, delivering, for once, what was almost a real sailing wind, and within three hours or so I was forced to go through the whole procedure in reverse.

I tried to forget about headsails, and instead applied another layer of lanolin to the spray hood in the hope of ensuring its total water-tightness for the whole of the voyage. I then sat in the hatchway and worked out a variant of the Dutchman's Log, that old trick of determining speed by throwing a scrap of something floatable over the bow and timing its progress to the stern. That seemed both unnecessarily energetic and wasteful. I came up with a simpler system which, in deference to the genteel manners of my native city, I called the Scouser's Log. This enabled me to calculate our speed without the need to move an inch from my comfortable position in the hatchway and with no more physical effort than a quick spit over the side. As long as I spat at right angles to the centreline, the distance the globule had to travel to the stern, once it was afloat, was eight feet. Some quick calculations came up with tables showing, for example, that if it reached the stern in two seconds, we were travelling at two point four knots. Should the reader wish to adopt this exemplary form of speedometer, a system which, apart from not costing a single penny to install, requires for its perfect and constant functioning nothing more than basic skills in expectoration and the ability to count, then the universal formula, summarising Mingming's First and Only Law of Motion, is:

$$x=0.6y/n$$

where x = speed in knots, y = distance in feet from the spitting position to the stern, and n = number of seconds it takes the globule to reach the stern. For those who go to sea in grander craft where the unit of measurement is the metre, the formula becomes:

$$x=2y/n$$

Any oligarch in possession of this formula can impress his guests on the lounge deck of his Mediterranean-based motor yacht with a surreptitious hoik over the side, a quick look at his watch, and an announcement along the lines of *Well now, at the 12.73 knots we are currently making, we should dock at San Remo at 6.17 this evening. More champagne, anyone?* It would be as well, however, if he remembers not to try this trick on the windward side, particularly if the mistral has set in.

On we crept towards the unseen mountains that loomed large only on my chart; for the moment their imminence was no more than an act of faith. I scanned the murk ahead. From time to time little variations in the density and patterning of the greyness had me wondering whether I now had the first hints of land in view, but these lines of darker coloration, usually lying low on the horizon, and therefore easy to misinterpret, soon merged back into the general palette.

A temporary return of my toothache had me once more examining my dental kit. It was clear that if the problem deteriorated the remedy would have to be medicinal rather than surgical. With just a single course of antibiotics on board I decided to hold off any prescription for the moment. A fishing boat crossed ahead and disappeared over the western horizon. A bout of misty rain came and went.

I scanned the murk ahead and at eleven on the morning of Wednesday the sixth of July, our fourteenth day at sea, made out the unmistakable tilting form of the headland Eggøya, fine on the starboard bow. The wind once more fell right away, but the fog and low cloud kept up a constant reorganisation, alternately clearing and thickening in horizontal folds, and thereby creating momentary striations of visibility through which, just a few minutes later, a long ridge of snow-capped peaks appeared. We lay to the heave of the ocean and I admired the stillness of those peaks rising from the mist, their angularity and their iciness softened by the humid air that in places trailed in wisps from the highest points. We too hung motionless and I was happy in our immobility. The land was there. It would come and go to the dictates of the shifting haze. The land was there, but for the moment it was ephemeral and dreamlike, elusive and light as air. Horizontal slices of snow and ridge showed and disappeared. Nothing was joined up; nothing gave a sense of the whole. I felt no urgency. The land was there and in time it may, perhaps, reveal itself, but why hurry? Nothing could be more stirring than these softly-focussed tableaux of rock and ice that hung disembodied over the strata of sea-bound fog.

We crept imperceptibly landwards, pushed on by the current and, from time to time, the tiniest breaths of wind. The mountains disappeared. A seal broke the surface and stared at us. A hundred fulmars snoozed in our non-existent wake. I lowered the mainsail. Another zephyr came in and I raised the mainsail. A slice of southern mountain showed through the mist and was gone. Midnight came. A little auk, all slippery energy, dived for his supper around the boat. With the wind now, it seemed, gone for good I once more lowered the mainsail and slept. The mountains of the southern capes were just seven miles to our north-west. I slept in the cradle of that crescent of pinnacles. There was a comfort in their unseen and unspeaking presence. For two hours I slept a deep and contented sleep while the mountains and the ocean and the mists of the air waited, in silence, for another day.

9

I go to sea to see the sea. It is the wide ocean itself that is always calling. The land has little purchase. Little, that is, until it thrusts skywards in the wildest and most improbable of places.

The great continents sliding their way east and west and north and south around the earth's sphere are, for all their mass and seeming solidity, the expression of a kind of geophysical accident, the sum of the irregularities of the cooling of the planet's mantle, the eruptions of transient and uneven pressures. Time was, once the steaming moisture of our atmosphere had condensed to form the sea, that there was little but the sea. Observed in geological time it is the land which is the inconstant; the ocean is always there, absorbing the rise and fall and shift of the temporary rock on which we live.

Yes, it is the sea which, for all its apparent restlessness, is the constant. The heart of the world is the ocean; to sail to the heart of the ocean is to know the essence of the world a little better. But these islands! Accidents though they may be, rock and lava forced by unimaginable pressures from the bed of the ocean to the topmost heights of a thinning atmosphere; provisional though they may be, falling back, in time, beneath the inexorable waves, or simply ground down and washed back whence they came; what a pull they exert!

Is it that a gravitational force can work on the mind as well as the body? Or is it their very improbability which acts as a magnet? Or is it their awful aesthetic, the raw but harmonious contrast of sea and pinnacle, which draws the eye and drags in the body? I had sailed away to see the sea, but was now pulled back to the bosom of this great island monolith.

Lying to the pulse of the swell in the lee and shadow of this line of half-seen peaks I felt a soft joy and an all-pervasive calm. For a moment or two all the rush and hurry of the world evaporated. There was nothing but the now, which was time without end.

Awake once more I came to the hatch and settled in to my vigil. A silver sea merged into the folds of mist. Mirrored fulmars, heads under wings, slept to the rhythm of the ocean's breath. I looked to the west, towards the land, and let out an involuntary *Oh!* High to port, and framed by trails of insubstantial vapour, was a chance tableau of the most ethereal beauty. A horizontal clear patch had formed in the mist, leaving the sky open along a short stretch of mountain top. In the bigger scene it was a tiny opening, the slightest window through to the peaks beyond, but the peaks sparkled softly in the early morning Arctic sunshine, sunshine which was denied to the rest of the world hereabouts. Not only was this singular hint of the island lit by the universal spotlight, and therefore favoured and distinct, it was wreathed in rainbow, or, one might even say, rainbows, for the sun acting on the multi-layered mist had thrown up a crown of interlacing spectra. There was nothing brash or strident about this wash of colours laid over the ground of mist and mountain; it was little more than a scarcely perceptible shimmer, white light split to its component parts and glinting through a million droplets of the finest vapour.

In accord with the stillness of the day the mists hugging the sea, and therefore veiling the lower buttresses of rock, withdrew, or perhaps dissolved, without any sense of movement or dynamic. Here was the revelation of an island by imperceptible degrees as the enfolding fog transmuted to clearer air. It was impossible to discern any instant of change; the scene was frozen; but here now were more patches of mountain, and to the south the last headland was gaining substance and solidity. The only pattern or logic that could be assigned to this slow withdrawal of the mists was that its general trend was from south to north.

It took many hours, perhaps half a day, for the skirts and veils of the island to dissolve, and there was indeed something of the tease in this stripping bare of the land. Hints of curves and contours hung insubstantial in the upper mists. Shoulders of rock suggested themselves. Midriffs of mountain showed through the folds, midriffs bold in the zebra patterning of descending and close-spaced snow gullies offset against black basalt.

A little breeze came up and I raised the sail to ghost in towards the hard flesh of the land; there was no choice but to come as near as propriety allowed. Borne on a placid sea and driven by the faintest of breaths *Mingming* moved quietly in towards the high peaks of the southern range. These peaks fell swiftly to the sea, meeting the water in a whole vocabulary of configurations. Here was a tall and abrupt cliff, mitred at its topmost point and for all the world recalling the north-west Icelandic headland Horn. Here were softer shoulders, worn by time to a smooth curvature and nudging gently into the sea. Most obvious were the stupendous gouges of defunct glaciers, ten-lane motorways scouring the land from peak to valley and pushing flat and level into the sea like gigantic slipways. There was a certain pathos to the emptiness of these glacier tracks, to the work of millennia now stripped of any utility. It was hard not to recall the exclamations of Lord Dufferin, perhaps the first man who came to this island without commercial intent, and who enthused over

'a lucent precipice of grey-green ice, rising to the height of several hundred feet above the masts of the vessel'.

The mists cleared slowly from the south, and for a while I harboured the hope that, in time, Beerenberg itself would be stripped bare. At one point a wide band of icy slope at several thousand feet of altitude, perhaps a third of the way up the volcano, showed through the cloud. It was more than had ever been revealed, and it raised my pulse a little, but it was still a paltry section of the whole.

We headed in towards the land, hard on the port tack, with scarcely wind enough to raise a gurgling at the forefoot, and as we moved in the mountains stood higher and starker, and the blackness of their composition diffused into a palette of greys and dark browns and even, on the softer slopes, unpitted by cliffs or gullies or geological collapse, a gentle olive green. Up close the zebra patchwork caused by the residual scattering of snow and ice was a more complex and irregular arrangement of light and dark. Towards the peaks it was white which prevailed, white broken only by an occasional sharp line of black where a ridge broke through. As the pattern descended the darker shades took the ascendancy, asserting themselves through the increasing diffuse patches of melting snow. Each snow patch was edged in subtle and fluid lines, tightly curving, that hinted at the uneasy contouring of the land.

We headed in towards the tiny horseshoe bay marked on my chart as Bratvika, and for a while I was convinced that there was a yacht anchored cleverly within its confines. I could make out a boxy white hull and a tall mast rising. It seemed to me to be an impressive feat of seamanship, speaking of boldness or local knowledge, or perhaps both, to bring a yacht to anchor in this half-moon gouge in the coastline. I conceived the idea of getting in close enough to sail across the mouth of the bay and giving the boat a hail; there was a good chance it was the same yacht which had overtaken us a few days before. This rather silly and pointless ambition soon faded; the ungainly hull resolved itself into a small white hut low on the shoreline with a radio mast alongside. Feeling more than a little foolish I bore away to the north.

10

The central portion of the island, much lower in elevation but decorated with all manner of unworldly humps and twisted eruptions of rock, was now all but clear of mist. The upper air had reverted to long trails of proper cloud, cloud broken by the occasional streak of blue that gave me a last hope that as we moved north I might yet glimpse the upper cone of Beerenberg. For the whole day I tracked the evolution of these patches, but it was no good; without fail they merged back to solid sky as they pushed in towards the mountain.

Beerenberg was hidden, then, and would remain hidden for the duration of our passage along the island. I had expected that if this were the case I would be deeply disappointed; I had, after all, devoted a large part of two summers' sea time questing for a good view of the volcano. Beerenberg was hidden but as we ghosted north, still angling in towards the land and thereby edging always closer to the headland Eggöya, all disappointment evaporated. It was enough to be within hailing distance of this mighty shore. Beyond Eggöya, itself an extraordinary compilation of canted and competing slabs of geological strata, the layering of its southern shoulder angled almost vertical and therefore hinting at the stupendous tectonic ructions hereabouts, the middle ground turned to a softly contoured alpine valley. This valley sloped gently upwards between two rounded ridges until the whole arrangement disappeared into the cloud base. I sailed in closer, drawn by this scoop in the land and the subdued green of its thin summer covering and its scattering of residual snow. I had many times walked up such valleys high in the Bernese Oberland, and here now was one brought down to the sea itself. We were sailing through the Alps.

The one counterbalance to this delicious illusion lay at the interface between sea and mountain. Along this stretch of coast the land was fringed with a low stratum of black lava scoured by sea and perhaps ice to a repeating pattern of smooth rock pierced by deep indentations into which the slight swell now broke. I had missed this feature during our previous pass up this coast. Now I could see it, and hear too the clamour of waves swirling and breaking within the tight vertical chimneys which somehow serrated the land's edge.

A little further on we came to the base of Beerenberg itself. An almost proper breeze had come in from the south-west, allowing me to abandon the steering lines I had been using for the hours of ghosting northwards and to hook up the self-steering gear. We were now easing off to the north-east to skirt the monolith little more than half a mile or so offshore. With a detailed chart at hand I named each bay as we passed: Jameson Bay, Turn Bay, Håp Bay. These were not bays in the accepted sense, being little more than the shallowest of curves between the occasional rocky protrusion, but the chart suggested that some could be used as anchorages. Perhaps, in centuries past, ships of the northern whale fishery had lain here from time to time. Had they done so, they would have seen a different order of glacier to those that we were now passing. Here was the Sörbreen, the South Glacier, no doubt once a monumental frozen cliff now reduced, at its lower edge, to thin tongues of ice made mucky by the black rock showing through from beneath and petering out well above the waterline.

This ice was wilting and somehow accusatory; it did not

invite too much examination. I was glad, then, when we suddenly became the focus of a burgeoning of fulmars. The brooding immobility of the land was offset by an eruption of hundreds and hundreds of birds. They attached themselves to our wake, all hot life and ceaseless movement, perhaps, eventually, several thousand of them engaged in a restless merry-go-round of take-off and land as they kept with us by sea and air. In all our miles of voyaging we had never attracted such an entourage. Whether they came from nearby breeding colonies or were part of a non-breeding population drawn in by waters rich in nutrients was impossible to say. For several hours, in a breeze that was once more failing and, as we came up to the towering cliff of the North-East Cape, becoming increasingly gyratory, *Mingming* led this parade of tightly-massed birds whirling and bobbing along our track. It was a privilege to be accorded such attention and to be thus escorted close along the island's shore, to share a moment of companionship that dissolved any sense of aloneness and offset the bleakness of the icy slopes to port.

The wind fell away to nothing and we were left bucking in a typical headland slop. A thousand wings took to the air in a sudden rush as a bottle-nosed whale surfaced close by. I studied the grey rock of the North-East Cape, rock that here had an unstable and dissolute look to it, for it had crumbled in parts to great falls of scree, leaving the topmost edge of the Cape projecting outwards in a treacherous-looking cantilever. It was a high bluff, this one, perhaps a thousand feet or more, in part overhung by the puffy undercarriage of the passing cloud. As we moved out to the north-east the final stretch of northern coastline, a long line of precipitous falls striped vertically with snow gullies and glaciers, and petering out to the long spit of the North Cape, came slowly into view, so that we now had the whole eastern side of the island laid out in a single sweeping panorama. There was no choice but to sit and admire the prospect, for I had lowered the mainsail to spare it slatting.

For the whole night we worked painfully offshore as short-lived blows from all quarters interspersed with holes devoid of wind. I had spent nineteen hours at the hatch absorbing every visible detail of the island. Now, in the calms, I slept.

Mount Beerenberg stood silent behind its veil of cloud. The bottle-nose whale still stalked us. The fulmars bickered, indefatigable. I slept, and as I slept my mind turned away from the land, away from the mountains, away from ice and rock, away from the illusory comfort of the hard and stable; that was once more behind us. For the second time we were pushing out into the Greenland Sea and were thus back to the main business of this voyage. It took until seven in the morning for a proper wind to establish itself, a brisk north-westerly that soon had us plunging to the north-north-east under four panels of sail. I stowed my Jan Mayen chart and pulled out Norwegian Chart 515: Svalbard to Greenland. With my dividers I measured off a few distances. Five hundred miles ahead lay the north-west coast of Spitsbergen. Perhaps more importantly, six hundred miles of sailing would now take us to my target of 80°North 10°East. That was if we sailed straight there. I still hankered after keeping on due north and sailing over the tip of the Vesteris Seamount. This was, as it turned out, a vain hope. Thus far we had had an easy time. That was soon to change.

11

Ah yes, the sea! The wretched marvellous sea! Always the damned sea! What needs a man more than a stiff breeze and a blank horizon curling onwards over the edge of the world? Why the singing heart as the high rock falls once more behind? Why this draw to the perfidious waves? What madness is it? Or what sanity beyond reason? Why always this searching?

We pulled out once more into a frigid ocean and my spirits soared. Ahead lay as blank and unprimed a canvas of deserted water as a man could hope for. Here there may be monsters, or undreamed of sirens, or many-volumed and unwritten catalogues of untellable tales. Here was possibility writ large: the dread expansiveness of life beyond the pale.

Yes, my heart sang as the great mountain fell behind, still squeezed low between sea and sky, its last glaciers suddenly all a-sparkle as the sunlight cleaved a path through the enveloping cloud. The land had pulled me in but its spell was now broken; I did not look back longingly or regret the leaving. The land was rock hard and seemingly immutable, dense and intractable, and therefore unsuited to the evanescence of real adventure; too stolid, too pedestrian, too damned down-to-earth.

Now we rose and dipped to the dancing of the waves. Nothing was fixed. Nothing was ordained. No movement was predictable. We skipped along on a shifting cradle of never-resting energy. The only certainty was uncertainty, and with uncertainty came freedom, or at least the most of that commodity that a man could hope for in a world that anchors him to the dull earth with heavy-duty cables and a criss-cross of extra lines for good measure.

Yes, it was the fleeting and the insubstantial that drew me on, the restless and the serendipitous, the inconstant, the capricious and the volatile. We skipped along over the dancing waves with no greater intent or ambition than to see what would be seen and to feel what would be felt. I grew light-headed with the prospect, and *Mingming* too seemed lighter of body, an illusion of transference of the buoyancy of the moment, no doubt, but no less uplifting for that. We skipped on towards the blank horizon, careless of purpose, just going, or going for the sake of going, just going to see where it would bring us to, and what it would bring to us.

As we went I breathed deeply the sharp air from the north-west. This was air that came off the ice and was crystal clear and cold. It was pure air scoured purer by its long passage over the sea. I breathed it deeply and felt purified by the intake. Here was pure air at the conjunction with an undefiled sea, or nearly so. Its coldness had me shivering, but it brought me too to acuteness and aliveness; I welcomed the chill of this air.

Beerenberg fell into the cloud astern and we were once more alone; now properly cut adrift, that is, from the idea of the mountain. For several days the sky above us had been overborne by the notion of Beerenberg's towering presence. I had not in any real sense seen it, nor could I swear that it really was there. It had weighed heavily on us through nothing more than the power of the mind's construction. The weight of that mountain, its leadenness, was now gone.

We skipped away, then, from this improbable eruption, the one stain of land on a wide and otherwise unblemished sea. To take a departure thus and strike out on the second stage of our voyage demanded a symbolic gesture or two by way of marking the moment. I shaved, and changed my underwear, and pulled on track suit bottoms in place of jeans, and added a woollen sweater to my upper body layering. I sat in the hatchway and thought about how good it felt to be sailing properly once more, to have a fulsome weight of wind driving us along, to be back once more to the dip and plunge of muscular progression in a robust sea. We were hard on the wind and therefore advancing only modestly, but in full engagement with the shifting geometry of every passing wave; for the moment the simple pleasure of this gentle roller-coasting outweighed any consideration of speed or direction.

A black guillemot appeared and attached itself to our wake, flying in low and fast to lunge-feed just a yard or two off the stern. A little later it zoomed past right alongside, a flash of black and white trailing blood-red feet.

For another night and another day we pulled away from the idea of the mountain, always working to windward in a north-north-westerly that was up and down but always adequate. I sang a round of shanties and reflected on the pathos of a dying glacier. I reviewed once more all the options for the route to take to the far north and back, and settled for an anti-clockwise circuit, thereby utilising the currents to maximum effect, a plan that was excellent in the abstract but unachievable in practice; unkind winds put paid to it. I studied a new gull that joined us briefly, its wings long and slender and pure white to the very tips: an Iceland gull. A flurry of spouts off the port quarter raised my pulse a little, and my hopes, for I had long had it in mind that these northern waters must surely be a-swim with whales. I stared at the sea, now rendered indigo-black by a temporary patch of clear sky pushing along overhead, and felt the heaviness of the air, cold and solid and, on this second evening away from the land, starting to build to something more purposeful.

Before long we were down to one panel, a reduction in sail that I noted at the time as being more precautionary than anything else. At midnight I settled down for an hour or two's rest. *Mingming* plugged slowly along through a rising but seemingly unthreatening sea. I slept. My dreams, if there were any, have long since gone. I would like to think that I drifted away through a seascape of ice and mirrored ocean and floated skywards and turned away from the world and fell through black space in a soft and endless fall lit only by the pinpoints of a billion stars.

12

The knockdown, when it came, fused its first moments into whatever I was dreaming. The initial roll to leeward forced my well-swaddled body gently against the inside of the hull and, at my midriff, the navigation locker. It was a movement experienced a hundred times previously, and as gravity took over and pressed my nose harder against the hull's lining of foam and carpet, I only half-woke. In a state of dreamy semi-consciousness I felt the rotation of *Mingming's* hull as whatever combination of wind and wave it was that now had her in its grip rolled her onto her beam ends. To be thus laid out on the horizontal plane was all in a day's work, and it was only the smooth and unhindered continuation of this rotation past the horizontal that dragged me fully out of my dreamworld.

Mingming carried on spinning until I was lying face down against the hull and starting to fall skywards, or at least in the direction I normally reckoned the sky to be. I don't remember whether this moment was accompanied by the crash and roar of a normal knockdown; somehow my aural senses had not quite got going again. There was a slight lurch in my stomach as *Mingming* turned over almost to full inversion, but in the few fractions of a second that the whole knockdown seemed to take, my overwhelming sentiment was one of curiosity as to the outcome. *Would we come back up? What would happen if we didn't?* These questions never reached such precise verbalisation at the time; they were little more than unformed interrogation marks somewhere in the depths.

The answers, in any case, came quickly. After the briefest moment of stasis in the upside-down position, a moment so fleeting that I had scarcely started to lift off from my bunk before being deposited back downwards, the motion reversed itself and *Mingming* regained her usual orientation to the ocean, mast aloft, keels alow, skipper abed.

The whole interlude was over so quickly that I could have been forgiven for having thought I had dreamed it, were it not for the clinical rearrangement of *Mingming's* interior. *Mingming* is always well-stowed for the sea. Everything aboard of any weight or consequence is appropriately lashed down, restrained, wedged, enclosed, harnessed, shackled or smothered. Or so I thought. This was by no means our first excursion away from the vertical, but it created opportunities for the self-liberation of bits of our sea-going inventory that I had never before thought possible. Deep shelves emptied themselves. My insulated mug somehow escaped its purpose-built holder and took to the air. The top step of the companionway, a hefty lump of mahogany that in the previous seventeen thousand miles or so of ocean voyaging had moved not so much as a millimetre, successfully broke away from its downtrodden place in the world and went off travelling. The carefully stowed cordage and timber of my bosun's store, an immutable mountain of *things that might come in handy*, comprehensively adjusted both its internal arrangement and its geographical location. My navigational instruments: dividers, compasses, pencils, parallel rules, Portland RIB plotter and the like, scattered to the four corners of the cabin. It was three weeks before I finally rediscovered the plotter skulking under a bunk cushion.

The tightly-packed and well-drilled order of the cabin had been destroyed, and it was clearly going to take a good while to reassemble *Mingming's* dislocated interior, but as far as I could tell there had been no physical damage. This was a misapprehension: when I tried to open the hatch to check the mast and assess the state of sea and sky, it would only open several inches. Something was blocking it. This was an interesting innovation, one that I had often thought about. If the single exit from the cabin would not open I would be trapped below. Whilst I was very much at home and supremely comfortable inside *Mingming*, and furnished, for a while at least, with all that was necessary for good living, I was unlikely to accept this imprisonment. If necessary I would have to re-engineer *Mingming* from the inside out and create another exit. I had the tools to do it. I shoved harder against the hatch and it opened a few inches more, enough to get a hand and forearm out. The copper pipe framing of the spray hood had been crushed downwards and inwards. A piece of the starboard framing had been bent to a tight V over the hatch. Using brute strength I was able to straighten it back up enough to open the hatch.

Outside it was blowing no more than half a gale, with a sea that, but for the knockdown, would not have raised the slightest concern. How we had managed to be so comprehensively upended was something of a puzzle. There had evidently been some force in the rogue wave that had rolled us: I now saw the second item of damage, this time to one of my new plywood panels holding the series drogue in its place on the cockpit seats. The port-side panel had fractured near one end; the sudden weight of the coiled drogue on it, as we went over, had clearly been too much to bear.

I lowered the last panel of the sail, lashed the sail bundle amidships and turned *Mingming* off the wind. With the self-steering set at a hundred and thirty-five degrees to the apparent wind we ran gently off to the south. It was heart-wrenching to be headed the wrong way, but I needed to draw breath. The decision to run off was in any case soon justified: within an hour or two an icy blast from the north, a good solid uncompromising gale, had the mast clanking and juddering in a seamless industrial cacophony. I pulled on my oilskins for the first time of the voyage and mentally rehearsed the sequence for launching the series drogue, should it come to that. The gale was already starting to back, though, bending us round to a more easterly and therefore marginally more acceptable heading, and suggesting too that maybe the blow would be short-lived. I used the toilet bucket without mishap below or above deck, and stowed my cameras in an empty watertight food container, just in case. I eased *Mingming* a little further off the wind as it reached its crescendo, a move that softened our motion, but also brought on an inadvertent gybe that took some minutes of irritating readjustment to correct. Whilst at the hatch I took the opportunity to splint the badly damaged spray hood strut with a short piece of thick dowel and some gaffer tape, a temporary repair that still serves.

My noon position showed that we had lost about seven and a half minutes of latitude over the twenty-four hours. It was galling to be thus set backwards, but matters could have been much worse. The disappointment was mainly that we were still forty or so miles from 72°North, the most northerly latitude we had previously reached. I was keen to be over this line; only then would I feel that we had broken free into unknown territory.

A little after midday on Sunday the tenth of July, our eighteenth day at sea, I raised half a panel of sail and brought us a little harder on a wind that was now losing its ferocity. It was still a cold wind, though, a nasty uncompromising brute of a wind, a devious wind too, that followed each feint towards the west with a reversal back to north, thereby damning all hopes of quick progress. I tried to restore some order to poor old *Mingming,* and wished I had her heart. She plugged on, indifferent to every break and tear and rend in her fabric; I, though, was of less stern stuff. I felt drained, and ill, and fed up. As evening came I stretched out on my bunk and found solace in a short and dreamless sleep.

13

It was the best of storms: very sharp and quickly gone, and in its wake came a hotchpotch of calms and swirling little breezes. These innocuous and inconstant draughts started out from all quarters, but as each day passed they settled in more firmly from the north. We struggled past 72°North and thus liberated ourselves from the known and the familiar, and struck out towards the heart of the Greenland Sea. Every mile was hard-won, accumulated one by one to post daily runs that almost without fail fell marginally short of satisfying: forty-two miles, forty-five miles, sixty-six miles, forty miles, forty-six miles and so on.

We were making progress and I could not complain about that, but for several days I was afflicted by a mix of nausea and lethargy, a debilitating combination that required some willpower to counteract. The temptation was to sleep, but heaviness bred further heaviness, and I fought to keep awake. I sat in the chill air of the hatch and forced myself to watch the endless procession of waves. I opened my notebook and wrote page after page of inconsequential prose. I drank an excess of water; it was likely that this bout of malaise was brought on by slight dehydration.

We pushed on across the Greenland Sea, our course skewed further to the east than I would have liked. Any hope of sailing over the Vesteris Seamount was abandoned. The days were not monotonous, even though in the generality there was little to distinguish one from the next. Every twenty-four hours brought its new round of minutiae: a patch of cold rain, a sudden drop in barometric pressure, a long-tailed skua, a flood of brilliant and warming sunshine, the happy realisation that Bjørnøya now lay two hundred and forty miles to our east, the finishing of my first container of trail mix, a thick fog constricting the world, the pulling on of a second pair of tracksuit bottoms, an hour with the wind free and *Mingming* striding due north, another calm. Detail piled on tiny detail to create the substance of our voyage. I started to feel a little better. A pod of killer whales hurtled by on our starboard beam, heading south. I ate another mint as each degree of latitude was crossed. I grew more comfortable with the cold and worried that my time may run out before we reached 80°North.

Yes, I was happy enough to be plodding along at such a leisurely pace; it was, after all, our adopted role in the world. But I could not quite dismiss the spectre of other less pliable timetables. We were falling well short of the daily average distance covered during our previous voyages. As each day passed that average was falling further. The basis on which I had planned the timings for the voyage was already seriously eroded. I was not unduly worried; conditions can change quickly and it only needed a good bout of fair winds to redress the balance. However an internal debate had started as to how much extra time I could allot to the voyage if our modest progress continued. It had not yet reached its full declamatory status, this debate; it was more that the outlines of a vague motion were starting to form in the back of my head, something along the lines of '*This house believes that sailing on north should take precedence over a few business obligations*'. Speakers were lining up on each side, preparing their notes and rehearsing their arguments, in case battle should be enjoined.

We pushed gently on towards Spitsbergen, with what little wind there was bending our course in a clock-wise arc towards the southern end of the island. There was only one consolation in this deviation from our ideal track: it was taking us more firmly into the north-going current. It was also moving us towards shallower water, and at three in the afternoon on the sixteenth of July, our twenty-fourth day at sea, as I was standing in the hatch engaged in some minor sail management, a black- and white-striped torpedo, some ten feet long, fizzed down our starboard beam just a couple of feet under the surface. A second missile followed, it too judging its near-miss to perfection. White-beaked dolphins! I had not seen any dolphins for several weeks, and now here they were again. Earlier that day I had been thinking about this long absence, and whether or not we were now beyond the limits of the dolphins' northerly range. My handbook had confirmed that it was the white-beaked dolphin that has the most northerly distribution, but that they were to be found in '*the cool, temperate and sub-Arctic waters of the North Atlantic*'. 75°North was somewhat beyond 'sub-Arctic'. I had given up hope of meeting these robust and acrobatic creatures, yet here they now were.

As is often the case with cetacean encounters, one pod leads to another. Within seconds a group of common bottle-nose dolphins, these even more distanced from their accepted range, came leaping in from square on the port beam, streaked underneath *Mingming* and continued straight on. It was strangely satisfying to be seeing all these animals where they are not supposed to be. It gave weight to the idea that we were sailing in waters which are virtually never visited; we were still well to the west of the normal route between northern Norway and Svalbard. It was quite probable that the textbooks were wrong simply because of a lack of data. Marine biologists are severely constrained in their ability to cover large tracts of remote sea. They are largely limited to inshore waters, or have to hire pelagic vessels for short periods at huge expense. *Mingming* and I were able to spend a protracted time well off the beaten track. Whilst my observations were no more than those of a rank amateur, they raised the status of our voyage from the frivolous to the quasi-scientific. From time to time during our voyages I had felt the first sprouting of Darwinian whiskers. Here they were again, decorating my cheeks with a thick white floss as I made copious and self-important notes and wondered at what point I would be able to start referring to myself not as a sailor, but as a *cetologist*.

We clawed out way onto the south-western reaches of my chart for southern Svalbard: Bjørnøya to Isfjorden. The nearest land, Sørkappøya, or South Cape Island, was now a little less than one hundred and fifty miles away, but for a few days more any prospects of making real progress, whether towards the sounds and ice-capped mountains of Spitsbergen, or whether towards our less substantial goal of the eightieth parallel, were diminished even further as the winds fell away to almost nothing. What breezes there were tended to the adverse and the fickle, sending us one way then the other in a series of dog-legs and banana curves, meanderings that racked up the miles but which in their Euclidean analysis, that is to say in their ultimate straight-line geometry in any meaningful direction, yielded paltry results. The Arctic high pressure system had us firmly in its grip, and for a while I despaired of finding enough motive power to bring us within sight of even the southern tip of Spitsbergen. We lay static beneath a warmish sun that soon burned off the last remnants of a mackerel sky and left a sea of patch-worked mirrors and cats' paws. I set the light weather jib, raising a bubble or two at the forefoot. We passed a kittiwake perched on a floating log. More dolphins played around at distance, one thrashing along in a series of a dozen or so stupendous breaches. I studied the chart and acquainted myself with regions and coastlines that heretofore had not figured in my plans and calculations: Sørkapp-Land, Wedel Jarlsberg Land, Hornsund, Bellsund. This was the geography of south-west Spitsbergen, and I could not warm to it; it was the north I was after. For a while, though, the north was unattainable, and my thoughts grew daily more capitulatory and treacherous. All I could hope for was, say, to sail into the mouth of the nearest fjord, the Bellsund, sixty miles to our east, before heading for home. Even that unwholesome turning point drifted out of reach as a slight breeze came up from that very quarter. It seemed that whichever way we turned the route was blocked.

14

It is no bad thing to lie unrequited beneath an Arctic sun, and to be thus forced to reconsider time and motion and direction. Why should a man always need to be going somewhere, to be forever getting on? Why should he be counting every minute and every mile, and fussing over the compass heading of his trivial little peregrinations? Is it not enough to be alive and to be by that very fact another body in motion, without worrying constantly at the what and wherefore of that motion? Is it not enough that a man can see the sun and feel the pulse of the sea and know the caress of an icy wind on his cheek? What matters it whether he is pointing this way or that? Who but a fool would forget that we are all hurtling along on our little sphere, spinning and falling at speeds beyond comprehension into a blackness without end?

Yes, impaled on a sea of soft-focus azure a thousand miles from home, I finally rid myself of the gnawing pettiness of temporal constraint and gave myself over to the moment. It had taken nearly a month to break free, but now my mind and intent was clear: I would take as long over this voyage as was needed. Having reached this far I would continue to 80°N, however long it took. Neither would I worry about our rate of progress. I had in any event come to the conclusion that two knots, or to give it its more effervescent form, one thousand bubbles per minute, is the decisive speed. As long as one is moving along at two knots or thereabouts, as an average, anything is possible and everything is tolerable. Two knots equates to two point three statute miles per hour, an easy strolling pace. What could be more satisfying than to range the oceans at a comfy walking speed, with scarcely leg or finger to lift in the process? Two knots is fast enough to get there, slow enough to miss nothing on the way: fifty miles or so a day, three hundred and fifty miles a week, fourteen hundred miles a month. The more I thought about it, the better it sounded. Two knots cuts a fair compromise between the desire for stasis and the need for momentum. One is still, but not too still; ambulant, but not too ambulant. Progress is made at a gentle rhythmic trot rather than an easy canter, or worse still, a breathless gallop. As long as one is making two knots one can maintain a justified optimism.

It may well be that thus new-found approval of two knots as an ideal average speed was no more than an adaptation to the facts of the voyage. This was the average towards which our daily runs were heading. I had no choice in the matter, so I may as well learn to live with it and tease out its positive features.

I reflected further on this minimal requirement and saw too how it relieves this kind of sailing of anything particularly skilful or meritorious. All that is required is a dogged commitment. All that matters is the next twenty-four hours, the next fifty miles. How they accrue into a long distance is little more than a side effect. A voyage of, say, two thousand four hundred miles is nothing more than an unchallenging fifty miles a day, repeated for forty-eight days; thus is a voyage structured.

Matters are made even simpler for the sailor whose inclination is to keep the sea, for he is spared the difficulties and dangers of coastal pilotage. With the wide ocean to roam on he can wander this way or that, careless of too much accuracy in his navigation. One position fix a day, enough to maintain a general heading in the right direction, is more than adequate. Thus can a man rid himself of the tyranny of instrumentation and leave himself free to consider matters of greater import: the pleasing curvature of a bottle-nosed dolphin's fin, for example, or the morphology of a krill-like crustacean evidently washed on board and left to dry on the cabin top.

It also occurred to me that to keep the sea, alone and incommunicado, in wilful isolation and without too much regard for the niceties of where one is or where one is heading, is more than just a liberation; over time it leads to a kind of transformation. The starting point for this change is the gradual shedding of the land-bound persona: not the losing of self itself, as it were, but the self as constructed by social and personal need. This self is by definition and necessity a largely artificial self. It is oneself as one is seen, and oneself as one would like to be seen. It is the self as a single and largely inflexible part of a communal machine and therefore a constricted and circumscribed self. It is the self which is held rigid by a web of social relations and constraints. It is the self which, in a thousand insidious ways, is numbered, classified, ranked, pigeon-holed, examined, filtered, surveyed, judged and ultimately entrapped. It is the passported self, the stamped, taxed and censored self, the bank accounted self, the credit and debit carded self, the Nationally Insured self, the Travelcarded, Senior Rail Carded, licensed, pensioned, passworded and user-named self; the self, that is to say, imprisoned by such cloying and invasive social constructs and conventions that its room for personal manoeuvre is severely delimited. It is also the spied on self, the internet tracked self, the closed circuit televised self, the national data-based self, the socially networked and mediated self, the politically pressured self, the self as the object of incessant scrutiny, the self as the object of incessant marketing, the self as one of seven billion sales opportunities.

It takes time and distance and a good dose of the tonic of wildness to slough off the hardened carapace of this particular self. It also requires total rupture with the land and with land-based things. This shell we carry, imposed though it may be, grows into the very flesh of the self; it becomes a part of us, subcutaneous. We learn to live with it, we learn to like it, in time we come to love it, for it is what we see as our true self; it will not yield easily.

Now, at last, I was losing this self. In these far reaches of the Arctic seas it had no relevance. The cage that held it tight and compressed it to shape and substance was gone. Off it sidled, over the southern horizon, to await its moment to pounce back and reassert itself.

For the moment, though, I was free of it, and I breathed more easily, and looked on the sea and the sky and the birds and the whales with a different eye. I saw things more simply, more clearly, perhaps a little more as they are. I was able to look and absorb with a vision free of the distorting filters of that manufactured persona. I looked more and thought less, and so I took in more, and felt a little more at home. I must not exaggerate: this was only a small shift, the slightest tilt in the perception of this oceanic world, but it seemed to bring me a little closer to it.

15

I gave myself up wholly to the moment, then, and buried the terrestrial past, and immediately found favour. The wind hauled to the north-east, freshening as it went and allowing us, at last, to plunge on due north. At one in the morning of Wednesday the twentieth of July, our twenty-eighth day at sea, we passed 77°N, and an hour later a rounded mountain top appeared low above the horizon almost square on the starboard beam. Spitsbergen! It was evidently one of the peaks at the north end of Wedel Jarlsberg Land, the Storgubben perhaps, or maybe the four thousand-foot Berzeliustinden. It was a moment of some satisfaction, to have brought *Mingming* to within sight of this distant rock.

I glowed warmly inside, which was just as well, for the wind now veered to the east, straight off the glacial heights of the nearby land, and ratcheted itself up a further notch or two. We were soon down to a single panel, but with the wind free and a disconcertingly robust swell that had somehow set in from the south-east putting its shoulder to our little wheel, we were frolicking northwards at a fine old pace. This was doubly pleasing, for as well as advancing us rapidly towards our goal it also had us heading towards a crescent of limpid blue sky that spanned the northern horizon. The heavens above and astern were choked with a stratum of heavy black cloud, cloud in which any lateral movement was indiscernible, but which nonetheless seemed to be slowly lifting and thinning out.

For a whole day we hurtled along. The single tooth of a mountain to starboard had long since fallen from view, and so for the moment we were back to unalloyed ocean. Something had changed, nonetheless; I knew that the land was there, somewhere not far ahead, and that we were closing it quickly. The northern section of Spitsbergen slants somewhat towards the north-west, and so our northerly course would, if held, bring an inevitable landfall. The day was charged, therefore, with expectation and tension and a sense that our voyage was now firmly back on track.

At six in the afternoon I cooked and ate my main meal, and was quickly back at the hatch. A close-spaced line of jagged peaks, seven of them, crisply delineated against the wash of faded blue that still held to the north, now topped the horizon fine on the starboard bow. The general look of each of these tips, still separated from each other by short spans of clear sea, apart from the two to the right that formed the conjoined and double apex of a large molar, was black and monolithic. Even at that distance, though, I could make out on one of them a vertical gully of snow or ice.

Almost simultaneously the wind began to ease. I was immediately at the main halyard, hauling up panel after panel. *Make sail! Make sail!* With a fair wind on the beam and a wild land ahead, my heart was singing. *More sail, lads! Pile it on, boys!* The peaks were pushing higher every minute, changing their shapes and relationships as they transmuted from individual pinnacles to subsidiary elements of a single range. To either side more tips were piercing the soft line between sea and sky. *Pile it on, lads! Stuns'ls, water sails, moonrakers, skyscrapers! Close those mountains!* On we gambolled though the joyful evening, all care gone, all eyes fixed on the frozen sierra raising its clefts and serrations from out of the very sea itself. Oh, it felt good to be alive! What better thrill than to plunge and roll through a distant sea under this loom of silent rock? What needs a man more than a lovely ship and a fair breeze and the ice-sculpted granite of the ends of the earth?

Yes, my heart was singing, but now the chorus rose to its great crescendo, for there, close on the starboard beam, was a sudden eruption of towering whale spouts. Four... five... eight... eleven... twelve. A forest of silvery trunks stood tall for a moment, then thickened and subsided and merged to a low cloud of drifting moisture. A long back or two, backs whose blackness and perfect curvature and stately rotation suggested that here was a good-sized pod of fin whales, rolled forward through the muscular swell. Then here too were dolphins, a pair of Atlantic white-sided, no doubt companions of the fin whales, who swapped allegiance for a couple of minutes and investigated *Mingming* from every underwater perspective. She was evidently not to their liking; they soon sped off to rejoin the leviathans.

I thought that nothing could be added to sweeten this conjuncture of fair wind and mountain and the company of whales, but I was wrong. The arc of pristine sky to the north had taunted us for a day, and seemed unattainable, but now some readjustment of the cloud cover, aided perhaps by our steady progress north, brought us, at last, into a spate of dazzling sunshine. The great fiery orb was still high in the sky, for it was only eight in the evening. It could do little, though, to reduce the chill of the failing wind that still blew straight off the land, but the brilliance it now added to the seascape and to the mountainscape were compensation enough. Fourteen spiky summits were now visible; the initial grouping of seven had formed a single block of contiguous mountain, but with each mile we advanced another tip or two poked skywards to left and right. It was fascinating, and addictive, to monitor this gradual apparition; it was impossible to abandon my vigil at the hatchway. From time to time my eyes were drawn away by lofty whale spouts to starboard and astern, but they were soon back to the unfolding and fiercely delineated topography ahead. I could not imagine a finer landfall. Not only were the peaks starkly clear in the immaculate Arctic air, and wondrously lunar in the strangeness of their shapes, but the constant readjustment of their relationships brought on by our approach created a kind of narrative. Would two adjacent peaks turn out to be linked by a shallow col, or was their closeness only a trick of the eye that on correction would show them to be distant and independent monoliths? Like all the best stories, it unfolded slowly, and was at first a little puzzling. It took a long while to arrive at a sense of the whole.

The pace was further reduced, for the wind was coming off rapidly. By one in the morning we were becalmed. The first sour note crept in; the swell from the south-east was unrelenting, making for an ugly, throw-about calm. I lowered the mainsail and lashed it firmly, and with a last longing look at the outlandish cordillera ranged ahead, went below to sleep.

16

There are days that are etched indelibly in the memory, days that spring out of the formless generality of the sea-going cycle, days so dazzling and affecting that in just a few hours they can anchor and define a whole month or a whole two months of voyaging. These are the days for which one goes to sea. They cannot be manufactured, these days, or planned or predicted. They arrive without fanfare or invitation, subtly evanescent, and then are quickly on their way.

Thursday the twenty-first of July, our twenty-ninth day at sea, was such a day. Even now, as I sit at my desk of a cold winter's dawn and close my eyes and replay the sequence of images somehow captured by the cells and ganglions of an ageing cerebrum, I can still sense the poise and charm that infused the span of that day. It was magical in the sense that here was a new and different world, a world whose strangeness and unlikeliness suggested that it had been conjured up by spells and incantations, that here was wizardry afoot. It was a kind of rebirth, too. The dull knowns of a past life dissolved. Here were sea and mountain, and in terms of their crude classification there was nothing startling in that. It was just that I suddenly seemed to be looking at both for the first time, not because I was, of course, but because their shape and mood and the nature of their juxtaposition, beneath an Arctic sun and all three therefore forming a triptych of earth, fire and water, were unlike anything I had known before.

But I must not run ahead.

The unwieldy calm did not last long. Within three hours we were under way again, pushed along nicely by a fair breeze that once again came up from the east. At five in the morning we crossed 78°N, and so were now sixty miles due west of the mouth of the Isfjorden, the fjord leading to Svalbard's principal settlement, Longyearben. That distant node of civilisation held no interest; I would, as ever, keep the sea. With each mile of northing yet more summits pushed over the north-east horizon, creating now a whole quadrant of alpine silhouette sharp and black against the wrung-out backdrop of polar air. Counting in an anti-clockwise direction, from south to north, that is, I totted up the peaks now in view. Seventy-three! Those at the margins still rose individually, but the central mass was now solidly conjoined across a good twenty or thirty degrees of arc. The cut-out starkness of outline of this main body of mountain made it difficult to ascribe any sense of depth or perspective to the lay-out. The sheer number and crowdedness of the peaks suggested that many of them were higher summits from far inland fused by the light into the more coastal ranges and thus exaggerating the anarchic toothiness of the whole.

Our trajectory north had quite by chance positioned us along the edge of the continental shelf. The contours of the sea-bed compressed and rose sharply below us, creating the upwellings of nutrients that now brought extraordinary concentrations of whales. Spouts were firing off in all directions, tall columns of fin whale breath in the main, with the occasional low rectangles of humpback exhalations mixed in. Black backs rolled forwards, creating momentary caricatures of the less rounded mountains behind.

It was a primeval scene, a scene of ineffable timelessness, or would have been, had not a small vessel appeared far on the eastern horizon. I studied it with my binoculars. It was more or less motionless and, given its distance and our own heaving in the swell, difficult to evaluate. It seemed to have a sort of gantry at its bow, or what I took to be its bow, which suddenly resolved into a harpoon platform. *Jesus, no!* The day was shattered. I felt sick. Here was a Norwegian whaling ship. The Norwegians still reserve to themselves the right to go after certain species of whale. What better place to do it than here, in waters rich in whale life and far from view? It was numbing and incomprehensible. How could anyone kill these creatures? What awful mentality does it take to fire an exploding device into the brain of a great whale? What poverty of imagination can drive such slaughter? What contempt of life can cry such murder? I had for years considered these questions in the abstract; now I could see them written on the sea before me, in flesh and in blood. Surely it could not happen, right here and now? I studied the vessel again, a mix of nausea and anger deep in my stomach. It began to move, and I realised that my fears, on that day anyway, were unfounded. The harpoon platform was in fact the stern gantry of a normal fishing boat. I had made a daft mistake of visual interpretation; the kind of mistake that distance and poor visibility and the difficulties of using binoculars on a moving platform can often create. Perhaps to the landsman it seems scarcely credible, to take the stern of a ship as its bow, and vice versa, but in my notebook I drew two sketches side by side, the first showing what I thought I had seen, the second depicting what I had actually seen. The two sketches are almost identical and equally valid.

I was much relieved to learn that, for the moment, the cetaceans feeding peacefully all around were not at risk of slaughter. I did not regret my mistake, though. It had triggered a deep-seated and visceral reaction that both knocked me off balance and laid the basis for a much more sharply honed view on the whole sordid business of whaling.

The thoughts raging round my head were brought into sharper focus just a few minutes later: we were joined by a minke whale. It surfaced quietly and almost breathlessly just a few yards off the starboard side, sleek and trim and not much bigger than *Mingming.* The minke is by far the smallest of the baleen whales, the whales that feed by straining out plankton and small fish through their baleen plates. Like all things miniature it holds a special charm, which in the minke is enhanced further by its inquisitiveness and its habit of lying alongside stationary boats. For a second or two it hung there and surveyed *Mingming*, a kind of mirror image in its pared-down equivalence. It rolled forward and disappeared and surfaced a minute later on the port side, pushing along its pike-like rostrum just an inch or two above the water. I willed it to stay. The breeze was once more failing. We could stretch out side by side under the Arctic sun and consider each other and reflect on life and this strange world. We could talk about how it once was and about how it might still have been. We could debate how this seascape of vibrant life was no more than a pale parody of what had gone before. We could reflect how the beating heart of the ocean had been ripped out, wilfully and in short shrift. We could whisper to each other that seas which not so long ago throbbed and pulsated and heaved with hot life now lie almost inert, semi-comatose, perhaps soon-to-be-moribund. Maybe my friend could give news of the Spitsbergen bowhead whale, reduced in just a few hundred years from around a hundred thousand to just twenty or so bleak specimens. How did they now fare, these long-lived behemoths? What refuge now beneath the polar ice?

My mind brimmed with questions, but the minke whale would not talk, or even stay. After one final look at us it was gone. In my heart I was glad to see it go; the minke is a favoured target of the Nordic whalers. Thus is the way of the world: the trusting shall be damned.

The fishing boat mooched slowly away over the eastern horizon, ridding the day of its one dark overtone, and for an hour or two we lay idly on the easing swell. A warmish sun beamed down. The sea, now a lightly ruffled and undulating meadow of forget-me-not blue, glinted and sparkled. Close-bound pods of fin whales foraged to port and to starboard. The mountains of Prins Karls Forland and Oscar II Land and James 1 Land and Haakon VII Land, as regal a fusion of ranges as a man could find on this earth, looked down from a fitting height. I ate my lunch of rye bread and cheese, a home-made flapjack and a crisp green apple, and as I ate I looked through the bull's-eye windows of my little dining room and admired the mass and solidity of those peaks. They were brass-bound and copper-hearted, those domes and teeth, ferrous and fierce, other-worldly, imperious. Only the millimetre by millimetre grind of a million tons of sea-bound ice could dent and smooth them. Even so, many of the summits had evidently shrugged off that great weight, shouldering the frozen rivers aside into their lower clefts and leaving their mitres and ridges still razor-sharp and unmollified.

A faint zephyr came up from the south, sending us once more on our way. I sat in the hatchway and hand-steered with the steering lines. The wind veered to the south-west and I reconnected the self-steering gear. I rummaged below and found my kiddies' sea-side fishing net and within a few minutes had caught one of the clumps of seaweed floating by. I laid it on the cabin top to dry; it might make a tangible souvenir of the day, if such were needed. A pair of guillemots fizzed by. The wind veered further and faltered.

17

For twenty-nine days I had been honing my statistical skills. There is a certain pleasure and satisfaction to be had from the accumulation and analysis of numerical data. The more arcane the data and the sphere of analysis, the greater is the gratification. For this voyage I had added several lines of statistical enquiry to those already built into my daily systems. The aim was simple: to substantiate impressions and gut-feelings with hard fact. I wanted to bring a little more science into this instinctive business of minimal ocean sailing. In particular I wanted to analyse my daily activity as it pertained to *Mingming's* particular rig and set-up. I had for a number of years been writing and talking about the ease of handling of the junk rig, and about the advantages of a principally cabin-based system of ship management. This was fine as far as it went, but it lacked a mathematical basis. It was about time that I started to prove my point with numbers.

Thus far I had kept a running tally, at the back of each year's log book, of the distance made good each day from noon to noon, and of the average daily run thereby produced. This enabled me to make analyses of the following kind: in 2010, on my voyage to the west of Greenland, I was at sea for sixty-six and a half days; the outward leg took thirty-four days, covering one thousand nine hundred and ninety-nine miles at a daily average of fifty-nine miles; the return leg took thirty-two and a half days, covering two thousand and ninety miles at a daily average of sixty-four miles; and that the whole voyage therefore covered four thousand and eighty-five miles at a daily average of sixty-one miles.

These statistics concerned themselves with speed and distance, nothing more. I had now added to that a numerical analysis of the two main aspects of ship management: sail handling and deck work.

For the former I made a mark in my log, rather in the style of a prisoner noting days on a prison wall, every time I altered the size of the mainsail. At midnight the previous twenty-four hours' worth of marks were totalled and added to my running analysis. I could now see at a glance, for example, that during the first twenty-nine days I had either reefed or made sail one hundred and four times, at an average of three point six times per day. On average I had therefore raised or lowered sail every six hours and forty minutes. The highest number of sail alterations per day was ten. This had occurred twice, on the fifth day and the twenty-eighth day. So far there were six twenty-four hour periods when I had made no changes at all.

As I had not made this kind of detailed analysis before I had no idea whether these figures were in line with those of previous voyages. I suspected that in the generally lighter weather we were now encountering I had less work to do; I was already starting to see some direct correlation in the numbers between heavier weather and increased sail handling. For much of this voyage only five panels of the mainsail were available anyway, which of itself reduced the number of sail alterations possible.

I was also keeping a separate log of each exit from the hatch, and the reason for that exit. I further subdivided these sorties on deck into those which were mandatory and those which were discretionary. In the main, mandatory exits were for making repairs and adjustments, discretionary for things like photography. I also considered anything to do with the setting and retrieval of the headsails as discretionary; there was no absolute necessity ever to use these sails.

During the first twenty-nine days I had exited the hatch a total of twelve times: once every two and a half days or so. However only five of these exits were mandatory. I had therefore only been *required* to go on deck once every six days. Each exit was for a different reason: re-tensioning the self-steering lines, lashing the sail battens together, altering the mast lift so that the boom set higher, adjusting the luff parrel downhauls, and checking and re-securing the anchor lashings. Of the other seven sorties, five were related to setting and gasketing headsails, while two were to photograph fulmars around the boat in calm weather.

It was too early yet to be sure what story these numbers told; as new statistics they hung in a kind of unreferenced isolation. I realised, though, that it would be possible to trawl through my log books of previous voyages and reconstruct similar analyses from my written notes. That would allow me to establish, perhaps, some meaningful patterns.

For the moment I was more concerned with my usual figures relating to speed and distance. During her five previous voyages *Mingming* had settled into a remarkably consistent average daily run of between sixty and sixty-five nautical miles. This had held good for sixteen thousand miles of sailing, in all manner of conditions. Early on in this voyage, whilst we were still being driven on by a boisterous south-westerly, our average had climbed to nearly eighty miles a day. Since then it had been whittled away. For our first twenty-nine days we had averaged a daily run of just over fifty-two miles.

The convenient abstraction of two knots of speed as an ideal rate of progress had become, more or less, a reality. Life was now imitating art, mathematical fact usurping idle speculation. The relentlessly elevated pressure of the high Arctic weather systems had, as it were, caught up with us. There was something a little incongruous about the delicacy of the airs hereabouts, zephyrs often little more than the exhalations of sleeping butterflies, soft caressing winds, cool, yes, but restrained. This was not in any sense a delicate place. The high summer suppressed, for just a few weeks, the hard and icy fists that no doubt flail these waters most of the year. I was starkly aware that we could not have it both ways; modest progress was the price of entry.

Nonetheless, the first faint suggestions of a novel idea were forming somewhere deep in my mind. We were now comfortably past 78°N, and one fact was clear; the further north we went the happier I felt. This was where I wanted to sail. That being so, perhaps I needed to reassess how I was going to do it.

18

I had been thinking about the mildness of these summer winds, and what it might mean for the future, and so was not surprised, as the afternoon progressed, to be once more ghosting into the faintest of breaths from the north-north-west. The sea settled to an almost imperceptible swell. The whales were gone; we had evidently left their feeding ground behind. Only the murmur at *Mingming's* forefoot and the occasional creak of her rigging now wove a subtle counterpoint around the silence of the day.

We were closing the land to the north of the Isfjorden, and as we moved nearer I began to make a little more sense of the confusing topography. The foreground was dominated by the high defences of Prins Karls Forland, an island only three or four miles wide but ridged to nearly two thousand feet along most of its thirty-five miles. It runs parallel to the mainland and is separated from it by the narrow Forland Sundet. At one point towards the north end of this sound the island is almost conjoined to the land behind; a causeway linking the two is awash by only a few metres of water. All that was of course hidden from us. To the south of Prins Karls Forland the intermittent peaks and shoulders of Oscar II Land stretched away, now losing themselves in a fug of moist air and low cloud that was rapidly forming.

Before long Prins Karls Forland too was bound up in a thick mist. Only the paler patches of snow gullies somehow penetrated the veil of cloud and maintained the close presence of the land. We were now just sixteen miles or so offshore. I had carefully marked the twelve mile limit on my charts. It was important to keep outside this line; to cross it would put us into Norwegian waters and the jurisdiction of the Governor of Svalbard. That fine gentleman with his enviable title would no doubt take exception to a foreigner sailing his coastline without first having presented himself at Longyearben and submitted to a raft of intrusive requirements. Not least among these was the provision of a bond, a sort of bank guarantee, against the cost of any environmental damage or the cost of rescue. The amount of this bond is entirely at the discretion of the Governor's Office. I had heard tell of various sums, the highest being a whopping fifty thousand pounds. Also required was a valid large bore firearms licence, the mandatory hiring of a suitable gun as a defence against polar bears, and the presentation of a detailed itinerary. I really could not be doing with all of that. I would keep a respectful distance; close enough in to see, far enough out to maintain my freedom and integrity.

The hesitant breeze eased off further. *Mingming* crept slowly forwards, now scarcely rippling the smoothing sea. It seemed that the world was near to total stillness, but some swirling atmospheric process was still under way; against all odds the late evening mist began to lift and disperse and there once more were the mountains. The sky, now clarified, assumed the split I had become accustomed to: a stratum of quiet cloud dominated, but only so far towards the north. The polar horizon was overhung with clear air. At this late evening hour the sun's altitude was still enough to keep it hidden just inside the northern fringe of the cloud, but from time to time a thinning of the cloud edge allowed a flood of stronger illumination. Just once or twice the sun itself pierced a momentary clear patch. The light, then, was in flux, and the shifts in its intensity and placement created a corresponding restlessness in the shape and the texture of the peaks and ridges and indentations now strung high just a few miles to our east. This unfolding narrative of shifting light kept me at the hatch. I had always to be checking, for each variation brought the mountains into a different relief, sometimes highlighting with a fall of stronger shadow the myriad complexities of the indents and crenellations of the steep-faced crags, sometimes throwing a spotlight, as it were, on a high sliver of snow or ice, or exposing the dessicated tongues of expiring glaciers licking seawards down their ancient moraines.

By ten in the evening of that self-same day, a day which had somehow brought us into a new relation with this outlandish corner of the globe, the last of the breeze had died, leaving us immobile on a silky sea. I lowered and secured the mainsail and maintained my vigil at the hatch. Sleep, for the moment, was impossible; there was too much to see, too much to think about. The light had by no means exhausted its possibilities: as midnight approached the sky took on a burnished, coppery glow. The air and the surface of the sea assumed in tandem this wash of deep gold, an infusion that perhaps gave a hint of warmth, but only grudgingly so; here was something too strange and metallic, like the very mountains themselves, for a full-blooded embrace.

We perched seemingly immobile on the water, fixed to the seascape with our usual entourage of sleeping fulmars, all these now of the darker northern phase type, but the sea itself was moving. The North Atlantic Current was still at work, carrying us without fuss to the north. This may have gone unnoticed, were it not for the gradual appearance, way to the north-east, along the clear horizon beyond the northern end of Prins Karls Forland, of yet another mouthful of incipient teeth. Here were the beginnings of the last ranges of north-west Spitsbergen, the peaks and glaciers of Albert I Land. It would be some hours before the irregular tips now sprouting here and there would combine into a continuous span of skyline. Even so, there was already an impression of a more exaggerated conicality in the shape of these peaks, and of a less interrupted mantle of snow and ice; these teeth were sparkling white. I fancied I could make out the inverted canine of the Kaffitoppen, four thousand feet high and Albert I Land's dominant height.

The day ended in total quiet, total suspension. Even the surrounding fulmars had reached some provisional truce in their constant bickering; they rose and fell to the rhythm of the faint swell, heads under wings, untypically pacified. The only body still seemingly in motion was the midnight sun, tracing its tight parabola being the static cloud. *Mingming* and I lay placid on the sea, the mountains held their pose, the birds slept. It was hard to reconcile this stillness to the spin and orbit of our greater, collective, fall. All that rush and revolution through the infinite void should, one would think, generate a typhoon of a wind, the mother of all gales, a right royal and unending hurricane, but there we sat, contained, by some quirk of physics, within our little pocket of immobile and beatific air. It was beyond comprehension, this fragile balance of force that allowed our brief flowering. It made no sense either. Why this sea? Why these mountains? Why any damn thing? And where lay the tug on my heart? What exactly was the incontrovertible beauty of the moment? Warm flesh and hot blood adrift in a frigid world; there was nothing more.

Midnight came. I stretched out below and took a short and deep sleep.

19

For ten hours we drifted north, riding free on the last of the thermohaline conveyor, the revolving flow of cool deep water heading southwards and warmer surface water returning northwards. *Mingming* too revolved slowly as she went, spinning through a clock-wise rotation. There was nothing regular or predictable about these gyrations, except for the direction of turn. For long periods she lay still, her attitude to the line of nearby mountains, the dominant reference point, fixed, before some slight eddy or a gentle push from a more muscular swell or some other unfathomable conjunction of forces encouraged her to resume her pirouetting. It was an odd way to progress to the furthest reach of open ocean, this stop-start twirling, totally passive and undirected. I had, in any case, little choice in the matter, unless I were to ship the oars and try rowing towards the ice. There was something seductive, almost mesmerising, about this lazy waltz, something cleansing in the surrender of all possible control. I gave myself over to the moment and allowed my mind too to swirl and drift through an aimless procession of idle speculations: the symbolism of the dark and jagged graph formed by the peaks and troughs of the nearby skyline, for example, or the reasons for the vivid salmon pink of a fulmar's gape, or the proposition that the trouble with land is *it gets in the way*.

By five in the morning the contours of Albert I Land

were laid out wall to wall, as it were; apart from one singular and as yet unconnected cone to the far north, the mountains were now fused to a continuous span. This distant line of severe undulations, occupying just a degree or two of the available sky above the horizon, did not quite project the darkened mass and solidity of the nearer Prins Karls Forland. The heightened iciness further north, or the positioning under a clearer sky, or the slight fuzziness imposed by distance, or some combination of all these factors, rendered these far peaks somehow less substantial; they glowed softly grey-pink from the inside out as if they were hollow, or translucent. This ghostliness seemed fitting; that *Mingming* and I were now within sight of such a northerly land mass verged on the unreal and the illusory.

A little breeze finally came in, sometime after breakfast, but it was a useless, feeble wind from the north-north-west, the kind of wind that had become the motif of this voyage, and a wind which forced us further in towards Prins Karls Forland. We were by now skirting dangerously close to the twelve-mile limit. For a while I stood on. The alternative, to tack and head out west, was for the moment too unpalatable. We were less than ninety miles from 80°N, a day's sail with a fair wind; progress anywhere but north was a hateful prospect.

Our noon position showed that we had covered just twenty miles over the previous twenty-four hours. Worse still, we were now right on the twelve-mile line. We had the sea to ourselves and I could perhaps have carried on, angling in towards the northern end of Prins Karls Forland and sneaking past in Norwegian waters, but it was a risk I could not take; in this fluky wind we could easily be left becalmed once more, defenceless and indefensible. I went about and sailed away from the land. The already low cloud dropped suddenly, blanketing the mountains almost to their base. We pushed slowly seawards, falling away to south of west as the faint breeze weakened once more. There was nothing to be done but to sail on and wait for a wind shift.

I thought about the mountains astern. They had drawn me in but had now become a kind of barrier; they blocked my ideal board. They were wonderful, these mountains, cold, imperious, monumental, but for the moment they were something of a nuisance. I hankered once more for nothing but a clear horizon and the unbridled freedom of the open sea. A planet free of land, now that would be something! An ocean without obstruction! Infinite sea! To sail on and on, round and round, forever, without let or hindrance! It was a breathless prospect; thrilling, vertiginous, crazy, not wholly unimaginable.

For several hours we ghosted seawards, our course divergent from the eightieth parallel and therefore a negative, backwards heading. The only consolation was that we were scarcely moving anyway. This reverse was short-lived; a merciful backing of the wind allowed me to tack and resume a northerly trajectory that just held us, as far as I could determine, to the western side of the line pencilled onto my chart and showing the division between the universal and the parochial. It was an unexpected and curiously powerful reminder, this arbitrary stroke of lead on paper, of the power of the nation-state and its crude possessiveness. *This sea is ours!* Ha!

I was pleased that I had taken the diplomatic course, nonetheless, as just a few minutes later a fishing boat, an uncompromisingly boxy affair, passed us half a mile on the port beam, heading slowly south. We struggled on the other way in a breeze that was yet again fading away. A pall of grey had almost completely hidden the land. Gangs of auks, mainly Brünnich's guillemots, whirred back and forth between the open sea and their presumed nesting colonies on the shrouded cliffs. At nine in the evening another position fix, checking that we were not trespassing, showed also that we were now seventy-seven miles from 80°N.

The few miles hard-won since noon, and the stuttering, meandering, stop-start nature of our progress were thrown into the starkest relief an hour later. A small ship that at first I took to be a fishing boat, but which soon resolved into a smart red expedition-type cruise ship, crossed ahead of us heading south-west. It had perhaps just exited one of the mainland fjords to the north of Prins Karls Forland, the Krossfjorden maybe, or the Kongsfjorden. The ship purred past with masterly precision. It seemed to have little connection with the ocean around it; its movement through the water was so straight and smooth and rapid, and so unhindered by anything so rude and elemental as wind or wave, that I fancied it was actually fixed to, and rolling along, some kind of sub-aquatic track. It was a very neat ship. Everything about it and its forward motion was tight and orderly and, no doubt, preordained. I imagined its starch-shirted officers of the watch on their darkened bridge deck, their sparing comments exchanged in hushed tones, their space-age consoles. Maybe they were now bound for Jan Mayen; it would not take long.

Within just a few minutes it was hull down and away. *Mingming* ghosted on north, her movement halting and uncertain, every inch wrung out from the vagaries of air and water. It was laughable, and pathetic. After a moment's reflection I realised that, though that may be so, I did not care. I would not for the world have exchanged my lot for a berth on that ship, with its itinerary laid down to the second. What man would value speed and certainty over the serendipitous and the unknown? Where is the poetry in the eternal thunder of an internal combustion engine?

As if to point up the contrast even further, the wind soon died again. The land was lost in mist. *Mingming* drifted on. I listened hard and teased out, just, the distant strains of the midnight silence.

20

I listened hard and I thought a lot about ships and about silence. I entertained the notion that the most rewarding travel is usually accomplished in the perfect stillness of a flat calm. Put another way, the man who moves too fast goes nowhere. Speed itself is an evasion; only by stopping can one take the first steps of the journeys that really count.

I thought about speed and about silence, but I thought too about ice. We were now within a few miles of 79°N, a truly Arctic latitude in anyone's book, and had so far seen no sign of any sea-ice. In many ways this was unsurprising: the weather was not unduly cold. The wind itself, whenever it deigned to blow, had a severe edge to it, but that scarcely bothered me; most of my time was spent below or well-sheltered by the spray hood. I had by now pulled on an extra sweater and was sporting thermal long johns under my doubled tracksuit bottoms. My heavy-duty Arctic gear, though, remained stowed away; it would in fact not be needed for this voyage.

The high Arctic weather was benign, then, even for July, but as we edged north I was increasingly wary about ice. We were now to the seaward side of calving glaciers. We were well into the narrow tongue of clear water that I had sketched from the ice charts five weeks earlier. It was reasonable to expect, but not certain, that the southern fringe of the Arctic pack-ice had receded further north since I had drawn its position. It was also reasonable to expect stray patches of ice, small or large, well away from the ice-shelf itself. Much depended on local winds and currents. For the moment the current was still unequivocally north-bound. I could only conclude that it was this which was keeping the sea hereabouts ice-free. Nonetheless, every mile of northing now brought us closer to the edge, in every sense. We were entering the final and most critical stage of our outward trajectory.

I laid down a couple of ground rules for managing this final push. First, from here on I would not sleep while under way to the north. If I had to sleep I would heave-to. Second, I would not sail beyond 79° 30'N in a wind with any south in it. I was acutely aware that we were sailing into a potentially very nasty trap; I needed to be as sure as was possible that I could sail out of it quickly if necessary. I also reminded myself that while it would be nice to reach 80°N, it was fundamentally of no importance whether I actually did so or not. It was a notable and clear-cut latitude, to be sure, but what is any latitude but a mental construct? There was no point in getting exercised, to the extent of taking undue risk, over a purely imaginary line of an arbitrary planetary grid.

It is often as well to lay down a few simple rules of engagement when approaching nodes of hazardous navigation. The temptation otherwise is to be seduced or drawn on by conditions that seem fine for the moment, but which may well contain the seeds of imminent destruction. When the breeze finally returned, at about three the next morning, it came in from the south-west. Not only that, it came in robustly: by eleven we were down to two panels. Here, at last, was the perfect wind, a lazy man's wind, an eighty or ninety mile a day wind, a wind that could power us easily to 80°N. After so many weeks of insipid headwinds it would have been so easy to let us hurtle on northwards, driven along by this fine quartering south-westerly. Instead,

I hardened up the mainsheet and settled *Mingming* to fore-reaching gently to the west.

I wanted to get a good look at this wind before continuing any further. For all I knew it might be the prelude to a proper blow. I had no precise idea how much sea room we had under our lee, how much open sea now lay between us and the ice-edge, that is, but if we had a real gale of any duration, it may well not be enough. There was also the difficult question of stray sea-ice; I did not want to be running into it in the conditions that were developing.

The wind backed a little further towards the south, accentuating the potential danger, and blew up harder. By noon we were just fifty miles from our target, punching slowly to the west in a building sea. I sat in the hatch to eat my midday apple. A humpback whale huffed and puffed its way along just a few yards off our stern under a milling crowd of birds. Three puffins almost landed in the cockpit, drawn in by an excess of curiosity. Tight-bound squadrons of little auks zipped here and there. I noticed that my watch strap was now a little loose; a month at sea had burned off body fat everywhere. By one thirty we were in half a gale and down to a single panel. Bouts of light rain drove in.

It was a long and dirty afternoon, an afternoon in which I could do little but hold our position, and an afternoon that merged seamlessly into the endless Arctic night. I slept in short spells and watched the sky. Sometimes there were hints that the scudding cloud might lift and break, but every time it came down again more thickly. I watched the sky and considered every variation in the wind and towards midnight sensed a change: the half-gale was easing and veering towards the west. I raised a panel of sail and eased *Mingming's* heading to bring her almost due north. Within an hour or two we were plunging along in a thick fog, driven on by a perfect beam wind and a following swell.

One thing was clear: if I wanted to keep sailing I could not sleep; from here on I could not leave the hatch. We were racing towards the ice, but if we met danger I could turn immediately and run back along our track. I settled in the hatch way and stared out into the fog, first one way and then the other, alert for the least signs of ice. The wind eased gradually, giving confidence that the blow had passed. By three in the morning we were back to five panels. *Mingming* surged forwards and my heart sang. We were nearly there.

21

How do I describe this last stretch of water and our rapid passage through it? The sea here was no different from the sea as it has always been and perhaps always will be. The wind played obliquely on the rhythms of a dying swell, as it always does. Moisture condensing and un-condensing made cloud-patterns in the sky, just as it should. The sun held to its track. Gravity maintained the alignments of every body, my own included. The laws of physics were no less and no more than before or after. Nothing in the objective world changed.

What did change, though, as we hurtled along through a thinning fog, and as I searched the northern arc for any sign of danger, was the keenness of my perception. Here was a moment bred of a year of expectation. Every mile brought us closer to a node of aliveness; I was awaking from the waking dream. I tingled, with cold, yes, but with a heightened coursing of life-blood too. My skin came alive and registered every least interaction with the swirling molecules of inanimate air; my eyes cleared, the world came into focus, every gradation of shade and tint and colour sharpened, every line and curve and pattern etched itself more precisely.

I saw the world more keenly, then, and felt it more strongly, and so it seemed different. It became more real, and therefore more unreal, for the real world, little though we can perceive it, is an unworldly place. The fog lifted and we raced on into this unreal seascape. The further we went the more magical it seemed, more strange, more remote, more singular. I was conscious that there was something illusory in all of this, that I was perhaps imposing a particularity on the moment. The sea and the sky were in essence no different; there was not even a single lump of ice to stamp some Arctic authenticity on the scene.

And yet, and yet... it *felt* different, and what other measure do I have to go on? The swell was coming off, the sea was smoothing, and with a fine fresh breeze as near as mattered square on the port beam our sailing was as fast and as invigorating as any we had known on this voyage. The sharpness of our sailing was matched by that of the wind: it was now blowing straight off the not-so-distant pack ice. It was a cutting wind, this one, a wind heavy with cold, a winter wind on a midsummer's day. The fog was receding too, and so the horizon was back where it should have been, somewhere near to the curve of the earth, opening up our patch of sea and reducing the chance of a sudden encounter with unseen ice.

As I now sit quietly and recall every detail of that final joyful gambol to the ends of the navigable ocean, two images predominate. The first is the sky. The fog had lifted and the residual clouds had formed themselves into long and low-hanging cylinders, great rolls of thick moisture oriented on a north-south axis and therefore parallel to our line of progress. The denser hearts of these outsize slugs of cloud had taken on the colour of heavily bruised flesh. That in itself was impressive enough, but it was the fringes of each cloud that transformed the picture into something arresting. Tendrils hung softly down from each overlapping band of cloud, wispy, sinuous tendrils that through some quirk of their arrangement somehow caught the sun, or at least some shafts of stronger light, and so showed themselves as argentine patterns against the blue-black backdrop. North to south the sky was striated with silver on slate.

Beneath this heraldic cover the sea and the air fizzed with life. It seemed fitting. My chart was nearly at the end of soundings. What depths were marked were now only widely-spaced. A little to the north they stopped completely. We were at the limit of man's encroachment and so, it seemed, at some celebratory explosion of unconstrained nature. The little auks had taken over. They were everywhere, tiny pied starlings zipping left and right, flying, floating and diving. It was a wondrous and a warming thing, to see this easy conviviality at such a latitude. Tight-packed flocks scorched in and out, perhaps from breeding grounds on the cliffs somewhere way beyond the south-east horizon. The sea surface twinkled with the dots of their starched-white bellies. Bigger cousins sometimes came and went: a black guillemot, a Brünnich's guillemot or two, a puffin. This was without question, though, the home and territory of the little auk, and so I too felt less distanced; there was a place here for the most unassuming of life.

The wind held true and we raced towards our endpoint. I had held the deck for twelve hours without a break, but cold and tiredness dissolved with each mile of northing. Regular consultation of my hand-held GPS was starting to confirm a startling possibility: we may well reach 80°N at exactly midday. That would be the crowning symmetry; not simply to attain that latitude, but to record it as our noon position.

The wind held true and on we surged, eating up mile upon mile, four or five every hour, hurtling on, for the moment free as a bird, our unthinkable target almost palpable over the lip of the sea. I prepared for the moment, readying cameras and a GPS and pumping up my foghorn, and laying out the requisite items along the bridge deck, everything close to hand.

The wind held and the ice held off, giving us free passage, and at exactly 1142 hours and 19 seconds, British Summer Time, on Sunday the twenty-fourth of July, after thirty-one days and nineteen hours at sea, we reached 80°N on the line of longitude 8° 3.243'E. I recorded the moment with still and movie cameras and let off a long blast of the foghorn, not so much to announce our arrival to the world, for the world hereabouts cared not at all, but to give voice to my own inner jubilation. I succumbed to an excess of anthropomorphism, patting *Mingming* on the bridge deck, her shoulder, as it were, and murmuring words of congratulation and endearment. *Well done, old girl! Mingming* plunged on, unmoved.

For a brief moment I considered carrying on north. Why not keep on sailing until we reached the ice? The wind was fair, the sea unthreatening. It was not a thought that gained any traction. I did not want to overstep the mark. We had reached our goal; we had a perfect wind to take us quickly south and away from danger; it was not the moment for an impulsive revision of our strategy.

I readied *Mingming* for going about, disconnecting the self-steering chain and reversing the settings on the steering gear, and taking over the steering with the steering lines. I brought her through the wind and settled on a reciprocal course due south. The few minutes of sailing north and south again beyond 80°N brought us neatly to midday, and so without a break in our stride I was able to enter our noon position in the log: 80°N 8.03°E. My daily calculations showed that we had made good one thousand five hundred and sixty-nine miles at an average of fifty miles per day.

It had been, by comparison with previous voyages, a slow passage. I held no illusions that our journey home would be any easier. Unless I could get far enough to the west and pick up the south-going East Greenland Current, we would be battling the whole way against the northerly stream of the North Atlantic Current. We may be lucky and pick up a spell of northerly winds, but further south the chances were of a predominance of south-westerlies.

For the moment, though, we were once more racing. I had not yet adapted to our new orientation; the sun and the light seemed all wrong. My elation was tinged with a darker undercurrent, too, for the ascent, as it were, was over. From here on everything was downhill, a shift back from the pure air of the wilderness to the fug of civilisation. I pushed these thoughts away and allowed myself a rare moment of self-satisfaction: as an afterthought I put an asterisk beside the noon position marked in the log, and at the bottom of the page wrote a short and crudely-turned addendum: *Good, or what?*

22

Yes, I felt pretty good as we hurtled back south in a breeze still holding fair from the west-north-west, and as the next day or so unfolded I felt even better. Everything I had seen and felt about Spitsbergen and its mountains and the teeming life of its waters was doubled and redoubled on our passage south. Ah yes, Spitsbergen! It was by no means done with us yet.

Let us first consider the whales. As we ran our course back along the edge of soundings we were subsumed into a sea of leviathans. The spouts started sporadically: a few to port, a few to starboard, nothing too overwhelming. We ran on through the night and I slept a little. At five the next morning I was back at the hatch and the world began to change. The cloud was lifting, revealing once more the jagged line of peaks to our east. Clear against the hills, and backlit to puffs of shimmering diamonds by the low slant of the morning sun, an unending sequence of whale spouts was firing off across the whole span of the sea. They were not just on our landward side either; the same density of flesh and spout stretched to the seaward horizon to our west. For four hours we sailed through this great convergence of whales; the dimensions of this gathering therefore measured a good fourteen or fifteen miles in the north-south axis, and at least three or four miles in the transverse, east-west direction. The whales were mainly finbacks, foraging in groups of five or six. The constituent members of each group surfaced simultaneously, spent a few minutes replenishing their lungs with four or five breaths, and then dived together for fifteen minutes or so. The tall fin whale spouts were interspersed with the occasional low and strangely rectangular blow of a humpback. Once in a while a group or a lone creature came close enough to photograph. Using the motor drive I was able to record a full surfacing sequence: the first explosion of vapour that thinned and drifted as a long back swivelled forward beneath it; the ineffably beautiful curve of the arching spine leading, at long last, to the always absurdly small crescent of the fin.

Just once a monster burst out from nowhere with a tornado roar of breath, close on the port beam, no more than fifty or sixty feet away. Despite the fright it gave me I managed a few third-rate photographs. It was only when examining them later, and comparing them with the fin whale sequences, that I realised that this fellow was in fact a sei whale; its skin was a much lighter grey than the darker fin whales, its back flatter and less pleasing in outline, its fin less delicately formed.

It was difficult to assess the number of whales with any accuracy. At any one time most were feeding in the depths. When they did surface their multiple blows could give a false impression of the number in a group. My best guess left a wide margin of error: somewhere between sixty and a hundred. By present-day standards this was a hefty crowd of cetaceans, and I felt deeply privileged to sail through them. And yet my heart yearned for the way it once was, for the time when the seas, not just hereabouts, but from end to end, buzzed and bristled with abundance. I thought once more about the Spitsbergen Bowhead whale, that massive ice-breaker in whose waters we were now navigating, reduced in just a few hundred years from plenitude to near-extinction. Like as not they will soon be gone forever; a million years of nurture lost, in the blink of an eye, to the lance and the try-pot and the infinitude of human idiocy. There was even something forlorn about the whales now ranging around us; their future was too uncertain to rejoice in their numbers. They themselves may now enjoy a modicum of protection against their would-be killers, but what use is that if there is nothing left on which to feed? The industrial extraction of every last living thing from the oceans, krill included, continues apace. How long before, in the warped logic of short-term gain, we will have created little more than a giant cesspool, over-acidified, toxic, empty of life?

The whale spouts slowly thinned out and I turned to happier thoughts. After a noon to noon run of seventy-six miles, our best for a long while, the gradual clearing of the cloud cover reached its glorious apotheosis; by mid-afternoon the sky had attained to perfection. Neither a single wisp of cloud nor the tiniest blemish marred the great bowl of pale and piercing blue that stretched from horizon to horizon. For once this blue held good right down to the lip of the sea, or, to the north-east, to the craggy rim of mountains ranged across that quadrant.

With each mile we sailed, the peaks sank further into the sea. I watched them longingly and in my notebook allowed myself a final and unbridled descriptive flourish in their honour:

Spitsbergen skyline: an expression of every possible variation on the conical: witches' hats, sharks' teeth, sperm whales' teeth, crocodile teeth, metronomes that adorn un-played pianos, inverted ice-cream cones, pop-star brassieres, the steel studs of Hell's Angel leatherwear and the collars of sexual deviants, cones of perfect regularity, cones distorted and bent, cones lob-sided and ragged-edged, cones that merge into other cones, cones free-standing, cones phallic, cones of limited tumescence, cones skulking low, cones that aspire to the cylindrical, cones collapsing towards the rectangular, cones black and naked, cones harbouring snow gullies and therefore vertically striated and pied cones, cones squeezing against glaciers and ice-fields, cones set linearly and forming the blades of giant rip-saws, cones scattered in random jumble; the most toothsome, ragged, protuberant, exuberant, demented, brazen, unworldly, quasi-lunar skyline you are ever likely to see. So I thought as the last few peaks, now spread by their height into a final gap-toothed, roofless grin, descended towards the north-eastern horizon.

The wind eased. Exhausted by whales and Whitmanesque hyperbole, I took to my bunk. I was quickly asleep and expected to remain so for quite a while. The Far North, though, held one last surprise. At two in the morning I was woken by heat. In my sleeping bag I was sweating heavily; the cabin was unbearably hot and stuffy. I opened the hatch to let in some cool air and found that *Mingming* now lay totally becalmed under a hot sun. It was scarcely credible. The sun was not high: it was ranging along the northern horizon at an elevation of no more than ten degrees. Without the cooling breeze off the pack-ice, though, its heat was palpable. I lowered and lashed the mainsail, took off a layer of clothing and sat in the hatchway to cool down. The sea had settled to the faintest undulation. The mirrored blue of water and sky was marred only by a band of orange haze now forming low on the horizon. I was tired, but I could not abandon the hatch; the moment was too strange, too perversely beautiful. I sat there in the high Arctic night, warmed by the sun, and listened for the faint breaths of whales. They were still there. Soft exhalations, little more than slight perturbations of the still and shimmering air, caressed their way over the surface of the sea. Tiny arrow-tips, the last of the Spitsbergen peaks, serrated the horizon astern. The sun glared down, boldly yellow and brilliant. *Mingming* lay silent while I, I considered this unlikely confluence, and waited, with neither urgency nor expectation, for anything that might call itself a wind.

Our voyage is long, and we really must be getting on. Can you blame me, though, for wanting to linger a little longer over this final moment of conjunction with wild mountains and whales and an Arctic sun? What stony heart would remain unmoved by such a simple and uncluttered précis of the world? Yes, in those few hours of immobility I saw the planet and the things that crawl on it and the great space of space scoured clean: sea and air and rock and flesh, unblemished and elemental, shining and awful.

The translucence of the moment was almost too much to take; after a while I felt blinded by the glare of the sun and the laying bare of the seascape and the unmasking of the retreating mountainscape. There was too much clarity, an excess of exposure; the world was shot through with too much light. It could make the eyes ache and the head pound, all this brilliance, and before long I hankered after something more subdued, perhaps more ambiguous.

I did not have to wait long. A firm breeze came in from the south-east, and with it a belt of solid cloud. I made sail and, as we moved off, the last of the peaks fell below the horizon. The wind swung to the south-west and I went about and hardened up *Mingming* on the starboard tack. Yes, we were soon back to our more usual world, plugging doggedly to windward in a sea of grey. Spitsbergen, for the moment, was gone, the whales too. The universe shrank back down, compressing us between a rising head-sea and a glowering sky.

I felt a kind of relief. Nothing was now in our favour. Ahead, no doubt, lay a tortuous passage. I took a deep breath and smiled inwardly. All was as it should be.

23

There is nothing like a headwind for making a man think and for forcing him to consider afresh the enormity of his own insignificance. The more capricious the headwind, and the more comprehensive its stranglehold on the progress of a voyage, the more it demands a reassessment of a lowly skipper's place in the world. A headwind is in no way comparable to a calm, apart from the obvious capacity of both to stifle the speed and direction of travel. Our voyage thus far had already been heavily laced with periods of calm, though nothing in comparison to the number and duration that were yet to come; I will have a lot more to say about calms. For the moment, though, I would summarise a calm as an absence of agency, a temporary suspension of all action. As such, a calm can be somehow life-enhancing; tranquility can refresh the mind; stillness can soothe the spirit. A headwind, by contrast, is agency incarnate. It is difficult, too, in a persistent headwind, not to consider that agency as somehow pernicious, to ascribe to it a will of its own, and a spiteful will at that.

It blew for a week, that wind, sometimes vigorously, sometimes with a dismissive half-heartedness. It sidled around between south and south-west. It threw up awkward little seas, seas to make a ship buck and stall, and it kept us pinned down somewhere off the south-west corner of Spitsbergen. Our daily positions huddled together on the chart, pencilled crosses seeking solace in proximity; one day our straight line distance made good totalled just sixteen miles.

Had I been a younger man I might have grown weary of that wind. I might have cursed it, or even shouted at it. I might have felt singled out, or persecuted, or hard done by. Where, after all, was the fairness in such a wind? Why should our passage home be thus thwarted before we were hardly on our way?

Yes, had I been a younger man I would soon have come to hate that wind and the smug grey cloud it brought with it. It was a tiresome, meddling wind, weak of character but totally effective in blocking our progress south. I did not hate it, though, or even allow it to bother me; nor, conversely, did I welcome it as some sort of test of my mettle. Old age and a lengthening wake were breeding a kind of indifference. Air moves the way it has to move. The trick is to be ready for it, expecting nothing. It may be better not simply to impute nothing to adversity, but to deny adversity itself.

The headwind blew, then, day after day, putting paid to any thoughts of getting to the west and into a more favourable current, putting paid too to my vague idea of another pass alongside Jan Mayen. I replenished my accessible stores from the more deeply secreted containers and made calculations about water; I still had more than enough for a lengthy passage home. I considered reducing my daily apple to a half only, but held that particular privation in reserve. I reduced my daily chocolate ration to two squares, though, and so felt that I was responding with commendable self-discipline to the stalling of our progress.

I found virtue, too, in the chewing of my morning and afternoon handfuls of nuts and dried fruit. For this voyage I had adopted a new method of consumption. Rather than slowly sucking and breaking down each component individually, I had gone to the other extreme. Now I assembled a handful of nuts: one almond, one Brazil nut, one walnut and so on, laced with dried cranberries, raisins and dates, and then stuffed the whole lot into my mouth in one go. This may sound a little gluttonous, but the subtlety of the methodology was yet to come. At this point my mouth was loaded with all kinds of shapes and textures. The technique was then to start chewing very slowly and patiently, and to count each clamping of the jaws. By gently rotating the mass of matter in my mouth, and giving each portion its appropriate amount of tooth time, as it were, the hard-edged bulk was gradually reduced to a soft paste. The pinnacle of taste came as the flavours merged. I kept chewing until every last particle of hardness had been eliminated. This usually took one hundred and twenty chews, or thereabouts. Only then did I start to swallow the resulting purée. This new-found technique in fact made me feel doubly virtuous. Firstly I was at last starting to heed those childhood admonitions to chew my food properly. Secondly I was giving my jaw muscles an excellent work-out and thereby compensating for my general lack of physical exertion aboard *Mingming*.

I soon had some real work, though. Coming to the hatch early one morning to tack yet again after a slight wind shift, I saw that the stitching of another seam had parted completely. It was an after seam in the fourth panel, easily accessible from the hatch with the sail partially lowered. I set to work with needle and palm, laying down first a line of straight stitches to pull the seam together, and then reinforcing these with a second row of overhand stitching. The needlework was massively crude; each stitch was about half an inch long. It did the job, though, and held for the rest of our voyage.

In particular, it helped us to 76°N. The almost frivolous decision to award myself a mint sweet for every two degrees of latitude sailed on the return leg had by now become the underlying reference point for our progress. The sixteen hundred miles of the return passage were broken down into sections of a hundred and twenty miles each. The crossing of each evenly-numbered line of latitude was now an event of some significance; the crew was assembled, speeches made, fanfares played, and the sweet itself presented and unwrapped with all the ceremony of state that could be mustered. 78°N had been traversed with relative ease; 76°N, for a while, seemed almost unattainable. The obliqueness of our lines of approach, as we tacked one way then the other in search of the favourable board, produced only the faintest convergence. We sailed and sailed. I trimmed the sheet and adjusted the self-steering gear. I raised panels and lowered panels and between times watched a sea now empty of whales and dolphins. I stared at the heavy sky, gunmetal grey and often threatening to descend to fog, and thought about the elusive flavours of mint and honey.

It took five days to cover those one hundred and twenty miles, and when we finally crossed 76°N, at four-thirty on the afternoon of Monday the first of August, our fortieth day at sea, a mere boiled sweet seemed scant reward. A boiled sweet! For five days hard work! There were murmurings in the forepeak, for there were those up there who felt that this was not good enough. There were those skulking up for'ard, lazy lawyerly types to a man, who considered that the least they deserved was a full-works Fortnum and Mason hamper, delivered there and then to *Mingming* by special helicopter, suitably wrapped and beribboned and enclosing perhaps a hand-written note from Her Majesty, taking great pleasure in informing the crew of their impending knighthoods and wishing them Godspeed for the rest of their Great Endeavour.

No helicopter came, but in its stead three Arctic skuas

loped by, three mean-looking hoodlums looking for trouble. They did not give a damn about *Mingming*, those three. They ignored her completely and carried on west, bouncing and chattering, feinting at each other with mock attacks, scouring the horizon ahead for well-filled gullets fit for emptying, effortlessly happy in their work.

24

An idea had been forming throughout the previous few weeks of this voyage, a treacherous kind of idea, previously unthinkable. It is there, though, plain to see in my notebook, resurfacing from time to time in the shape of sketches and lists and little memos to myself.

It is tempting to skirt around this idea, to ignore it for the moment, and in so doing to distort the chronology of its appearance. It would certainly be more comfortable for me to keep this new and rather startling line of thought for later; perhaps to withhold it entirely from this particular narrative. I have decided, though, that I must come clean on it. The guiding principle in writing about these voyages has been one of uncompromising honesty. Truth, or at any rate my perception of that elusive concept, however uneasy or unflattering it may be, takes precedence over convenience.

The fact is that I was now starting to think about a successor boat to *Mingming*. Along with that thought, inevitably, was the possibility that this current voyage might be our last major adventure together. I had approached this possibility rather obliquely, over a period of time. It was a thought which brought with it a measure of guilt. It smacked of infidelity. It was difficult to fault *Mingming's* sea-keeping ability and her fitness for purpose. She was as gutsy a boat as I could hope to sail on and as easily manageable a yacht as I could hope to create. I loved her dearly. Why then, should I be even thinking of replacing her? It needs some explanation.

The more immediate reasons are to do with the practicalities of sailing in the high Arctic. Our brief stay off the coast of Spitsbergen had convinced me that this is where I wanted to be navigating: as far north as possible, whether it be here, or further to the east, in the region of Franz Josef Land, for example, or back in the Davis Strait and the approaches to the North West Passage. This was the unequivocal orientation of my plans for the future. To make these voyages in the brief window of the summer months would mean covering long distances in predominantly light airs. *Mingming* could certainly do this, as she had already shown, but only just. The reality was that with her waterline length of only sixteen feet, the natural limitations to her speed meant that although she could reach these destinations in the time available, she could not do so and leave time to spare for further exploration. Put differently, if I wanted to spend more time at these high latitudes, I would have to be able to reach them a little more quickly.

This is not to say that the requirement for extra boat speed was particularly significant. My calculations suggested that another three or four feet of waterline length, with the extra half to three-quarters of a knot that this would generate, would be more than adequate. Over a typical northern voyage of sixty or so days this would give somewhere between seven hundred and a thousand miles of additional distance, more than enough for my purposes.

In terms of basic requirements for high Arctic sailing, there were two other major considerations, both related to ice navigation, and both much more contentious than mere waterline length. The first was whether I would need some kind of engine. This was as heretical a thought as a man could muster, but it needed examination. I could see the benefit of having some motive power beyond sweeps if becalmed in ice, and of also having the capacity to explore a fjord or two. The downsides, though, of weight, complexity, fuel, pollutive capacity and so on, in what would still be a very small yacht, were considerable.

There was also the question of hull material. I spent many hours thinking about steel, its pros and cons. These were neatly balanced. The additional strength comes at a huge cost as regards weight. More weight requires a bigger rig, itself creating more weight and less manageability. Could a steel hull be made unsinkable? I calculated the kinds of flotation volumes required; the sums were not encouraging.

Beyond these rather tedious practical considerations, though, I could sense another motivation in all of this: I wanted to create my final yacht. *Mingming* was nearly it, but not quite. I wanted to start again and use everything I had learned in order to produce, as it were, my last word on the matter. The urge to create was getting the better of me. I could see it in the doodles and drawings starting to fill up pages of my notebook. Six long voyages in *Mingming* had created a deep well of experience and reflection. The urge to translate that into something physical was growing stronger. Every winter for six years I had worked away on *Mingming*, tinkering and improving; she had always been a work in progress. Now I wanted to start again, with a clean sheet, or at least a bare hull, and build my last ocean-going yacht from the bottom up.

She would not be radically different from *Mingming*, simply a more complete and knowing development of the same principles. One of the many lists I had compiled was of potential names for a new yacht: *Blackfish, Saddleback, Squidhound, Vaquita, Great Northern, Snowgoose, Cachalot, Ice Hunter, Razorback, Arctic Whale, Beluga, Sea Canary, Arcticus, Narwhal, Glacialis, Orcinus, Delphinus* and so on and so forth. The thrust was obvious. I had rolled these around my tongue and my head for a week or two, a necessary stage in the process, before settling on the first and only real contender: *Mingming II.* The yacht I had in mind, although at this early point still a set of ideas rather than a fully-formed concept, would be a natural progression from *Mingming*, and therefore the true and incontrovertible daughter of her mother.

The chances were that, like her mother, she would be created from an existing hull. At home I had a whole series of designs made over the years, many of them worked through in all their hydrodynamic detail. I doubted, though, that I would be able to find the time and energy to build a new boat from scratch. There would be a pleasing symmetry to it if I could: I had, after all, built my first ocean-going yacht in its entirety. I wondered, though, whether the world needed yet another new boat. There seem to be already far too many under-used craft clogging up every river and harbour and marina. It would be a nobler enterprise to revive an old and unloved hull. It would also be quicker. I wanted to be sailing rather than boat building. If I could find a suitable hull to refashion as *Mingming II* it would, I imagined, take me two years' work to have her sea-ready. I could commence a new series of voyages in 2014. By then I would be sixty-seven years old. With the right yacht and a willing body I might be good for another ten or twelve years of ocean work.

That was all very well, and it gave me a lot to think about as I sat in the hatchway and waited for a fairer wind. We were still a thousand miles from home, though, with work to do; the priority, as ever, was the here and now.

The long nights were growing more opaque; there was now a twilight feel about them. I thought about switching on the navigation lights in the dimmest early morning hours, but held off for a while longer. *Mingming* pitched on into the greying night and I thought about yachts and whales and the mountains lost to our wake astern.

25

Whales and mountains. The further they fell away behind, the larger they loomed in my mind. There was an obvious correspondence here, some relationship between these living masses within the sea and the inanimate bulk of the land; a relationship, yes, but somehow the dysfunctional one of a fine story all gone wrong. It took a while to strip away everything peripheral to this story, the overlays of culture and conditioning and the crippling anthropocentric mindset, and to start then to see these whales and mountains, and their long parallel narrative, in a clearer light.

I came back to a thought that had been taking shape for a while: in a perfect world there would be no land. Those parts of the earth's crust thrust up above the waves are not the norm, but the aberration, the fault lines of a cooling mantle. The natural, at-rest state of the planet, were it not for the inconsistencies and imperfections of its geology, would be oceanic. We tend to think of the sea, with the perpetual movement of its surface and with its tides and its currents, as the unstable secondary medium. In the larger spans of geological time, though, it is the land which, for all its seeming solidity, is the transient phenomenon. It cracks apart; it slides around the oceans; it accrues on one side and crumbles on the other; it tilts and tips and grinds. The mountains, squeezed skywards by the colliding plates, only to be worn back down to the sea they came from, in marches of time too protracted to contemplate, are the most blatant expression of this transience. No land mass has guaranteed permanence; the sea, though, until, no doubt, the death throes of our sun when it will most likely boil merrily and evaporate to nothingness, will always be there.

It is logical, therefore, that the primary life of the planet is the life of the sea. Thus has it always been. That is where it started; it only crawled out into the air and colonised the shifting land mass, the eruptions and pustules and inflammations of the tectonic plates, that is, as a kind of afterthought. Some of that life came back home, though, back to the sea, the whales, or at any rate their precursors, amongst it.

I thought about those early whales, the *archeocetes*, finding their way back into the water they came from, perhaps fifty or sixty million years ago. Try to imagine it! Fifty million years! Two million human generations! Two million! How can one even begin to conceive of the time that the whales have roamed the oceans? I thought about my own life, all sixty-four years of it. That meagre timeframe has elapsed more than seven hundred and eighty thousand times since the whales took once more to the sea. To conceive properly of the age of the whales I would have to relive my life more than three quarters of a million times.

It made me feel strange, and breathless, and somehow lightheaded, this attempt to grasp the essence of geological and evolutionary time, and thereby to sense a little more firmly the age of the whales. As a young man I had many times lain under the stars in the Australian outback and stared for hours into the blackness of space and tried to comprehend the scale of infinite distance. It was beyond me, but just once in a while the faintest sensation of that scale took a hold, making my head spin. This later-life scratching at the edges of time was similar; the dullness and immediacy of mere human perception created a kind of dark prison. Only a rare shaft of light penetrated its high and tiny window, bringing with it a brief moment of dazzling disorientation.

I thought about the age of the whales, then, and the primacy of the ocean, and the ephemerality of the land and the mountains, and that brought me to the bi-ped life now teeming and proliferating on that land and on the foothills of those mountains. I began to see it all from a different perspective. I was not, and never could be, an ocean-dweller, but months of quiet communion with the sea, allied with hundreds of hours of observation and reflection, had brought me, almost literally, to a different viewpoint. In a halting way I could start to see the land as one who was not of it, and the life on that land as one not bound to it. This was only the slightest shift in perspective, and momentary at that, but it was enough, nonetheless, to create a disconcertingly different picture.

What now seemed clear, blindingly obvious in fact, was a grotesque asymmetry. The world, and the life on it, was completely out of balance. The natural progressions had been skewed to an alarming disproportion. Consider this: the whales lived peaceably in the oceans for over fifty million years; one relatively new land-based species as good as annihilated them in three hundred. Consider this too: this same Johnny-come-lately now extracts from the sea something like ninety million tons of ocean life a year. With its talent for euphemism this same lot has invented terms that reduce this unthinkable pillage to bloodless management speak: all that those clever chaps from up there on the land are doing is 'harvesting biomass'. Say it quickly and it rolls innocuously through the mind, scarcely disturbing a sleepy brain cell. Think about it more carefully, though, and try to place it not in the timescales of mere years or decades or even millennia, but in the true planetary cycles of millions of years, and it becomes clear that what is happening is not simply genocide on the grandest scale, but something even more alarmingly unnatural: a kind of blithe matricide.

The primary life of this planet is the life of the oceans. This life is the mother of all life; the sea is its amniotic fluid. To kill and poison the life of the oceans is to kill and poison the womb of all life. Matricide carried to excess soon becomes suicide.

These were dark, disturbing thoughts, made worse as I thought about the inherent innocence of life within the sea. For here was another paradox, another inversion of good sense, yet another crazy imbalance. It takes great intelligence to be able to industrialise the mass extinction of life; it also requires monumental stupidity to actually do it. How can this supposed intelligence and this crass stupidity coexist within the same organism? Or is intelligence, in human terms anyway, an illusion? Is the logic this: we think, and we know that we think, therefore we think that we are intelligent? Nothing much in human history would suggest universal intelligence. Nothing much that one sees today gives much hope for an intelligent reversal of human behaviour.

Maybe that would not matter, were it not that, as well as ourselves, we are destroying too the real wisdom of innocent life. I realised, as I thought about it, why I had reacted so strongly to the almost simultaneous appearance, in the very shadow of those imposing but provisional mountains, of what I thought was a whaling vessel, and an inquisitive minke whale. There, right under my nose, was as good and palpable a metaphor for the whole sorry narrative: on the one hand the bristling artifice of rapacious but limited intelligence, on the other, the unknowing and quiet wisdom of innocence. In the short term this is an unequal confrontation. In the long term there seems little doubt where the victory will be. The problems lie in the collateral damage along the way.

26

The liberation, when it came, was quick and complete. The wind veered to west-north-west, stuttered a little, veered a little further, then blew up hard. *Mingming*, unbound, a fair breeze on her favoured starboard quarter, leaped forward with a will. A day's run of seventy-nine miles was followed by an eighty-fiver. Two and a half degrees of latitude in two days! At this rate I would soon grow fat on Murray mints.

I was by now too accustomed to the contrariness of the weather, though, and therefore wary of allowing too much expectation to settle in. Here was the most bounteous of winds, by now almost a full northerly, and along with it a fine following sea. Everything was set fair. I thought that it could not last long, but it did.

For eleven days we rode that northerly. This was an Arctic summer breeze, and it was therefore in constant flux. It veered and backed and eased off and strengthened, but it kept up from a northerly quadrant and, in the main, it blew good and hard. As each day passed, the crests pushing us on from astern grew taller and more muscular. The sky, too, gave up on dullness and went for something more mobile and more vibrant. Colossal rain squalls interspersed with brief periods of unalloyed blue. It was a restless sky, mixing and merging, separating and reconstituting, a constant rotation of every permutation of cloud and clear patch.

This instability kept me constantly at work. I was forever

adjusting the mainsail, not just in terms of complete panels but, in the heavy following wind, in fractions of a panel. One and a half panels set would be reduced to one panel, then a third, then a half, than a quarter, then back to a half, and so on. The optimum setting, the setting, that is, that gave the best compromise between speed and balance, was elusive in that up-and-down wind. This difficulty was compounded by having the breeze, most of the time, directly from astern. Even with the self-steering gear set at a reasonable angle to that wind, somewhere round about a hundred and thirty five degrees, for example, and thereby putting it firmly on our quarter, the sudden wind shifts combined with a boisterous sea led to regular gybes. I was constantly unpicking these gybes and resetting us on course. From time to time I could achieve some stability by sailing by the lee, an attitude well-suited to the junk rig, and somehow locking the contrary forces in balanced opposition.

My occasional toothache had long since settled down, forcing the ship's aspiring medicos, that hovering assortment of would-be doctors, dentists, brain surgeons, bone-setters and blood-letters, into a muttering redundancy. Their hopes of employment were raised for a while; early one morning I leaned forward while doing something at the chart table and cricked my lower back. This happens from time to time, with differing degrees of severity. This was a bad one, by far the worst I had known at sea. No movement was possible without intense pain. The only way I could escape that pain was by lying flat out on my back, but forcing myself back to a seated position or onto my feet was an exercise in protracted agony.

I have learned, over the many years that I have been graced with occasional back pain, that the best remedy, or at least the best reaction to it, is not to capitulate, but to carry on with normal activities as far as is possible. There were those aboard *Mingming*, though, the lazier fellows skulking up for'ard in particular, who would jump at any excuse to spend a day, or a week, or if they had half a chance a whole lifetime, lying a-bed in supine self-pity. Old Ahab, that implacable skipper, knew a thing or two about these types, and was not slow to issue two commands to all members of crew, Ship's Boy and his cronies included:

1. All usual shipboard duties will be undertaken promptly and without regard to personal discomfort.
2. No crew member, on pain of cancellation of all rights, privileges, occasional treats, shore leave and any other form of bonus, compensation, incentive or remuneration, shall henceforth utter the word *Ow!*, or any substitute thereof, or any expletive, vulgar or otherwise.

The first edict was to ensure that there was no morale-sapping shirking from any aspect of routine ship management. The second was based on the premise that vocalisation of discomfort suggests an element of self-pity, and self-pity of any kind, or of any degree, has absolutely no place aboard a short-handed sea-going vessel. *Just grin and bear it, Sunshine, and get on with your work.*

I made one small concession to the severity of the initial moments, taking a couple of pain-killers. They had no effect and I did not bother with pills from there on. The more I thought about it, anyway, the more suspect it seemed to attempt to anaesthetise the pain. What is pain, after all, but the primary indicator of life? Show me the man without pain and I'll show you the man who is well and truly defunct.

All in all it was an eventful day. At five the same morning a small blue container ship, the *S.Rafael*, passed close on our port side, heading west. It seemed fitting; we had just exited the Arctic Circle and so were once more drawing closer to the norms of human commerce. Just on cue, too, a Leach's petrel ghosted past in the grey dawn. A little later I tested our southerly progress by trying the short wave radio. Some crackly and barely discernible cricket commentary came through, followed by the first Shipping Forecast I had listened to in ten weeks. There was something comforting in the seemingly timeless normality of cricket, and the weather, and the prospect of gales in Thames and Dover.

Here the wind was slipping away. Our downwind idyll, eleven days that had brought daily runs of up to ninety-five miles, despite an adverse current, and which had seen us across well over ten degrees of latitude, was nearing its final hours. Those eleven days had transported us back to a different world. The depths of the night had reassumed their blackness; the air had re-found its balm; Whitehills lay just five hundred miles ahead.

The next morning, somewhat reluctantly, but encouraged by this proximity and the feeling that perhaps I should start the process of preparing myself for life back on land, I listened to a news bulletin. It was not a pleasant experience: rioting in the streets; financial markets in turmoil; Europe on the brink of economic collapse; a strange and somehow disembodied litany of intelligent madness. None of this maelstrom of constant human crisis seemed to have anything to do with the real world. It was a kind of parallel construct, self-generating, powerful, all-consuming but ultimately irrelevant.

The pain in my back was reinforced by a deep ache of regret in my heart. This year's voyage would soon be over; the wilderness would soon be behind us. I need not have worried. There would time enough before, on a black night with the mother of all storms on our heels, Whitehills finally hove into view. The weather was about to change. Our voyage was on the brink of a new and puzzling phase.

27

Late on the evening of Thursday the eleventh of August, our fiftieth day at sea, the noble wind that had driven us across six or seven hundred miles of ocean finally expired. It was a drawn-out, hesitant departure, well-laced with last gasps and occasional attempts at a miraculous revival. In the end, though, nothing could save that wind, and an hour or so before midnight I accepted the inevitable and lowered the mainsail, not just to half-mast in recognition of the dear-departed, but all the way. The wind was gone; all motion, save our rolling to the easy swell, was gone too. For eighteen days winds contrary and winds favourable had kept us progressing, in some fashion or other, through the water. A million or two million or maybe a billion bubbles and foamy perturbations marked our winding track across the ocean. It gave me pleasure to think that the energy of all that air had been converted, via the medium of *Mingming's* modest advance, to a snake of water-borne and provisional sculptures, an ephemeral art-trail, unviewed and uncontrived and therefore the best of creations.

Now, though, we were once more at rest, and so I busied myself with tasks held off for just this moment. I exited the hatch, for only the second time in nineteen days, and reattached the outboard end of the mainsheet to the after rail to minimise chafe. Later on I went out again and re-tensioned the self-steering lines.

Activity down below was centred on keeping my ancient body functioning and presentable. The Ship's Doctor had set up a daily skin-care clinic. Applying cream to what seemed like patches of fungal growth on my hands, and to areas of solar keratosis on my face, scarcely qualified as doctoring, but it gave the fussy fellow something to do, and kept his hand in should he be called upon for a nice amputation or an on-board heart transplant. He had also come up with a nice line in quack physiotherapy, and regularly had me stretching forward, head between knees, to help relieve my back pain. I reluctantly had to admit that he was on to a good thing here; for once one of his remedies actually seemed to be working.

I had not seen a soul for over seven weeks, but I still maintained my regime of shaving every other day. Long practice, and the regular changing of my razor blade, enabled me to effect a good shave with just a tablespoonful of water. What with the slightly astringent smell of the shaving soap, and the rasp of steel on smoothing skin, and the inevitable dribble of water down my neck, and the final rub-down of pink and sparkly flesh with a small towel, it was always a welcome and invigorating ritual. Along with the shave, I gave my teeth a good scrub and cleaned my fingernails and so, despite the months spent in a kind of barely-controlled grubbiness, I felt, for a while at least, dashing and debonair and superbly laundered.

Outside, strange things were happening. The first patch of calm, which pulled our daily run down to just nineteen miles, and which was only a kind of trial run for what was to come later, transformed rapidly into a half gale from the south-east. It did not last long, this blow, but it brought with it a mass of hot summer air that had me gasping and sweating. It also brought with it, in its aftermath, some unexpected birds: a heron, flying purposefully west low over the water and bound, by the look of it, for Iceland; and a few hours later, somewhat more poignantly, a juvenile wagtail. This fellow landed in the cockpit, and for fifteen minutes or so we contemplated each other. He had no doubt been blown seawards, by the recent gale, from the Norwegian mainland a hundred and fifty miles to our south-east. I do not know what he made of this odd life-form staring at him from just a few feet away. The bird was clearly exhausted and distressed. It was scarcely more than a baby; the patterning of its plumage and the yellow at the base of its bill suggested that it was only a few months old at most. Unless it was possessed of extraordinary stamina and a very accurate sense of direction, it was unlikely to survive much longer. There was nothing out here for a ground-feeding wagtail to eat, nor could it land on the water to rest. It was condemned to keep to the air until hunger and exhaustion forced it down to the sea, where it would soon drown.

I admired the beauty of the wagtail's plumage. The flow and pattern and fineness and the exquisite detailing of its down and of every wing feather, seen from so close, was all of a most extraordinary subtlety. The tendrils of down crisscrossed and overlaid each other in the finest of filigrees, transforming, at the same time, from the soft grey-white of its under-parts to a shimmering mix of olive-grey-blues above. Beneath its bill and its out-size ebony eye, hints of lemon yellow merged into the dark mayoral chain of a bib that identified the bird for what it was: a first summer white wagtail.

I was struck by the overriding and impersonal cruelty of it all. Just a few months earlier this bird had been no more than yolk warming in an egg. It had then exploded into this extraordinary composition of flesh and feather, an amazing flying machine, stupendously well-engineered, heart-achingly beautiful. Inside this bird hot blood flowed and a beating heart throbbed and a constrained consciousness struggled to make sense of anything. Here were a few grammes of aliveness that formed a life that surely warranted, for all its brevity, some sort of record in the chronicles of the world, or a prominent statue or a memorial stone engraved in monumental and thickly-gilded lettering. I looked into the eye of the wagtail and considered its short existence, lambent and pointless. In a few hours it would be dead. Its death would, no doubt, fuel other cycles in the merry-go-round, and so would not be a total waste. Those gorgeous feathers, though! The perfectness of it! And along with that, the complete and utter dispensability!

I stared at the bird and wondered whether it had any intimation that it was very soon to die. I doubted it, but that thought did not bring much comfort; it raised, rather, the inscrutable pathos of the moment. Yes, the innocence of that bird made its imminent death a far, far worse thing to contemplate.

I stared helplessly at the helpless bird. There was nothing I could do for it. It fluttered up onto the windward side of the coach roof and for a few moments cowered in the fading breeze. Then it was gone. I did not see which way it went, or whether there was any strength or purpose to its flying.

Midday came. From noon to noon we had covered just twelve miles.

28

How many words can a sea-going writer expend on an endless calm? For day after day we scarcely moved. For day after day the mainsail was lowered, sometimes for eighteen hours out of the twenty-four. A great wedge of static air had, according to what I could deduce from the occasional weather forecast I listened to, forced its way up from the Azores. This sliver of puffed-up pressure had insinuated itself to the west of Norway and taken up a kind of residence. Nothing could budge it. Gales from the west bounced off it and expired. To the south-east, down Skagerrak way, vigorous winds whirled around in their own little vacuum, disconnected from their westerly cousins by this imperious finger of rigid atmosphere probing gracelessly up the North Sea and into the welcoming sheath of the Norwegian Basin.

Our course took us straight down the line of this finger, and so our progress did not so much falter as teeter on the very edge of oblivion. I did not complain about this; by going nowhere I was gaining another life. Every hour and every minute of each hour now took on a different, more swollen proportion. Inaction and stillness exerted their own relativity, a counter-intuitive one, filling the days with more time and more space than a short-lived man merited. Yes, as we edged our way south, forcing a course to keep us clear of the Shetlands to our west and the agglomerations of oil rigs to our east, often sailing limply for just a few hours a day as a slight readjustment of the atmospheric pressure created a gentle shift of air from here to there, but more often than not lying inert on a mirrored sea, mainsail lashed and all movement arrested, the hours bulged and swelled and grew fat and dispensed their own particular bounty; a superabundance of time. The heartbeat of the world slowed to the faintest pulse and so we lay there, day after day, suspended in a soft and Proustian stasis.

Our escort of fulmars, ever-faithful, crowded in closer and more intimately. They circled *Mingming's* hull, inspecting it carefully and pecking at what I assumed were edible morsels now attached to it. The scrapings and dull rat-tat-tats of their bills as they scoured the topsides set up a hard-edged descant to the silence of the sky. I leaned over the side and watched them closely, nose to nose as it were, my own fleshily curved, theirs the strangest configuration of calcified and brittle-looking tube. With a new lifetime now at my disposal I worked patiently away with my camera to try to capture the definitive fulmar portrait. Despite their unabashed closeness and their fascination with the camera lens they were hard to pin down, these subjects; they refused to sit still and to hold their heads just so as regards the light. One abandoned its photo-call entirely when it spotted a small jellyfish just below the surface. After some excited manoeuvring it lunged down and grabbed it. The fulmar paddled off with its prize but was soon set on by a melee of squawking companions. The jellyfish was torn apart and devoured by a fighting mass of hooked and implacable bills.

For one whole day we lay there as two fishing boats trawled back and forth from horizon to horizon, infusing the air with a dull and steady throbbing. One of them eventually made a close pass astern of us, and so I was able to determine that she was the *Bressay Bank*, out of Boulogne-sur-Mer, BL 900470.

We were closing the four hundred metre contour, and that brought with it more fishing boats and along with them, away on our port beam, the Magnus oil rig and then the Heather oil rig. I would have preferred to have been further to the west but for well over a week had had scarcely any say in the matter.

Little changed. Calms interspersed with faint zephyrs and we stuttered our way south. On Sunday the twenty-first of August, our sixtieth day at sea, we drew level with Unst, the most northerly Shetland Isle, thirty nautical miles to our west. Ten days of intermittent sailing had brought us two hundred and forty miles closer to Whitehills; two hundred miles still remained. I marked our position on the chart and measured distances and computed the chances of our arriving on a Saturday or a Monday or a Tuesday, but by now all this calculation and temporal fixation was no more than habit born of long repetition. After two months at sea I had been subsumed into a wider time-frame and a different sense of space. I had grown to suspect that an obsessive measurement of time robbed time of its greatest attribute: its timelessness. To calibrate and subdivide time is to hurry it on. For a while, aided by the permanent daylight of the far north and these more recent days of balmy immobility, I had grown less sensitive to the persistency of the clock.

And what significance, if any, was to be found too in those two hundred remaining miles? Their only relevance was in their relationship to our future speed, our physical displacement in time, that is, and since that was unknowable there was not much more that could be said.

I thought again about the great shearwaters we had encountered the previous year, and the sooty shearwaters and the black-browed albatross, all of them voyagers on an epic scale and yet impervious to the least concept of distance and untroubled by any notion of time; the navigational contrivances of the modern world seemed curiously inept and lumbering by comparison with such innate skill. Sixty days in the wilderness had drawn me, just a little, towards a less mechanistic view of the world, to a less rigidly rationed and compartmentalised assessment of time and space.

Now, though, as we approached the land once more and prepared for what was potentially the most threatening phase of our voyage, there was no escaping the humdrum imperatives of conscientious navigation. I fussed with the dividers and walked them across the chart in a procession of what-ifs. What if it blows up from the north-east? We could be home in a couple of days. What if this ridge of static air persists? We could be at sea for another week. What if we have a real south-westerly gale, right on the nose? We might be out here for another lifetime.

For the moment we were squeezed between the solid islands to our west and the even more ephemeral protuberances to our east, the giant gnats of the oilfields. This lack of space was underlined by a delightfully tubby and picturesque fishing boat that trawled across our track and forced a change of course. A few minutes later, as another noon arrived, we were becalmed once more, and alone, and had covered just twenty-two miles.

29

The contrasts between the first and final stages of a voyage cannot be overstated. The departure from port is relatively easy. The movement is from a fixed point towards a seascape of infinite possibility. The moment of leaving can be precisely chosen to give the best set of conditions for getting quickly off soundings and away from traffic. The further one sails from port the greater the sets of options, the more expansive the freedom.

For the return, though, the opposite is true. The closer one sails towards home the narrower the vectors, the more constrained the options for manoeuvre. After roving freely across a million square miles of ocean, the ship must be brought to a harbour entrance just a few feet wide. What's more, this must be done with little choice as to the prevailing conditions.

As we forced our way south, finally passing 60°N and so completing twenty degrees of latitude of our return leg and, in the process, putting ourselves to the east of the Fair Isle Channel, I grew more acutely aware of these limitations. For a start our sea room was now severely compromised, with dangers at all points bar due north. Worse still, we had lost our pelagic depths. This meant shorter, more dangerous seas in heavy weather. It also excluded the possibility, in the worst of cases, of deploying the series drogue. *Mingming* was now at her most vulnerable.

The north-east coast of Scotland is an iron-bound, pitiless littoral. There are no natural, easily-accessed havens. The fishing ports are hewn out of rock, heavily walled, and lethal in onshore winds. I knew well enough that if conditions went against us in the final stage of our voyage I would have no choice but to keep the sea. I also knew that with the encircling hazards of land and oil rigs, and with a severely constrained repertoire of heavy weather tactics at my disposal, that this would be a severe test.

We were firmly into this critical phase of our voyage and now, at last, the weather began to change. It was not that the winds grew stronger, or less fickle; if anything the blandness of each day increased, but it was a curiously threatening blandness. The high pressure that had kept us pinned down for almost two weeks was dissipating, but the usual flow of the weather systems had been so disrupted by this barrier of static air stretching up the North Sea and beyond, that they seemed at a loss as to how to re-establish their rhythm. Little pockets of low pressure formed and almost as quickly disappeared. Air swirled around slowly but uneasily. Nasty-looking strands of high cirrus packed the upper atmosphere, crowning layers of strange and gently shifting cloud. Sometimes an anaemic sun pierced through, but there was nothing bright or summery about these interludes; it only added to the air of strained expectancy.

I listened to the Shipping Forecasts and could find no reassurance. At six-hourly intervals the structure of the weather was reinvented. Nothing seemed to carry through. Confidently described lows and their likely movements were quickly replaced by newer narratives. It was evident that it was beyond the gift of the forecasters to unravel the meteorological anarchy of the moment. The only thread that seemed to have any consistency was that the nodes of low pressure were now moving north rather than east, and that their principal highway was the North Sea. Weather in Wight was expected, by same time, in Fair Isle.

I stopped speculating on the weather and instead examined my hands. Their palms were beyond redemption. Two months without hot water, soap and a good scrub had allowed dirt and accumulated detritus to settle firmly into all their whorls and indentations, creating a complex mucky-brown engraving. The lack of hygiene was not absolute: I regularly anointed my rough old mitts with antiseptic gel, the type now ubiquitous in hospital wards, in the hope of keeping the lid on all the microbes, bacteria and other unpleasantnesses that had colonised their hills and dales. My fingertips too were in a sorry state; their skin had adopted a process of constant renewal, sloughing off layer after layer and leaving a kind of terracing between the raw areas at the extremities and the fully-skinned bases. I stared at my crusty palms and flexed and un-flexed my fingers. These hands were by now so battered and ill-used that they scarcely seemed my own.

I thought too about *Mingming*, she almost another bodily extension, equally scarred and worn. My hands would just have to keep going, but perhaps I had asked enough of *Mingming*. We were near the end of our sixth voyage together. She had taken me across the best part of twenty thousand miles of ocean. She had done as much as I could ask of her. I took out my notebook and wrote a clear and unequivocal message to myself that this was to be our last adventure together.

I went to the hatch and bore off for a short while to let an orange ship, the *Eagle Turin,* in ballast and for some reason with great curtains of water cascading over its after bulwarks, pass ahead.

We struggled on, still hampered by a round of calms and little headwinds and fairly placed zephyrs that never came to much. Whitehills was now less than a hundred miles ahead, then eighty, then sixty. More oil rigs towered over the port horizon and glowed hotly at night: Claymore, Tartan, Scott. The weather forecasts still ebbed and flowed, and became more sinister. A deep depression, imprecisely placed, was heading north. Northerly winds, the worst for the approaching coastline, became the theme for Cromarty. Force 7s were replaced by Force 8s than downgraded to Force 7s. A more unbuttoned forecaster on a domestic channel confessed that the weather systems bubbling around the UK were so unstable that any accuracy was impossible. The north-heading depression, though, was *winding itself up* as it went.

We passed close to the east of the Captain Oil Field, the final tight-packed compilation of lofty structures and service vessels and the long and low hulk of what looked like some sort of ship but may have been an odd kind of platform or wellhead. I exited the hatch and replaced the yard-hauling parrel with its spare. After almost three thousand miles of heavy usage the original was badly chafed at its top portion. We were now less than fifty miles from Whitehills, but I had to be ready for the worst of weather.

We had entered the final patch of clear water between the oil rigs and the northern coast of the Moray Firth, and I was faced with a serious problem of navigational tactics. The closer we came to that implacable coastline, its stubby headlands stretched east-west along the seventy miles or so from Fraserburgh to Inverness, the more I put *Mingming* at risk. The closer we came to Whitehills, the fewer the options should a northerly storm strike. It ran against every fibre in my body to approach land with severe onshore weather in prospect. I needed sea room and deep water. Whatever I did, though, I would have neither. I studied the chart and considered all my options for a range of possible winds. Should it blow hard from the north or the north-west, as seemed likely, I needed to be in a position where I could still run off to the south-east and clear of Rattray Head. Should the storm come in from the north-east, a grim prospect, I would have to try to hold position by fore-reaching to the north-west across the wide mouth of the Moray Firth.

I chose and marked on the chart a box about fifteen miles square. It was the best spot I could find to meet a storm, with just enough distance from the land and from the oil rigs to give the maximum flexibility. Should it come to it, I would fight as long as possible to keep *Mingming* within that tight sector. Flight from it would be the last resort.

I shortened sail and altered course. Whitehills was less than thirty miles ahead but, for the moment, I did not dare strike out across that final stretch of water. All I could do was slow down, and hold position, and wait.

30

Imagine it! Not long after noon on Friday the twenty-sixth of August, our sixty-fifth day at sea, the air cleared a little and unveiled, just a mite above the southern horizon, the easy contours of the Banffshire hills. The wind had once more fallen away and so we lay there, unmoving, our relationship with the land ahead now doubly ambivalent. Here was home, and here too was palpable danger. Here was the haven I now yearned for, or at least was ready for, and here too was all that was hard and inimical. In the calm of a summer's afternoon I was caught fair and square between the pull of everything wild and innocent that lay astern and the tug of that other world on land. For the moment, though, I had lost the freedom of the former, and dared not approach the latter, and so was caught in a kind of no-man's-land, a void which was neither one thing nor the other, and a void on which, it now seemed certain, all manner of fury would soon be visited.

It was the worst of all positions, made no better by the balminess of the afternoon. A warm sun shone. We rolled softly to a delicate swell. I fussed over the chart, measuring and calculating, and waited for something to happen. Sixty-five days had brought us full circle and to the cusp of our sternest test. The next hours may well define the two preceding months. I stared at the low line of hills to our south, and loved them for their deceptive softness in the grainy summer air, and for their undeniable hold on a land-born creature, but wished too that they and all of the protruding earth would dissolve away and leave us to a clear and infinite ocean.

For a long afternoon we slatted limply under a sky now thickening, at its upper reaches, with a veil of cirrus. There was no mistaking the message in those horses' tails; nothing good would come of them.

At six in the evening I decided to run in to Whitehills. This was a change of tactics I had not thought possible, brought on by two slight but, in combination, significant shifts in the actual and the expected. A fair wind had sprung up from the east, a wind that, if it held for just seven or eight hours, would be enough to bring us home. It did not figure in the forecasts, this easterly, but there it was. I could not ignore it. The early evening Shipping Forecast still held to its mantra of strong north-westerlies, but with a slight variation: there would be an introductory period, as it were, with just a moderate Force 4. I balanced what we actually had with what we would supposedly soon get, and concluded that here was the tightest possible window for reaching port.

There is no question, in retrospect, that this was the right thing to do. The storm that was unleashed just a few hours after our arrival was far worse than anything predicted, in both its strength and its duration; it would have tested *Mingming's* sea-keeping to the limits. Despite that, I still feel a little uncomfortable about the decision. For every mile that we closed the coast the stakes were raised. A safe haven was nearer, yes, but so too was potential danger. Every mile reduced our options in the worst of cases.

Put simply, once I had made the decision to head in to harbour, there was no turning back. The starkness of this proposition was underlined within several hours: without preamble the easterly breeze swung round to the north-west.

I had no doubt whatsoever that this was the start of the weather that had threatened for several days. If it remained light I could, if necessary, sail into Whitehills with it; the entrance channel lies on a north-west axis. If it blew up quickly, though, the inverse would apply; the entrance channel would be impossible to negotiate. Nor would there be any other viable havens along that stretch of coast.

Yes, it was a bold move to make a dash into Whitehills, but it teetered on the very edge of good seamanship. It could just as easily have been construed as stupid, or desperate. I am not being unduly hard on myself here, for the north-westerly was not slow to get going. Within as little as two or three hours after making port the entrance was impassable.

I knew none of this as we sped in to the darkening coastline. I called the generous-spirited Martin Wibner, skipper of *Calloo,* and made an early morning rendezvous at the harbour entrance. I called Jimmy Forbes, staunch helpmeet and Harbour Commissioner, to let him know that I was on my way in.

We settled to the final few miles, the sixty-five unhurried days in our wake now transformed to an urgent sprint. A black sea melded to a black coast beneath a black sky. It was not unrelieved, this blackness: the tight-packed lights of Macduff and Banff, yellow and festive and strangely alien, drew us in to the unseen land. A mile or two off, in a wind already hinting at the violence to come, I hardened up a little to run parallel along the coast to Whitehills. The shoulder of Knock Head obscured the village lights tucked beneath its eastern side. I ran in closer, now steering *Mingming* with the tiller lines. The first low lights of Whitehills showed ahead. Shallow water and an increasingly purposeful wind combined to throw up a boisterous sea. I felt intensely vulnerable. This was not our kind of sailing. I went about, for no reason other than to test the angle of our other, offshore tack. The wind had enough west in it to allow us to claw off, if need be, with relative ease. I went about again and once more angled in shorewards. Whitehills opened up ahead and there in the jumble of lights was the red flash of the harbour beacon.

We had made good time in the freshening breeze and so were early for our rendezvous. I went about again and settled into a rhythm of reaching back and forth, one tack to the east and slightly seawards, the other to the west and angled in to the land. Away from the land; back to the land; we rocked back and forth under what was now a well-reefed mainsail. On each landward tack I came in a little closer; familiarity with the lights of Whitehills and an improving judgement of distance gave increasing confidence. I wanted to be as close in as possible when Martin came out. Time was becoming critical. The wind was ratcheting itself up by the minute. It was clear that there was now only a short window for negotiating the harbour entrance.

At exactly four-thirty the masthead lights of *Calloo*, dipping and rolling in the sharp swell, moved seawards along the narrow harbour channel. *Mingming* was just a hundred yards or so off. I lowered and lashed the mainsail, hauled myself on deck and prepared a towing line. By now there was a fine old sea running. *Calloo* edged closer. Both yachts were rolling heavily. In the strong wind passing a line would not be easy. As *Calloo* came alongside, fifteen or twenty feet away, I saw through the gloom that there was a second person on board. *Bertie!* It was Bertie Milne, the Harbourmaster. Unasked, unbidden, he had roused himself in the middle of the night to give Martin an extra pair of hands. They were welcome, those hands, and needed. It took two difficult passes alongside to get a line aboard *Calloo* and secured. Martin turned landwards, and with *Mingming* pitching happily in his wake, towed us once more home through those last few precious yards between wall and rock.

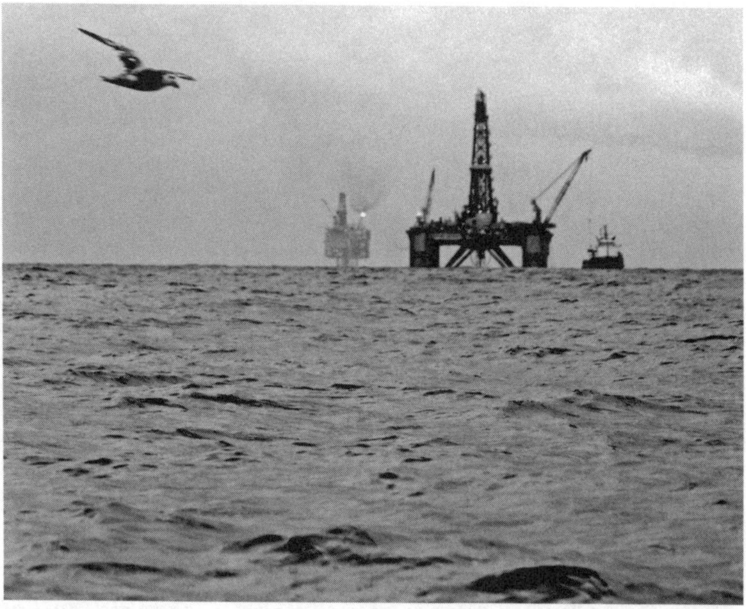

'... the steel islands of the Clair oil field...'

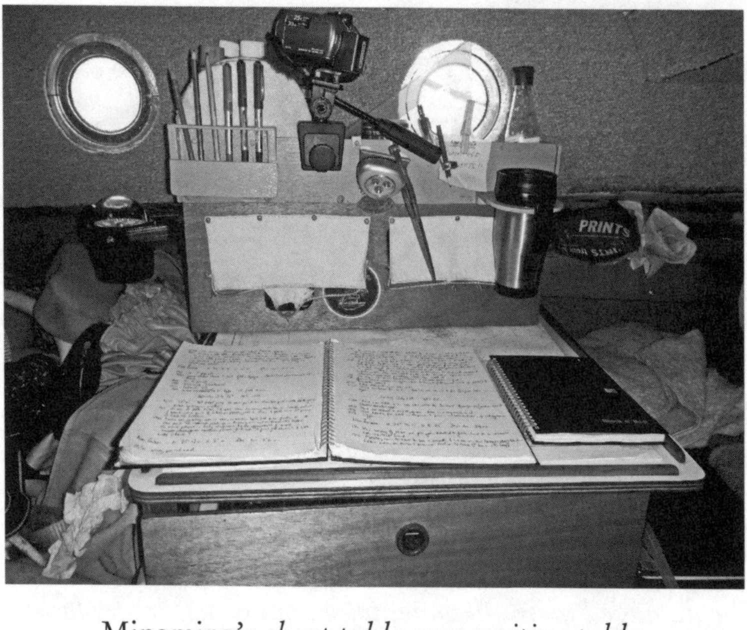

Mingming's *chart table cum writing table.*

A young long-finned pilot whale surfaces close to its mother's fin.

The damaged mainsail panel taken out of service by lashing together two battens.

Mingming's *cat's cradle of cockpit lines when under way.*

The mountains of southern Jan Mayen peak through the morning mist.

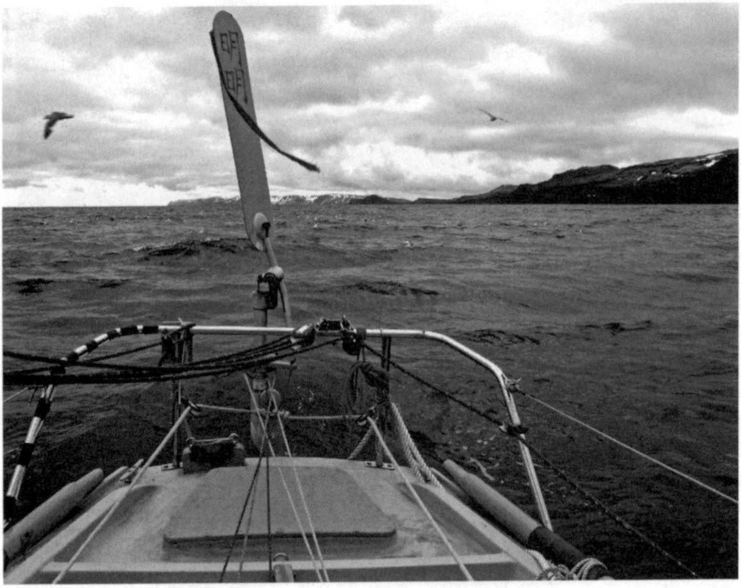

Looking astern along the eastern coast of Jan Mayen.

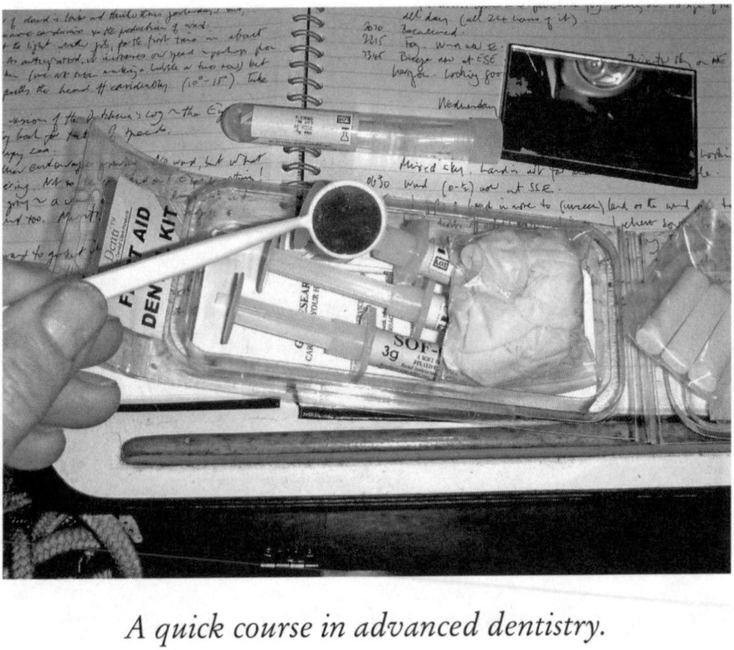

A quick course in advanced dentistry.

Landfall at Spitsbergen.

Becalmed off Prins Karls Forland.

The mother of all noon positions.

A fin whale surfaces close by.

78°North – becalmed at 0200 hours under a hot sun

'I stared helplessly at the helpless bird...'

Mingming *safely back at Whitehills.*

Three of the finest mates a man could have: from l. to r. Bertie Mills, Whitehills Harbourmaster; Jimmy Forbes, Harbour Commissioner; Martin Wibner, ex-oil rig helicopter pilot and skipper of Calloo.

The entrance to Whitehills Harbour just a few hours after our return.

APPENDIX

Statistical analysis of voyages

Voyage	2010	2011
Destination	Baffin Island	80°North
Days at sea	67	65
Distance sailed *	4085 miles	3036 miles
Average daily run	61 miles	43.1 miles
Highest daily run	100 miles	93 miles
Lowest daily run	24 miles	12 miles
Total sail area changes	237	228
Average daily sail area changes	3.54	3.51
Maximum daily sail area changes	11	13
Total exits from hatch	17	20
Mandatory exits from hatch	13	10
Discretionary exits from hatch	4	10
Headsail set	2x	4x
Wet weather gear worn	4x	1x

* Total straight line noon to noon distances. All distances in nautical miles.